Applied International Finance

Applied International Finance

Managing Foreign Exchange Risk and International Capital Budgeting

Thomas J. O'Brien

First published in 2014 by
Business Expert Press, LLC
222 East 46th Street, New York, NY 10017
www.businessexpertpress.com

ISBN-13: 978-1-60649-734-0 (paperback)
ISBN-13: 978-1-60649-735-7 (e-book)

Business Expert Press Finance and Financial Management Collection

Cover and interior design by Exeter Premedia Services Private Ltd., Chennai, India

First edition: 2014

10 9 8 7 6 5 4 3 2 1

Printed in the United States of America.

I thank Shmuel Baruch, Reid Click, Martin Glaum,
John Griffin, Alain Krapl, Steve Magee, Chris Malone, and
Dev Mishra for their helpful comments and discussions.

Abstract

This text is designed for use in a course in applied international corporate finance for managers and executives. Instead of the "encyclopedic" approach, the text focuses on the two main issues of interest to managers who deal with overseas operations. The first main issue is how uncertain foreign exchange (FX) rate changes affect a firm's ongoing cash flows and equity value, and what can be done about this risk. The second main issue is the estimation of the cost of capital for international operations and the evaluation of overseas investment proposals. Numerous examples of real-world companies are used.

The text is divided into two parts based on the two main issues. Each part includes a case that unifies the ideas. In Part I, the case company has overseas operations and is faced with ongoing FX exposure in corporate revenues. The decisionmaker estimates the FX exposure and considers financial hedging using foreign currency debt and currency swaps. The accounting implications are also considered. In Part II, the case company evaluates a proposal to expand production for a foreign market, with location alternatives being the home country, the foreign market country, or a "cheap-labor" emerging market country. The text presumes an introductory foundation in FX rates and FX valuation, as in Thomas J. O'Brien, *Introduction to Foreign Exchange Rates*, BEP Press, 2013.

Keywords

FX exposure, operational hedging, FX translation exposure, foreign currency debt, hedge accounting, currency swaps, cost of capital, hurdle rate, political risk, international capital budgeting

Contents

PART I

Managing Foreign Exchange Risk

CHAPTER 1

Foreign Exchange Operating Exposure

Many companies operate globally, taking raw materials from some countries, producing parts in other countries, assembling in still other countries, and competing to sell final products in markets at various places in the world. Many other companies operate only in their home country or have only limited international operations. But regardless of the scope of a firm's international operations, volatile foreign exchange (FX) rates can impact profitability and growth.

The risk that future FX rate uncertainty poses to a company is determined by both how volatile the FX rate is and the company's *FX exposure*, which is the sensitivity of its operating and financial results to the FX rate changes. In 2001, for example, the unexpected depreciation of the euro severely affected the revenues and earnings of a number of U.S. companies, including DuPont, Merck, Minnesota, Mining and Manufacturing (MMM), Johnson & Johnson, and Proctor & Gamble. In general, the FX exposure we will cover is more complex than the FX transaction exposure of single foreign currency revenue or disbursement, which is covered elsewhere.[1]

A recent study of approximately 2,400 companies from 55 countries finds that 76% of the firms report that they are exposed to FX rate changes. The study finds that 63% of purely domestic firms are affected by FX rate changes. Of the firms engaged in international trade—exporting, importing, or both—at least seven of every ten report that they are exposed to FX rate changes.[2]

A 2003 UBS study of U.S. companies reported that the industry with the highest FX exposure was automobiles and components. The industries with the next highest FX exposures were, in order, materials, energy, and health care equipment. Also with substantial FX exposures were household products, consumer durables and apparel, pharma and biotech, technology hardware, capital goods, telecommunications, and food, beverage and tobacco. At the low end of estimated FX exposures were retailing (lowest); semiconductors; transportation; hotels, restaurants, and leisure; commercial services; and media.[3]

It will be useful for us to measure FX exposure to a foreign currency as an *elasticity*: the percentage change in the firm's variable of interest (cash flow, earnings, equity value, and so forth), measured in the *home currency*, given the percentage change in the home currency (HC) price of the foreign currency (FC), which means that the FX rate is measured in direct terms from the perspective of the home currency, HC/FC. This elasticity definition is consistent with the notion of FX exposure as a regression coefficient.[4] We'll use the symbol ξ to denote FX exposure.

FX Operating Exposure

In this chapter, we specifically tackle *FX operating exposure*, which is the effect of FX rate changes on a firm's on-going operating cash flow stream, measured in the firm's home currency. The notation $\xi_{O\epsilon}^{\$}$ denotes the FX operating exposure to the euro, measuring the operating cash flow in U.S. dollars. The O subscript indicates that the FX exposure is the FX *operating* exposure; other letters will be used later to denote other types of FX exposure. The ϵ subscript indicates that it is changes in the euro FX rate that causes the FX exposure. The superscript denotes the currency in which the financial results are expressed, which in this case is the U.S. dollar.

Thus, $\xi_{O\epsilon}^{\$}$ denotes the following elasticity: the percentage change in the operating cash flow, measured in U.S. dollars, given the percentage change in the spot FX price of the euro. Let $\%\Delta O^{\$}$ denote the percentage change in the operating cash flow, measured in U.S. dollars, $(O_1^{\$} - O_0^{\$})/O_0^{\$}$, and let $x^{\$/\epsilon}$ denote the percentage change in the spot FX price of the euro, $(X_1^{\$/\epsilon} - X_0^{\$/\epsilon})/X_0^{\$/\epsilon}$. FX operating exposure to the euro, from the perspective of U.S. dollars as the pricing currency, is thus shown in equation (1.1).

FX Operating Exposure

$$\xi_{O\epsilon}^{\$} = \%\Delta O^{\$}/x^{\$/\epsilon} \qquad (1.1)$$

For example, assume that operating cash flow (in U.S. dollars) tends to rise by 10% when the euro appreciates by 5%, and tends to fall by 10%

when the euro depreciates by 5%. According to equation (1.1), we'd say the FX operating exposure to the euro is 0.10/0.05 = 2.

A U.S. company expects an operating cash flow (measured in U.S. dollars) of $5 million, given a current spot FX rate of 1.25 $/€. Assume the company has an FX operating exposure to the euro, $\xi_{O€}^{\$}$, of 0.80. If the euro unexpectedly depreciates by 20% (relative to the U.S. dollar), all else remaining the same, what is the firm's new expected operating cash flow, measured in U.S. dollars?

Answer: The expected operating cash flow drops by 0.80(20%) = 16%. So the new expected operating cash flow is 0.84($5 million) = $4.2 million.

A company with a positive FX operating exposure is sometimes said to have a *long* FX operating exposure. A long FX operating exposure often characterizes an exporter, where the revenues are in the foreign currency but operating costs are primarily in the home currency. The European airframe manufacturer Airbus is not an exporter, but has a long FX operating exposure to the U.S. dollar anyway, because the revenues are in U.S. dollars. See the box "Airbus." Another type of firm that usually has a long FX operating exposure is one that has a foreign subsidiary that makes and sells products in the foreign country.

Airbus

The large European aircraft manufacturer, Airbus, prices its commercial aircraft in the standard currency of the industry, U.S. dollars. With manufacturing, production, subassembly, and assembly primarily in Europe, Airbus's operating costs are largely in euros.

In 2005, Airbus's management estimated that a 10% drop in the U.S. dollar relative to the euro would be enough to wipe out <u>half</u> of the company's annual operating income. Using operating income as a "proxy" for operating cash flow, this estimate is the same as saying that Airbus's FX operating exposure to the U.S. dollar, from the point of view of euros, denoted by $\xi_{O\$}^{€}$, is −0.50/−0.10 = **5**. That's a high number, but Airbus perhaps has the highest FX operating exposure of any company in the world.

Domestic firms can also have a long FX operating exposure to a foreign currency. One classic scenario is a domestic company with one or more foreign competitors. For example, say a U.S. company with no foreign operations competes against a Japanese firm in the United States. If the yen appreciates (U.S. dollar depreciates), the Japanese firm is inclined to lower output in the face of falling revenues when measured in yen. So the U.S. firm's share of the market, and its operating cash flow, will rise. The reverse scenario happens when the yen depreciates (U.S. dollar rises). Even though the U.S. firm has no international operations or foreign currency transactions, the firm has a positive FX operating exposure to the yen because the U.S. dollar cash flow rises when the yen appreciates, and vice versa.

A domestic company may have a long FX operating exposure in other ways. For instance, the firm could be a supplier to one or more firms with a long FX operating exposure to a given foreign currency. An example is the Canadian firm, Finning Inc., which distributes heavy equipment to Canadian customers, many of which sell goods primarily in the United States with prices fixed in U.S. dollars. So when the U.S. dollar depreciates relative to the Canadian dollar, Finning's customers experience lower cash flow in Canadian dollars, and their orders for Finning's products tend to drop. Thus, Finning has a positive FX operating exposure to the U.S. dollar, even though Finning's sales are in Canada and in Canadian dollars.[5]

Not all companies' FX operating exposure is positive. A negative FX operating exposure often characterizes an importer, because as the foreign currency appreciates, an importer's operating costs rise, and so the operating cash flow drops. A firm with a negative FX operating exposure is said to have a *short* FX operating exposure. Short FX operating exposures may be found in other scenarios as well. For example, consider a U.S. company whose Swiss subsidiary manufactures products that are sold primarily in the Eurozone. Because the subsidiary's operating costs are mainly in Swiss francs, the U.S. parent company will have a short FX operating exposure to the Swiss franc, in addition to the long FX operating exposure to the euro.

"What if" Analyses

Although many companies have FX operating exposure, actually quantifying that exposure is extremely difficult to do with precision. To help you better understand the idea of FX operating exposure, we'll look at a few hypothetical examples using a "what if" sensitivity analysis with simple *pro forma* cash flow statements. In the examples, measuring the exact FX exposure looks easy. However, this is not to suggest that the process is easy in reality, only to help you understand the idea. In reality, you sometimes may be able to form only a rough guess of FX operating exposure, not a precise estimate.

Our hypothetical company is a U.S. exporter named United Pipe Fittings Co. (UPF), which produces aluminum pipe fittings in the United States.[6] All sales are in the Eurozone, predominantly to construction companies. This year, UPF expects to sell 400 fittings at a local currency price of €1 per fitting, generating expected foreign revenues in euros, R^{ϵ}, of €400. Excluding aluminum, the variable production cost is $0.40 per fitting. So the total variable production expense for the expected output of 400 fittings is $160. Like many metals, aluminum is priced globally in U.S. dollars, and the price is currently $0.75 per pound of aluminum. Each fitting requires one-third of a pound of aluminum, so the cost of the aluminum per fitting is $0.25. The total aluminum expense for the expected output of 400 fittings is $100. Assume fixed operating costs of $40.

Now assume the spot FX rate is currently 1.25 $/€. In our examples, we'll base the initially expected revenues and expected operating cash flows on the current spot FX rate. At 1.25 $/€, UPF's expected revenues of €400 convert to $500, implying an expected operating cash flow in U.S. dollars, $O^{\$}$, of $500 − 160 − 100 − 40 = $200. UPF's projected operating cash flow statement, given the current spot FX rate of 1.25 $/€, is shown in Exhibit 1.1a.

What happens to UPF's operating cash flow if the spot FX rate unexpectedly turns out to be a rate other than 1.25 $/€? For now, assume for simplicity that UPF would make no output or price adjustments if the FX rate changes. That is, UPF expects to sell 400 fittings at €1 per fitting,

Exhibit 1.1a. UPF Initial Expected Operating Cash Flow ($) $X^{\$/\epsilon}$ = 1.25 $/€

Revenues ($R^{\$}$)	$500 (€400 @ 1.25 $/€)
Variable Production Expense	160
Aluminum Expense	100
Fixed Operating Costs	40
Operating Cash Flow ($O^{\$}$)	$200

Exhibit 1.1b. UPF "What if" Operating
Cash Flow ($) $X^{\$/€} = 1\ \$/€$

Revenues ($R^\$$)	$400 (€400 @ 1 $/€)
Variable Production Expense	160
Aluminum Expense	100
Fixed Operating Costs	40
Operating Cash Flow ($O^\$$)	$100

regardless of the FX rate. Thus, UPF's foreign currency revenues, in euros, do not change when the spot FX rate unexpectedly changes.

What if the spot FX rate unexpectedly drops to 1 $/€? At 1 $/€, the local currency revenues of €400 would convert to only $400. The variable production expenses, the aluminum expense, and the fixed operating costs would not change. UPF's new operating cash flow in U.S. dollars is only $100, lower because the revenues in euros are not worth as much in U.S. dollars, and the operating costs are not affected. UPF's projected cash flow statement in U.S. dollars, given the new spot FX rate of 1 $/€, is shown in Exhibit 1.1b.

The "what if" spot FX change represents a 20% depreciation of the euro, from 1.25 $/€ to 1 $/€. UPF's operating cash flow (in U.S. dollars) drops by 50% (from $200 to $100) when the euro depreciates by 20%. So we see that UPF's FX operating exposure to the euro, $\xi_{O€}^\$$, is $-0.50/-0.20 = \textbf{2.50}$, indicating that given a 1% change in the euro, the operating cash flow, measured in home currency, will change in the same direction by 2.50%.

It is important to see that the measurement of UPF's FX operating exposure does not depend on the hypothetical spot FX rate used in the "what if" analysis. The next example confirms that we'd find that the FX operating exposure is 2.50 using a different "what if" spot FX rate.

Confirm UPF's FX operating exposure to the euro of 2.50 by showing that a 20% appreciation of the euro (from 1.25 $/€ to 1.50 $/€) would result in a 50% increase in operating cash flow.

Answer: At 1.50 $/€, UPF's new operating cash flow in U.S. dollars will be $600 − 160 − 100 − 40 = $300. The percentage change in operating cash flow is $300/$200 − 1 = 0.50, or 50%, in response to a 20% appreciation of the euro, representing an FX operating exposure to the euro of 0.50/0.20 = 2.50.

Now let's look at an example of a company with a short FX operating exposure. BNP Corporation is a hypothetical U.S. manufacturer of scientific instruments, with sales entirely in the United States. BNP sells each instrument for $500 and expects to sell 2,000 instruments next year. BNP sources specialized components from Japan, with prices fixed in yen. For each instrument, the specialized components will cost ¥10,000. Other variable production costs, incurred in the assembly of the instruments in the United States, are $125 per instrument, and the fixed operating costs are $300,000.

Assume today's spot FX rate is 100 ¥/$. Because the expected revenue is $500(2,000) = $1 million, and the cost of the specialized components from Japan is ¥10,000(2,000)/(100 ¥/$) = $200,000, the initially expected operating cash flow is $1 million − 200,000 − $125(2,000) − $300,000 = $250,000. If the yen appreciates by 25%, what is BNP's new operating cash flow? Note that the new spot FX rate is 80 ¥/$, <u>not</u> 75 ¥/$, which would be a 25% depreciation of the U.S. dollar. In U.S. dollars, the new cost of the specialized components is higher, ¥10,000(2,000)/(80 ¥/$) = $250,000. Thus the new operating cash flow is lower, $1 million − 250,000 − $125 (2,000) − $300,000 = $200,000. The operating cash flow drops by 20%, from $250,000 to $200,000, when the yen appreciates by 25%. Hence, BNP's FX operating exposure to the yen, $\xi_{O¥}^{\$}$, is −0.20/0.25 = −0.80.

Note again that our measurement of BNP's FX operating exposure does not depend on the spot FX rate used in the "what if" analysis. The next example confirms that BNP's FX operating exposure to the yen is −0.80 for a different "what if" spot FX rate.

Confirm BNP's FX operating exposure to the yen of − 0.80 by showing that a 20% depreciation of the yen would result in a 16% increase in operating cash flow.

Answer: A 20% depreciation of the yen means a "what if" spot FX price of the yen of 0.008 $/¥, which is equivalent to 125 ¥/$. In U.S. dollars, the new cost of the specialized components is lower, ¥10,000(2,000)/ (125 ¥/$) = $160,000. BNP's new operating cash flow will be $1 million − 160,000 − $125(2,000) − $300,000 = $290,000. The percentage change in operating cash flow is $290,000/$250,000 − 1 = 0.16, or 16%, in response to the 20% depreciation of the yen, representing an FX operating exposure to the yen of 0.16/−0.20 = −0.80.

Operational Hedging

If a firm with a positive FX operating exposure stabilizes some or all of its operating costs in the currency to which the revenues are exposed, the firm is said to be doing *operational hedging*. The purpose of operational hedging is to mitigate the effects of FX operating exposure. Let's look at a scenario where UPF relocates some latter stages of production from the United States to the Eurozone. The headquarters and the earlier production stages remain in the United States, but to help clarify the example, we'll assume the entire company takes on the new corporate name of EPF.

After the restructuring, the variable production costs (excluding aluminum) are in the Eurozone and are €0.32 per fitting, for a total expected variable production expense of €128 for 400 fittings. Because aluminum is priced globally in U.S. dollars, the aluminum cost is stable in U.S. dollars at $0.75 per pound and thus $0.25 per fitting. Also, EPF's fixed operating costs are still incurred in the United States and are still $40, and EPF's sales volume and price are not affected by FX changes. EPF's expected operating cash flow statement, given an initial spot FX rate of 1.25 $/€, is shown in Exhibit 1.2a.

As we see in Exhibit 1.2a, at a spot FX rate of 1.25 $/€, EPF's expected revenues of €400 convert to $500; the variable production expenses of €128 convert to $160; and the expected operating cash flow in U.S. dollars is thus $500 − 160 − 100 − 40 = $200. What happens to EPF's operating cash flow if the spot FX rate unexpectedly changes from 1.25 $/€ to 1 $/€? With output and price unaffected, EPF's revenues and variable production expenses are stable in euros

Exhibit 1.2a. EPF Initial Expected Operating Cash Flow ($) $X^{\$/€} = 1.25$ $/€

Revenues ($R^{\$}$)	$500 (€400 @ 1.25 $/€)
Variable Production Expense	160 (€128 @ 1.25 $/€)
Aluminum	100
Fixed Operating Costs	40
Operating Cash Flow ($O^{\$}$)	$200

Exhibit 1.2b. EPF "What if" Operating Cash Flow ($) $X^{\$/\epsilon} = 1$ *$/€*

Revenues ($R^{\$}$)	$400 (€400 @ 1 $/€)
Variable Production Expense	128 (€128 @ 1 $/€)
Aluminum	100
Fixed Operating Costs	40
Operating Cash Flow ($O^{\$}$)	$132

and so fall in U.S. dollars. The aluminum expense and fixed operating costs are stable in U.S. dollars. Exhibit 1.2b shows that at the "what if" spot FX rate of 1 $/€, EPF's new operating cash flow is only $132. So if the euro depreciates by 20% (from 1.25 $/€ to 1 $/€), EPF's operating cash flow (in U.S. dollars) drops by 34% (from $200 to $132). Thus, the FX operating exposure to the euro, $\xi_{O\epsilon}^{\$}$, is –0.34/–0.20 = **1.70**.

The reason why EPF's FX operating exposure to the euro is lower than UPF's (2.50) is that some of EPF's operating costs "match currency" with the revenues, whereas all of UPF's operating costs are stable in U.S. dollars. Figure 1.1 depicts the FX operating exposures to the euro for UPF and EPF.

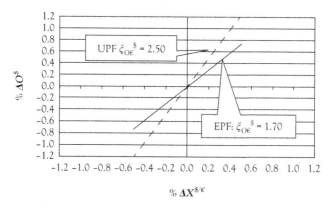

Figure 1.1. Operational hedging and FX operating exposure: FX operating exposures to the euro for UPF and EPF. The slope shows FX operating exposure. For UPF, which does no operational hedging, the FX operating exposure is 2.50. For EPF, with variable production costs in the Eurozone, the FX operating exposure is only 1.70.

Assume that in addition to variable production costs of €0.32 per fitting, all of EPF's fixed operating costs are in the Eurozone and are €32. All other assumptions are the same as in the text. Find EPF's FX operating exposure to the euro.

Answer: At 1.25 \$/€, the fixed operating costs of €32 convert to \$40. Thus, EPF's initial expected operating cash flow in U.S. dollars is still \$500 – 160 – 100 – 40 = \$200. At 1 \$/€, EPF's operating cash flow in U.S. dollars will be \$400 – 128 – 100 – 32 = \$140. The percentage change in the operating cash flow (in U.S. dollars) is \$140/\$200 – 1 = –0.30, or –30%, in response to a 20% depreciation of the euro. This represents an FX operating exposure to the euro of 1.50, which is lower than in the text example, because here EPF has more of its operating costs doing operational hedging.

Airbus: Operational Hedging

In December 2005, Airbus decided to begin assembly operations in China. In addition to the relatively inexpensive labor, the purpose was for operational hedging of Airbus's huge FX operating exposure to the U.S. dollar, because the Chinese yuan is pegged against the U.S. dollar. If the Chinese government were to discontinue pegging the yuan to the U.S. dollar, the assembly operation in China would no longer be an effective operational hedge of Airbus's FX operating exposure to the U.S. dollar, and Airbus would have a **negative** FX operating exposure to the yuan.

United Technologies Corporation: Operational Hedging

Carrier Company, a division of United Technologies Corporation (UTC), makes air conditioners. Consider Carrier's European subsidiary, which sells air conditioners in the Eurozone, and the price is stable in euros. Carrier can choose where to source compressors, which account for about 30% of the cost of producing an air conditioner. One alternative is to produce the compressors in the United States. The other choice is Ireland, which is in the Eurozone, so the cost of making a compressor would be stable in euros. Assume that all other inputs, especially labor, in the production of air conditioners by Carrier-Europe are incurred in Europe and have unit costs that are stable in euros.

Carrier's (and thus UTC's) FX operating exposure to the euro depends on where the compressors are sourced. If Carrier-Europe gets compressors from Ireland, the entire cost of producing an air conditioner for the European market is stable in euros. From the U.S. dollar point of view, this option makes maximal use of operational hedging. If Carrier-Europe gets compressors from the United States, the cost of producing an air conditioner for the European market is 70% stable in euros and 30% stable in U.S. dollars. From the U.S. dollar point of view, the FX operating exposure to the euro would be higher than if the compressors are sourced from Ireland. Of course, there are other considerations in the decision on where to source the compressors, such as cost and quality.

A domestic firm with a positive FX exposure to a currency due to foreign competition can also practice operational hedging, by buying parts and materials from the exposure country. But this is not a good method for a firm with a negative FX operating exposure to practice operational hedging. In principle, an importer could try to enter the market in the country where the import costs are based. But this strategy may not be realistic. One strategy an importer may consider, however, is to diversify FX risk by developing import channels in more than one country. If the importer can get half of the needed inputs from Country A and the other half from Country B, and if the FX price of the two currencies is negatively correlated, you can see that the diversification strategy would reduce the importer's combined FX operating exposures. This strategy is likely to work better when the imported material is a more of commodity and less of a specialty item.

FX Pass-Through

Whether the FX operating exposure to a currency is positive or negative, a firm may be able to control some of the FX risk by adjusting the product's local currency selling price in response to FX changes. We measure *FX pass-through* as the proportion of an FX rate change that a company passes through to the customer. For example, a firm may pass through 20%, 60%, or even 100% of given FX changes. Of course, a firm would prefer to pass through 100% of any adverse FX change if sales volume were not affected. High FX pass-through is possible when competition is weak, or in other situations. For example, the Japanese tractor manufacturer Komatsu is happy for its U.S. parts suppliers to fix prices in U.S. dollars, which is equivalent to 100% FX pass-through. Komatsu's strategy is the operational hedging of its U.S. revenue. As the Dow Chemical Europe box suggests, different products allow different FX pass-through levels, when the FX pass-through strategy includes avoiding changes in sales volume

When the product's selling price is in a foreign currency, you have to multiply the FX pass-through percentage by the percentage change <u>in the home currency</u> to get the percentage change in the product price in the foreign currency. For example, say a U.S. exporter sells a product in the Eurozone and has an FX pass-through policy of 30%. Assume the euro depreciates by 20% relative to the U.S. dollar, so that the U.S. dollar appreciates by 25% relative to the euro. (Note: $(1 + x^{\$/€})(1 + x^{€/\$}) = 1$.) The product price in euros will be adjusted by 0.30(25%) = 7.50%. If the initial price is €100, the new price is €107.50.

Say EPF's FX pass-through policy is 40%. If the euro depreciates by 10%, from 1.25 $/€ to 1.125 $/€, what is the new fittings price in euros?

Answer: First, we need to know the percentage change in the U.S. dollar, given the 10% depreciation of the euro. Using $(1 + x^{\$/€})(1 + x^{€/\$}) = 1$, we find that the U.S. dollar appreciates by 11.1% when the euro depreciates by 10%. So EPF would change the price of pipe fittings in euros by 0.40(11.1%) = 4.44%, from €1 to €1.0444.

Dow Chemical Europe

Dow Chemical assesses the FX pass-through potential for its Eurozone products using a rating of local currency price stability in the face of FX changes. The lower the local currency price stability, the higher is the FX pass-through, with no assumed impact on sales volume.

Eurozone marketing managers are asked to rate the stability of the local currency prices (in euros) of each product, using a price stability rating of 0 to 100. A stability rating of 100 means a product's price in euros is 100% stable. The price is unaffected by changes in the spot FX rate, and Dow cannot or does not pass through spot FX changes to the customer. A price stability rating of 0 implies that the product's price in euros has zero stability when the spot FX rate changes. Spot FX changes are entirely passed through to Eurozone customers in the product's local price in euros.

Most Dow products have a stability rating between 0 and 100. Some examples of Dow's Eurozone price stability ratings are: (1) Magnesium is rated 0, implying 100% FX pass-through. (2) Caustic soda, by contrast is rated 60, implying less responsiveness of local prices to spot FX changes. (3) Propylene glycol and agricultural products are rated 80 and 90, respectively, suggesting that FX changes have little effect on local prices.[7]

A company with a negative FX operating exposure to a currency, like an importer, may also be able to reduce the risk by using FX pass-through. A domestic importer's price adjustment is a bit easier to calculate than an exporter's, because the price is in the home currency rather than in a foreign currency. So the percentage change in the price is simply the FX pass-through percentage times the percentage change in the foreign currency. In the BNP example, if the yen appreciates by 25%, and BNP's FX pass-through policy is 20%, the home currency product price changes by 0.20(25%) = 5%.

Note that BNP passes through some of the <u>favorable</u> FX change to its customers in the form of a price reduction. BNP would seemingly make more money by not passing through favorable FX changes, only unfavorable ones. But if customers are willing to accept some of the unfavorable results of FX changes, they will want to share in the favorable ones. So we treat FX pass-through as a strategy that is symmetric for both favorable and unfavorable FX changes.

Changes in Sales Volume and Operating Leverage

FX economic exposure is a term that is sometimes used as a synonym for FX operating exposure, in the sense of referring to the impact of FX rates on a firm's real cash flows rather than reported financial statement accounting items. (We cover the impact of FX changes on accounting items in Chapters 2 and 3.) Other times, FX economic exposure refers specifically to a subcategory of FX operating exposure where the causes are of an economic nature. Typically, these economic situations involve a change in sales volume.

One potential economic influence on sales volume, and thus on FX operating exposure, is an income (or wealth) effect. Sometimes when an economy's own currency appreciates, buyers in that economy increase their purchases of foreign goods, and vice versa. So, for example, if the euro appreciates relative to the U.S. dollar, a U.S. exporter to the Eurozone may see a rise in product demand. Not all economic effects result in a positive FX operating exposure. When the home currency depreciates, an air carrier tends to experience a drop in demand by home country citizens who want to travel internationally, because the overseas purchasing power of the home currency has dropped. Because the carrier's demand and cash flows drop when the foreign currency appreciates relative to the home currency, air carriers tend to have a negative FX operating exposure to foreign currencies.

Another economic effect can result for commodities and products that have a *currency habitat of price*, which is a term used to indicate the currency in which, due to the particular economic circumstances, the price of a good is effectively set. An example of this idea is that the price of aluminum is always in U.S. dollars. In fact, the U.S. dollar is the currency habitat of price for metals generally, including gold. Similarly, you saw the currency habitat of price idea for a product (airframes) when we discussed the FX exposure of Airbus. If the currency habitat of a good's price is the U.S. dollar, the good's price changes for a non-U.S. dollar buyer when the FX rate changes relative to the U.S. dollar. So if the euro depreciates against the U.S. dollar, the German air carrier Lufthansa must pay a higher price in euros for the aircraft bought from either Boeing or Airbus. The result of a depreciation of the euro could be a drop in the demand for goods whose currency habitat of price is the U.S. dollar. Non-U.S. metal mining companies, such as Australia's Western Mining Company, face this kind of FX exposure when they sell in countries other than the United States.[8]

Of course, the impact of price changes on sales volume usually depends on the product's *price elasticity of demand*, which is the percentage change in product demand, given the percentage change in the product's price. Thus, price elasticity of demand is inherently negative, but we'll express it as a positive number. For example, a price elasticity of demand of 2 says that if a product's price is lowered (raised) by 10%, the volume demanded would rise (drop) by 20%.

When changes in sales volume are considered, there is a "rule of thumb" that **for an exporting firm with no competitors, the optimal FX pass-through policy is approximately equal to the percentage of variable operating costs that are <u>not</u> denominated in the exposure currency.**[9]

So, for example, because 100% of UPF's variable operating costs are denominated in U.S. dollars, UPF's optimal FX pass-through policy would be 100%, meaning that UPF would pass through 100% of any given FX rate change into the fittings price in euros. Similarly, you see in Exhibit 1.2a that EPF's proportion of non-euro variable operating costs is 100/260 = 0.385. So EPF's optimal policy would be to pass through 38.5% of any FX rate change into the fittings price in euros. In the next section, we'll take into consideration the potential impact of the price change on the volume of product demanded.

For a numerical example, assume that 1.70 is the price elasticity of demand for fittings in the Eurozone. Because UPF's optimal FX pass-through policy is 100%, UPF will raise the fittings price in euros by 1(11.1%), to €1.111, if the euro depreciates by 10%, from 1.25 $/€ to 1.125 $/€. Given that the price elasticity of demand is 1.70, UPF's sales volume would drop by 1.70(11.1%), or 18.9%. So UPF's sales volume would drop to (1 − 0.189)400, or 324 fittings. UPF's "what if" operating cash flow is (1.125 $/€)(€1.111)324 − 0.40(324) − 0.25(324) − 40 = $154.36, a drop of 22.8% from the initial operating cash flow of $200. When price elasticity of demand is considered, the "what if" estimate of UPF's FX operating exposure is −0.228/−0.10 = **2.28**.

Assume the price elasticity of demand for fittings is 1.70. Find a "what if" estimate of EPF's FX operating exposure to the euro for a 10% depreciation of the euro, given that EPF's FX pass-through policy is 38.5%.

Answer: If EPF raises the fittings price in euros by 0.385(11.1%) = 4.27%, to €1.0427, sales volume would drop by 1.70(4.27%), or 7.26%. So sales volume drops to (1 – 0.0726)400, or 371 fittings. EPF's "what if" operating cash flow is (1.125 $/€)(€1.0427)371 – (1.125 $/€)(€0.32)371 – 0.25(371) – 40 = $168.89, a drop of 15.6% from the initial operating cash flow of $200. EPF's FX operating exposure is –0.156/–0.10 = 1.56.

Other things the same, a higher price elasticity of demand implies a higher FX operating exposure. For example, assuming a price elasticity of demand of 2, UPF's sales volume would drop by 2(11.1%), or 22.2%. So UPF's sales volume would drop to (1 – 0.222)400, or 311 fittings. UPF's "what if" operating cash flow is (1.125 $/€)(€1.111)311 – 0.40(311) – 0.25(311) – 40 = $146.56, a drop of 26.7% from the initial operating cash flow of $200. UPF's FX operating exposure is –0.267/–0.10 = **2.67**.

When sales volume changes as a result of an FX rate change, the FX operating exposure also depends on the *degree of operating leverage*, which describes the company's operating cost structure in terms of fixed versus variable operating costs. To see the impact of the operating leverage, suppose UPF were to restructure its production process, such that the non-aluminum variable operating cost drops to $0.20 per fitting, so that the expected variable production expense drops from $160 to $80. Also, the fixed operating costs rise from $40 to $120, so that the expected operating cash flow is still $200. Given the price elasticity of demand of 1.70, UPF's "what if" operating cash flow is (1.125 $/€)(€1.111)324 – 0.20(324) – 0.25(324) – 120 = $139.16, a drop of 30.4% from the initial operating cash flow of $200. The "what if" estimate of UPF's FX operating exposure is –0.304/–0.10 = **3.04**.

If, instead, UPF's additional fixed operating costs were incurred in euros, say €64, which is equivalent to $80 at the initial spot FX rate of 1.25 $/€, UPF's FX operating exposure would be lower than the previous example, because the new fixed operating costs are doing operational hedging. In this case, UPF's "what if" operating cash flow is (1.125 $/€)(€1.111) 324 – 0.20(324) – 0.25(324) – 40 – (1.125 $/€)(€64) = $147.16, a drop of

26.4% from the initial operating cash flow of #200. The "what if" estimate of UPF's FX operating exposure is –0.264/–0.10 = **2.64**. This FX operating exposure is higher the one before the cost restructuring, 2.28, because of the increase in operating leverage, but is lower if the additional fixed operating costs are doing operational hedging than if not.

Assume that EPF restructures its production costs such that the euro-denominated variable production cost drops from €32 to €16 and U.S. fixed operating costs rise from $40 to $120. In U.S. dollars, EPFs expected variable operating expense drops from $160 to $80, and expected operating cash flow remains at $200. Find a "what if" estimate of EPF's FX operating exposure to the euro for a 10% depreciation of the euro, given that EPF's FX pass-through policy is 38.5%.

Answer: If EPF raises the fittings price in euros by 0.385(11.1%) = 4.27%, to €1.0427, sales volume would drop by 1.70(4.27%), or 7.26%. So sales volume drops to (1 – 0.0726)400, or 371 fittings. EPF's "what if" operating cash flow is (1.125 $/€)(€1.0427)371 – (1.125 $/€)(€0.16)371 – 0.25(371) – 120 = $155.67, a drop of 22.2% from the initial operating cash flow of $200. EPF's FX operating exposure is –0.222/–0.10 = 2.22. EPF's FX operating exposure is higher because of two reasons: the degree of operating leverage is higher and the extent of operational hedging is lower.

Competition and FX Operating Exposure

Earlier in the chapter, we mentioned an example of a U.S. company that competes domestically against a Japanese exporter. If the yen appreciates, the Japanese firm would typically reduce output in the face of falling revenues, resulting in a rise in the U.S. firm's share of the market and its operating cash flow. The reverse scenario happens when the yen depreciates. By the same token, a U.S. exporter competing in a foreign market against a local company would usually have a higher FX operating exposure to the foreign currency than if there were no local competitors.

This section delves further into how competition affects a firm's FX operating exposure. One driver is how the currency denomination of the firm's variable operating costs compares with the industry average:

> A firm whose proportion of variable operating costs denominated in the exposure currency is <u>lower</u> than the industry average will have a <u>higher FX operating exposure</u> than with no competition.

> A firm whose proportion of variable operating costs denominated in the exposure currency is <u>higher</u> than the industry average will have a <u>lower FX operating exposure</u> than with no competition.

To better see how competition affects FX operating exposure, assume that UPF and EPF compete to supply pipe fittings in the Eurozone. As above, UPF produces entirely in the United States, with variable production cost of $0.40 per fitting and $40 in fixed operating costs. EPF has variable production costs in euros of €0.32 per fitting and fixed operating costs of $40 in the United States. Both firms pay $0.25 per fitting for aluminum. To address the question of how competition affects each firm's FX operating exposure, we assume that the competitors produce a homogeneous product, and so customers are indifferent between UPF's and EPF's fittings. At the initial spot FX rate of 1.25 $/€, the two firms have the same variable production cost per fitting ($0.40 when expressed in U.S. dollars). So both firms initially expect to sell the same number of fittings, given the initial spot FX rate of 1.25 $/€. Assume both firms initially expect to sell 270 fittings and the fittings price is €0.85. Expressed in U.S. dollars, both firms initially expect revenues of €0.85 × (270)(1.25 $/€) = $286.875. UPF initially expects operating cash flow of $286.875 − 0.40(270) − 0.25(270) − 40 = $71.375. By design, EPF's initially expected operating cash flow, expressed in U.S. dollars, is also $71.375, given the initial spot FX rate, 1.25 $/€.

An unexpected change in the euro FX rate will affect the competitive balance in the industry. A depreciation of the euro weakens UPF's relative competitive position. Now with lower variable operating costs than UPF, EPF takes some of UPF's market share. "What if" the euro depreciates by 10%, to 1.125 $/€, and the following changes occur: (a) the price per fitting rises

7% to €0.85(1.07) = €0.91; (b) UPF reduces production from 270 fittings to 223 fittings; and (c) EPF reduces production from 270 fittings to 253 fittings. The industry's overall fittings production drops by 12%, from 540 to 476, consistent with a price elasticity of demand for fittings of 1.70. The "what if" operating cash flow statements for UPF and EPF in U.S. dollars, given the new spot FX rate of 1.125 $/€, are shown in Exhibits 1.3a and 1.3b.

In Exhibit 1.3a, we see that UPF's new revenue in U.S. dollars is $228.30. UPF's new operating cash flow is $43.35, a drop of 39.3% from the expected operating cash flow of $71.375. So UPF's FX operating exposure to the euro, $\xi_{O\epsilon}^{\$}$, is −0.393/−0.10 = **3.93**.

In Exhibit 1.3b, EPF's new revenue in U.S. dollars is $256.96. EPF's new operating cash flow is $64.68, a drop of 9.4% from the initially expected operating cash flow of $71.375. So EPF's FX operating exposure to the euro, $\xi_{O\epsilon}^{\$}$, is equal to −0.094/−0.10 = **0.94**.

If the euro instead unexpectedly appreciates, it is UPF that would gain in competitive advantage, and EPF would be at a disadvantage because its variable operating costs would be relatively higher. The effects are the reverse of the example above. UPF would substantially increase production, and EPF would change production by a more modest amount.

Exhibit 1.3a. UPF "What if" Operating Cash Flow ($)
$X^{\$/\epsilon}$ = 1.125 $/€

Revenues ($R^{\$}$)	$228.30 (€0.91 × 223 @ 1.125 $/€)
Variable Production Expense	89.20 ($0.40 × 223)
Aluminum	55.75 ($0.25 × 223)
Fixed Operating Costs	40.00
Operating Cash Flow ($O^{\$}$)	$43.35

Exhibit 1.3b. EPF "What if" Operating Cash Flow ($)
$X^{\$/\epsilon}$ = 1.125 $/€

Revenues ($R^{\$}$)	$259.01 (€0.91 × 253 @ 1.125 $/€)
Variable Production Expense	91.08 (€0.32 × 253 @ 1.125 $/€)
Aluminum	63.25 ($0.25 × 253)
Fixed Operating Costs	40.00
Operating Cash Flow ($O^{\$}$)	$64.68

An example would still show that UPF's FX operating exposure to the euro is substantially higher than EPF's.

In competition, UPF has a **higher** FX operating exposure, 3.93, than as the sole firm in the market, which we estimated in the prior section as 2.27. In contrast, EPF will have a **lower** FX operating exposure, 0.94, than as the sole firm in the market, which we estimated in the problem in the prior section as 1.56.

Why would EPF's FX exposure be <u>lower</u> when competing? First, recall that the only effective difference between the two competitors is that EPF does more operational hedging than UPF. Second, note that the Eurozone fittings market has an FX economic exposure that is driven by the price elasticity of demand for fittings. In competition, UPF bears the majority of the market's inherent FX risk due to its lower operational hedging. Correspondingly, due to its higher operational hedging, EPF's reactions to FX changes are smaller than UPF's, and smaller than even than if EPF were the sole firm. Thus, in competition with UPF, EPF does not bear as much FX risk as it would as the sole firm.

Another point to see is that if UPF and EPF were identical in their operating cost structure currency denominations, both firms would have the same FX exposure to the euro in competition as each would have as the sole company in the market. That is, competition does not affect firms' FX operating exposure per se, only the allocation of the FX economic exposure of the fittings market, given the competitors' relative operating cost structure currency denominations.[10]

ABC Company is a U.S. manufacturer of precision instruments. Initially, ABC's exports to Australia had virtually no competition. Recently, another U.S. company has built a plant in Australia to produce and sell similar instruments in the Australian market. (A) Which company has a higher percentage of variable operating costs denominated in the local currency? (B) ABC's FX operating exposure to the Australian dollar has likely (a) increased; (b) decreased; or (c) not changed.

Answers: (A) The new competitor; (B) (a) increased, because the new competitor has a higher percentage of variable operating costs in the local currency.

The U.S. component manufacturer, CAB Co., has a subsidiary in New Zealand that produces locally with no competition. Another U.S. company starts exporting similar components to the New Zealand. (A) Which firm has a higher percentage of variable operating costs denominated in the local currency? (B) CAB's FX operating exposure to the New Zealand dollar will likely (a) increase; (b) decrease; or (c) not change.

Answers: (A) CAB; (B) (b) decrease, because CAB has a higher percentage of variable operating costs in the local currency.

Note that we could also think of either UPF or EPF as a Eurozone firm, with a home currency of euros and an interest in measuring FX exposure to the U.S. dollar. Say EPF is a Eurozone firm. With no competition, EPF would have a negative FX operating exposure to the U.S. dollar, because of the aluminum costs being in U.S. dollars. However, competition with UPF will create a positive influence on EPF's FX operating exposure <u>to the U.S. dollar</u>, for the same reason that the competition has a negative impact on EPF's FX operating exposure to the euro. To see this point, note that an asset's FX exposure to the euro from the U.S. dollar's point of view, $\xi_{O\epsilon}^{\$}$, plus the asset's FX exposure to the U.S. dollar from the euro point of view, $\xi_{O\$}^{\epsilon}$, sum to 1.[11] That is, $1 - \xi_{O\epsilon}^{\$} = \xi_{O\$}^{\epsilon}$. So if EPF's $\xi_{O\epsilon}^{\$}$ of 0.94 is lower than if EPF is the sole firm, 1.56, we have that EPF's $\xi_{O\$}^{\epsilon}$ of 0.06 is higher than if EPF is the sole firm, –0.56. You can verify these FX operating exposures by simply viewing the operating cash flows in euros rather than in U.S. dollars. For example, if the euro depreciates by 10%, from 1.25 $/€ to 1.125 $/€, and EPF's operating cash flow drops from $71.375 to $64.68, as in Exhibit 1.3b, the equivalent operating cash flow in euros <u>rises</u> by 0.69%, from €57.10 to €57.49, and the U.S. dollar appreciates by 11.1%, from 0.80 €/$ to 0.889 €/$. The FX operating exposure to the U.S. dollar is 0.0069/0.111 = 0.06.

This scenario seems typical: the local firm has more local currency operating costs than an exporting foreign competitor. In this case, competition typically implies both a higher exporter's FX operating exposure to the local currency and a higher local firm's FX exposure to the exporter's currency.

That said, it is instructive to consider a less typical scenario where UPF is a Eurozone firm and EPF is a U.S. firm. UPF produces the fittings in the United States, and then imports the fittings for sale in the Eurozone, with no operating costs denominated in euros. EPF exports unfinished fittings from the United States to the Eurozone and then incurs significant variable operating costs denominated in euros. In competition with EPF, UPF's FX operating exposure to the U.S. dollar would be –2.93, given that the FX operating exposure to the euro is 3.93. This FX exposure to the U.S. dollar is lower than if UPF were the sole firm in the industry, which would be –1.04, based on the $\xi_{O\epsilon}^{\$}$ = 2.04 result seen earlier. So, in this scenario, competition implies both a lower exporter's FX operating exposure to the local currency and a lower local firm's FX exposure to the exporter's currency. Here, the U.S. exporter, EPF, has more operating costs denominated in the local currency than the local Eurozone firm, UPF.

DET Ltd. is a UK manufacturer of precision instruments. For some years, DET's local UK sales had virtually no competition. Recently, a U.S. competitor began exporting similar instruments to the UK market. (A) Which firm has more variable operating costs denominated in the local currency? (B) DET's FX operating exposure to the U.S. dollar has likely (a) increased; (b) decreased; or (c) not changed.

Answers: A) DET; B) (a) increased; if DET were a subsidiary of a U.S. parent, the FX operating exposure to the pound would be lower under competition, because DET produces locally and is competing against a U.S. exporter that presumably has lower variable operating costs incurred in pounds. But DET is a UK firm, so the perspective of the FX exposure is to the U.S. dollar.

UZN Company is a U.S. manufacturer of precision instruments. For some years, UZN's exports to New Zealand had virtually no competition. Recently, a New Zealand company began producing and selling similar instruments domestically. (A) Which firm has more variable operating costs denominated in the local currency? (B) UZN's FX operating exposure to the New Zealand dollar has likely (a) increased; (b) decreased; or (c) not changed.

Answers: (A) the New Zealand competitor; (B) (a) increased. It does not matter whether the new competitor is a New Zealand firm or a U.S. firm, but whether the new competitor has more variable operating costs in the local currency.

Regression Estimates of FX Operating Exposure

Volvo

The Swedish auto manufacturer, Volvo, exports substantially. As a result, Volvo has a high FX operating exposure to the U.S. dollar. This FX operating exposure was at one time estimated by regression analysis to be around 5.[12]

Vulcan Materials

Vulcan Materials used regression to estimate its UK subsidiary's FX operating exposure to the British pound, from the U.S. dollar point of view. To the managers' surprise, the estimated FX operating exposure was practically 0. In analyzing the regression result, the managers realized that, measured in U.S. dollars, Vulcan UK's sales revenues did not fluctuate with changes in the $/£ spot FX rate. The reason is that Vulcan UK sells metals like aluminum whose prices in British pounds are indexed to the $/£ spot FX rate, so that the price is essentially stable when viewed from the perspective of U.S. dollars. Moreover, the market price for the raw materials (scrap metal) is also relatively stable in U.S. dollars. Because both the revenues and costs of Vulcan UK are relatively stable when viewed in U.S. dollars, the approximate FX operating exposure to the pound is 0, even though the subsidiary's sales and production are totally in the United Kingdom.[13]

Summary Action Points
- A firm's FX operating exposure to a currency depends on its business, the currency location of its operating costs, its competition, and so forth. Some FX operating exposures are positive and some are negative.

- Operational hedging reduces a positive FX operating exposure by matching operating costs and revenues exposed to the same currency. Locating production in a country with the same currency to which revenues are exposed is one form of operational hedging.
- FX pass-through is another operational strategy that a firm may be able to use to manage FX operating exposure. The viability of an FX pass-through strategy depends on the product's price elasticity of demand and the extent of local competition.
- When firms compete and have different strategies for operational hedging, the firm that does less operational hedging will have the higher FX operating exposure to the local currency.

Glossary

Competitive FX Exposure: A type of FX economic exposure that focuses on the impact of competition.

Currency Habitat of Price: Term used to indicate the currency in which, due to the particular economic circumstances, the price of a good is effectively set.

FX Economic Exposure: A type of FX operating exposure that focuses on the impact of economic variables.

FX Operating Exposure: A type of FX exposure that focuses on the variability in a firm's ongoing operating cash flow stream caused by uncertain FX rate changes.

FX Pass-Through: The change in product price in response to an FX rate change, such that some or all of the FX change is passed along to the customers.

Operating Leverage: The use of fixed operating costs instead of variable operating costs.

Operational Hedging: The arranging of a firm's operating costs to match the currency to which its revenues are exposed.

Price Elasticity of Demand: The percentage change in a product's volume of demand, given the percentage change in the product's price.

Discussion Questions

1. Explain why an exporter tends to have a positive (long) FX operating exposure to a currency, and why an importer tends to have a negative (short) FX operating exposure to a currency.

2. Explain a scenario where an exporter does *not* have a positive FX operating exposure to a currency, and a scenario where an importer does *not* have a negative FX operating exposure to a currency.

3. Explain the role of operational hedging when an exporter competes with a local firm.

4. Explain how increased competition can cause a firm's FX operating exposure to a currency to be (a) higher and (b) lower.

Problems

1. A U.S. company has $500 in expected operating cash flow measured in U.S. dollars, given the current spot FX rate of 0.90 $/A$. The company has an FX operating exposure to the Australian dollar, $\xi_{OAS}^{\$}$, of 0.60. If the Australian dollar unexpectedly appreciates by 20% (relative to the U.S. dollar), what is the firm's new operating cash flow in U.S. dollars?

2. A U.S. company has $500 in expected operating cash flow measured in U.S. dollars, given a current spot FX rate of 0.90 $/A$. The company has an FX operating exposure to the Australian dollar, $\xi_{OAS}^{\$}$, of −0.60. If the Australian dollar unexpectedly appreciates by 20% (relative to the U.S. dollar), what is the firm's new operating cash flow in U.S. dollars?

For 3–5: UWK Co. produces components in the United States for sale in England. At the current spot FX rate of 2 $/£, UWK expects to sell 500 components at £1 each. Each component requires half a pound of aluminum, at $0.80 per pound. Other than aluminum, each component's variable production cost is $0.80. Fixed operating costs are $200. UWK is owned by the U.S. multinational, ABC. ABC's management wants a "what if" scenario of

UWK's operating cash flow measured in U.S. dollars, given 20% depreciation the British pound.

3. (a) What is UWK's initial expected revenue in U.S. dollars? (b) What
   is UWK's initial expected operating cash flow in U.S. dollars?

4. UWK's managers tell ABC that if the British pound depreciates by
   20%, to 1.60 $/£, UWK would not adjust the local currency com-
   ponent price nor the volume of components produced. What is
   UWK's FX operating exposure to the British pound?

5. ABC suggests to UWK that it can pass through 25% of FX rate changes
   into the local currency component prices without affecting demand. If
   so, what would be UWK's FX operating exposure to the British pound?

For 6–8, extend problems 3–5: ABC ponders moving UWK's production
from the United States to England. At the current spot FX rate of 2 $/£,
the company would still initially expect to sell 500 components at £1 each.
Other than aluminum, each component's variable production cost would
be £0.40. Fixed operating costs would be £100. As before, each component requires half a pound of aluminum, at $0.80 per pound. ABC wants a
"what if" scenario of UWK's operating cash flow measured in U.S. dollars,
given a 20% depreciation of the British pound.

6. (a) What is UWK's initial expected revenue in U.S. dollars? (b) What
   is UWK's initial expected operating cash flow in U.S. dollars?

7. UWK's managers tell ABC that if the pound depreciates by 20%, to
   1.60 $/£, UWK would not adjust the local currency components
   price nor the volume of components produced. Find UWK's FX
   operating exposure to the British pound.

8. ABC suggests to UWK's managers that they can pass through 25% of
   FX rate changes into the local currency component prices without affecting demand. Find UWK's FX operating exposure to the British pound.

For 9–14: ZXC Corporation makes and sells scientific instruments in the
United States. ZXC sells each instrument for $100 and expects to sell
200,000 instruments. ZXC sources instrument components from Japan. The
cost of the components is fixed in yen. For each instrument, the components
cost is ¥2,000. Other variable production costs, incurred in the assembly of

the instruments in the United States, are $25 per instrument, and the fixed operating costs are $5 million. Assume today's spot FX rate is 80 ¥/$.

9. What are ZXC's initially expected revenue and expected operating cash flow (in U.S. dollars), given today's spot FX rate is 80 ¥/$?

10. If the yen appreciates by 25%, what would be the new operating cash flow, given no FX pass-through?

11. What is ZXC's FX operating exposure to the yen, given no FX pass-through?

12. If the yen appreciates by 25%, what would be the new instrument price, given that ZXC's FX pass-through policy is 20% and that the FX pass-through does not affect sales volume?

13. If the yen appreciates by 25%, what would be the new operating cash flow in U.S. dollars, given that ZXC's FX pass-through policy is 20% and that the FX pass-through does not affect sales volume?

14. What is ZXC's FX operating exposure to the yen, given that ZXC's FX pass-through policy is 20% and that the FX pass-through does not affect sales volume?

For 15–20: GXC Corporation is a U.S. manufacturer of scientific instruments. GXC's sales are entirely in the Eurozone. GXC's selling price per instrument is currently €100. GXC expects a sales volume of 2,000 instruments. GXC sources components from the Eurozone. The cost of the components is fixed in euros. For each instrument, the components cost is €20. Other variable production costs, incurred in the assembly of the instruments in the United States, are $25 per instrument. The fixed operating costs are $50,000. Assume today's spot FX rate is 1.25 $/€.

15. What are GXC's initially expected revenue and expected operating cash flow (in U.S. dollars), given today's spot FX rate is 1.25 $/€?

16. If the euro were to depreciate by 20%, what would be the new instrument price in euros if GXC passes through 100% of the FX change?

17. If GXC passes through 100% of FX changes with no change in customer demand, what is GXC's FX operating exposure to the euro?

For 18–20: Still at time 0, GXC is worried about customer reaction to the full FX pass-through policy, so GXC decides to pass through only 60% of any spot FX change to the customers. The customers have indicated they will not change their order levels in the face of these changes in instrument price.

18. If the euro were to depreciate by 20%, what would be the new instrument price in euros?

19. If the euro were to depreciate by 20% (from 1.25 $/€), what would be the new operating cash flow in U.S. dollars?

20. What is GXC's FX operating exposure to the euro?

For 21–23: TBR Company is a U.S. exporter of a small motor component to the Eurozone. The price per component is €10 and TBR expects to sell 1 million components, given the present spot FX rate of 1.30 $/€. The variable cost of producing in the United States is $6 per component, and the fixed operating cost is $1,000,000. After the product reaches Europe, the variable cost of distributing the components is €2 each and the fixed operating cost is €1,000,000. When the spot FX rate changes, the production and distribution costs are stable in the currency in which the cost is incurred.

21. Find TBR's optimal FX pass-through policy assuming that sales volume changes when price changes, based on the price elasticity of demand.

22. Assume TBR decides to pass through 70% of any FX change to the customers. Find the new component price if the euro depreciates by 10%.

23. Assume the price elasticity of demand for TBR's product is 1.50 and that TBR has no competitor. Find the FX operating exposure to the euro using a "what if" scenario where the euro depreciates by 10%.

24. GBT is a U.S. multinational. GBT's subsidiary in the UK produces locally. For a few years, GBT's British subsidiary had virtually no competition. Over the recent past, however, another U.S. company has started exporting similar products to the British market, and has proven to be a credible competitor. (A) Which firm has more operating costs denominated in the local currency? (B) Over time, GBT's FX operating exposure to the British pound has likely (a) increased; (b) decreased; or (c) not changed.

25. ABC is a U.S. manufacturer. For a few years, ABC's exports to the United Kingdom had virtually no competition. Over the recent past, another U.S. company has built a plant in England to produce and sell similar products in the British market. (A) Which firm has more operating costs denominated in the local currency? (B) Over time, ABC's FX operating exposure to the British pound has likely (a) increased, (b) decreased, or (c) not changed.

26. ABC Company is a U.S. manufacturer of precision instruments. For a few years, ABC's local U.S. sales had virtually no competition. Over the recent past, an Australian company has proven to be a credible competitor in exporting similar instruments to the U.S. market. (A) Which firm has more operating costs denominated in the local currency? (B) Over time, ABC's FX operating exposure to the Australian dollar has likely (a) increased, (b) decreased, or (c) not changed.

27. DET Ltd. is a UK manufacturer of precision instruments. For some years DEK's exports to the United States had virtually no competition. Over the recent past, however, a U.S. company has proven to be a credible competitor in producing and selling similar instruments in the U.S. market. (A) Which firm has more operating costs denominated in the local currency? (B) Over time, DET's FX operating exposure to the U.S. dollar has likely (a) increased, (b) decreased, or (c) not changed.

Answers to Problems

1. $560.
2. $440.
3. (a) $1,000. (b) $200.
4. 5.
5. 3.75.
6. (a) $1,000. (b) $200.
7. 2.
8. 0.75.
9. Expected revenue is $100(200,000) = $20 million. The cost of the components is ¥2,000(200,000)/(80 ¥/$) = $5 million. So the expected

operating cash flow is $20 million – 5 million – $25(200,000) – $5 million = $5 million.

10. In U.S. dollars, the cost of the components is now higher, ¥2,000 (200,000)/(64 ¥/$) = $6.25 million. Thus the operating cash flow is now lower, $20 million – 6.25 million – $25(200,000) – $5 million = $3.75 million.

11. The operating cash flow drops by 25%, from $5 million to $3.75 million, when the yen appreciates by 25%. Hence ZXC's FX operating exposure to the yen is $\xi_{O¥}^{\$} = -0.25/0.25 = -1$.

12. The selling price for instruments is adjusted higher by 0.20(25%) = 5%, to $105.

13. The new operating cash flow is $21 million – 6.25 million – $25(200,000) – $5 million = $4.75 million.

14. Operating cash flow drops by 5%, from $5 million to $4.75 million, when the yen appreciates by 25%. Hence ZXC's FX operating exposure to the yen, $\xi_{O¥}^{\$}$, is –0.05/0.25 = –0.20.

15. $R^{\$}$ = (1.25 $/€)(€100)(2,000) = $250,000; $O^{\$}$ = $250,000 – €20(2,000)(1.25 $/€) – $25(2,000) – $50,000 = $100,000.

16. €125.

17. If the euro depreciates by 20%, new $O^{\$}$ = $250,000 – €20(2,000)(1 $/€) – $25(2,000) – $50,000 = $110,000; So operating cash flow rises by 10%, when the euro depreciates by 20%; FX operating exposure to the euro = –0.50.

18. €100(1.15) = €115.

19. $O^{\$}$ = €115(2,000)(1 $/€) – €20(2,000)(1 $/€) – $25(2,000) – $50,000 = $90,000.

20. –0.10/–0.20 = 0.50.

21. Convert the euro variable operating cost per component to U.S. dollars: €2(1.30 $/€) = $2.60. The ratio of non-euro variable operating cost to total variable operating cost is $6/8.6 = 0.70. The optimal FX pass-through policy is 70%.

22. The product price will change by 0.70 times (1/(1 – 0.10) – 1), or 0.70(0.111) = 0.078, or 7.8%. So the new price will be €10.78.

23. TBR's initial expected operating cash flow in U.S. dollars is (1.30 $/€) (€10)(1,000,000) – $8.60(1,000,000) – 1,000,000 – 1,300,000 = $2,100,000. If TBR raises the fittings price in euros by 7.8%, to

€10.78, sales volume would drop by 1.50(7.8%), or 11.7%. So TBR's sales volume drops to $(1 - 0.117)1,000,000$, or 883,000. TBR's "what if" operating cash flow in U.S. dollars would be $(1.17 \ \$/€)(€10.78)883,000 - \$6(883,000) - (1.17 \ \$/€)(€2)(883,000) - 1,000,000 - (1.17 \ \$/€)€1,000,000 = \$1,602,706$, a drop of 23.7% from the initial operating cash flow of $2,100,000. The "what if" estimate of TBR's FX operating exposure is thus $-0.237/-0.10 = 2.37$.

24. (A) GBT. (B) (b) Decreased. Because the new competitor exports products made in the United States, whereas GBT produces locally in the UK, GBT has more operating costs in local currency. So GBT is like the EPF firm in the text, and GBT's FX exposure will be lower, given the new setting where GBT competes with a firm with no operating costs in the local currency.

25. (A) The new competitor. (B) (a) Increased. This is the complementary scenario to the previous problem. In this case, the new competitor has more operating costs in the local currency, so the first company's FX exposure is higher in the competitive setting than with not competition.

26. (A) ABC. (B) (a) Increased. ABC has more operating costs denominated in the local currency (the U.S. dollar). So if ABC were the U.S. subsidiary of an Australian parent that measures FX exposure to the U.S. dollar, competition would make that FX exposure lower. But ABC measures its FX exposure to the Australian dollar. From that currency perspective, competition makes ABC's FX exposure higher.

27. (A) The new competitor. (B) (a) Increased. The new competitor has more operating costs denominated in the local currency, so DET's FX exposure to the U.S. dollar will be higher in competition than with no competition.

CHAPTER 2

FX Exposure: Business, Equity, and Translation

This chapter looks at three more types of FX exposure. The first is *FX business exposure*, which is the effect of FX rate changes on an operation's *business value*. Business value is what an operation would be worth if it has no debt and no cash and marketable securities. The second is *FX equity exposure*, which is the sensitivity of a firm's equity share value to unexpected FX rate changes. The third is *FX translation exposure*, which is the accounting impact of FX rate changes on the reported financial results, particularly the equity book value, of a firm that owns a foreign business operation.

Business Value

Finance theory tells us that a firm's intrinsic business value is the present value of the firm's future expected operating cash flow stream. Let $V_B^{\$}$ denote business value in U.S. dollars; $E(O_t^{\$})$ the expected operating cash flow in U.S. dollars at time t; $k^{\$}$ the discount rate to apply, based on the risk of the operating cash flows; and N the number of years that operating cash flows are expected. The present value in U.S. dollars of the expected operating cash flow stream is thus $V_B^{\$} = \sum_{t=1,N} E(O_t^{\$})/(1 + k^{\$})^t$.

For simplicity, we'll use the standard *constant growth model*, which assumes that the cash flow stream is expected to grow at a constant rate into perpetuity. Given that a firm's operating cash flows (measured in U.S. dollars) are expected to grow perpetually at a constant rate, $g^{\$}$, and letting $E(O^{\$})$ be the initial operating cash flow, the intrinsic business value is shown in the formula in equation (2.1).

Constant Growth Model

$$V_B^{\$} = E(O^{\$})/(k^{\$} - g^{\$}) \qquad (2.1)$$

For example, assume RPC Company's future operating cash flows are expected to start with $200 and grow perpetually at an annual rate of 6%. RPC's managers estimate the business's discount rate, or cost of capital, in U.S. dollars is $k^\$ = 11\%$. We can apply equation (2.1) to find the intrinsic business value in U.S. dollars: $\$200/(0.11 - 0.06) = \$4,000$.

ANC Company expects future operating cash flows of $1 million initially and a growth rate of 5% per annum. The discount rate is 7.5%. What is ANC's intrinsic business value in U.S. dollars?

Answer: $1 million/$(0.075 - 0.05) = \$40$ million.

FX Business Exposure

We know that if a firm has FX operating exposure to the British pound, the operating cash flow (in U.S. dollars) changes as the spot FX rate for the pound changes. A change in the spot FX rate tends to also affect the forecast of future spot FX rates, which in turn affects the expected future operating cash flows (in U.S. dollars). So a change in the current spot FX rate will affect the expectation of the *entire stream* of future operating cash flows and thus their present value. The term *FX business exposure* describes the elasticity of the business value to changes in the spot FX price of a foreign currency. We'll use the notation $\xi_{B\pounds}^{\$}$ for the FX business exposure to the British pound.

For simplicity, we assume from here on that an operation's FX business exposure is the same number as its FX operating exposure. That is, $\xi_{B\pounds}^{\$} = \xi_{O\pounds}^{\$}$. One way to justify this assumption is to say that when the spot FX rate changes, the expected level of <u>all</u> future expected operating cash flows changes by the same percentage as the first operating cash flow, and that the discount rate is not affected by FX rate changes.

Suppose for example that a U.S. firm has an expected operating cash flow stream of $1,000 per year into perpetuity (zero growth) and the discount rate is 10%. Thus the intrinsic business value is initially $\$1,000/0.10 = \$10,000$, using equation (2.1). Assume further that the firm's FX operating exposure to the British pound, $\xi_{O\pounds}^{\$}$, is 1.20. So we know that if the British pound unexpectedly depreciates by 15%, the new initial operating cash flow (in U.S. dollars) will change by $1.20(-0.15) = -0.18$, or will drop by 18%, and thus will be 0.82($1,000) = $820. Given the expectation that each future operating cash flow will also be lower by 18%, the new expected future operating cash flow stream will be $820 per year into perpetuity. Given that the discount rate is unaffected by the spot FX change, the new intrinsic business value is $820/0.10 = $8,200. Thus, we see that the percentage change in the intrinsic business value is $8,200/$10,000 − 1 = −0.18, or −18%, the same as the percentage change in the initial operating cash flow.

A U.S. firm expects an operating cash flow stream that starts with $100 and grows perpetually at the constant rate of 5% per year. The discount rate is 10%. The firm's FX operating exposure to the British pound, $\xi_{O\pounds}^{\$}$, is 0.90. Assume that when the spot FX rate changes, all future expected operating cash flows change by the same percentage. (a) Find the initial intrinsic business value. (b) Find the FX business exposure to the British pound. (c) Next assume the pound appreciates by 10%. Find the new intrinsic business value and the percentage change in the intrinsic business value.

Answers: (a) Using equation (2.1), the initial $V_B^{\$}$ is $100/(0.10 − 0.05) = $2,000. (b) The FX business exposure equals the FX operating exposure, 0.90. (c) Each component of the expected future operating cash flow stream will change by 0.90(10%) = 9%, so the new expected operating cash flow stream is a perpetuity of $100(1.09) = $109 per year. Given the discount rate of 10%, the new $V_B^{\$}$ is $109/(0.10 − 0.05) = $2,180. The percentage change in $V_B^{\$}$ is $2,180/$2,000 − 1 = 0.09, or 9%.

MANY SMEs FAIL to GRASP FX RISK

A study by the Association of Chartered and Certified Accountants and Kantox, a foreign exchange provider, found that finance officers in small and medium-sized enterprises (SMEs) do not usually understand or sufficiently hedge foreign exchange risk. The report profiled 119 SMEs in 15 countries that had median revenues of about $200 million and traded about 19 per cent of revenue a year in foreign currencies. A third of the respondents reported gains or losses exceeding $1 million.

Philippe Gelis, chief executive of Kantox, said, "Finance officers know they have an exposure, but knowing and managing that exposure is not really their core business. They focus on selling and planning cash flow, but not so much on protecting their margins. Unless companies have suffered a significant FX loss, they do not hedge. While they know there is a risk, they do not have a formal policy. It's really reactive. Sales are nice, but if the profit margin on those sales is lost in poor FX management, then it's a pity. It's nice to grow, but nicer to grow profitably."

Source: *Financial Times*, September 16, 2013 (Liz Bolshaw)

Business Value and Enterprise Value

Business value is similar to *enterprise value*, which is equal to *equity market cap* plus *net debt*. Equity market cap refers to the market capitalization value of the firm's equity, which is equal to the market price per share times the number of shares outstanding. Net debt is debt minus cash, where cash includes marketable securities. For example, assume GCH Co. has 10 million shares outstanding. The share price is $40, so the firm's equity market cap is $400 million. The firm has $100 million in cash and $250 million in debt, so the net debt is $150 million. The enterprise value is $400 million + $150 million = $550 million. The difference between the firm's enterprise value and its total value is shown below in Exhibit 2.1.

Exhibit 2.1. **GCH Co: Value Balance Sheet**

Cash	$100 million	Debt	$250 million
Enterprise Value	550 million	Equity	400 million
Total Value	$650 million	Total Capital	$650 million

ABC Company has 20 million shares outstanding. The share price is $30. The company has $100 million in cash and $200 million in debt. Find ABC's enterprise value.

Answer: The firm's equity market cap is $600 million. The net debt is $100 million. The enterprise value is $600 million + $100 million = $700 million.

Researchers have found that the average U.S. industrial firm's cash balance grew steadily since the 1980s, and by 2006 the cross-sectional average net debt was zero.[1] In fact, these days it is more and more common for a company's risk management strategy to include little or no debt and a relatively large cash balance. If a firm's cash exceeds the firm's debt, then net debt is negative, but the arithmetic for enterprise value is the same. For example, assume HGC Co. has an equity market cap of $400 million. The firm has $100 million in debt and $250 million in cash, so the net debt is −$150 million. The enterprise value is $400 million − $150 million = $250 million.

Because firms differ in their debt and cash levels, both business value and enterprise value are meant to strip those choices out and give an idea of the value of a business, ignoring debt and cash positions. But in principle, there is a difference between a firm's business and enterprise values. The difference is that enterprise value includes the value of the firm's debt tax shields, but business value does not. In academic corporate finance circles, business value is sometimes called the operation's *unlevered value*, while enterprise value is called its *levered value*.

For many years, the tax shield value of debt interest was a standard theme in academic corporate finance, following the famous theory of Miller and Modigliani and despite Miller's extension that debt tax shield values are likely to be lower than originally theorized.[2] Also, the recent U.S. corporate trend toward reduced net debt levels suggests that firms do not think that debt tax shield value is critically important. For these reasons and to focus more clearly on international finance issues, this text ignores debt tax shield value, and so regards business value and enterprise value as generally the same. That said, we will cover some aspects of debt and taxes in the next chapter.

FX Business Exposure of a Multinational

Many real-world companies have multiple operations, and each operation may have a different FX business exposure to a given currency. The overall company's FX business exposure to the currency is thus a combination of the FX business exposures of the individual operations.

Consider GGT Company, a hypothetical U.S. multinational consisting of three different business operations that sell industrial materials in three different countries: the United States, Italy (in the Eurozone), and Spain (also in the Eurozone). Assume that the U.S. operation, UST, has a business value of $35 million, and UST's FX business exposure to the euro is –0.20, due to the importing of parts from the Eurozone. The Italian subsidiary, IRT, sells materials in Italy that are produced entirely in the United States. IRT's business value in U.S. dollars is $5 million. From the U.S. dollar perspective, IRT's FX business exposure to the euro is 2.50. The Spanish business, SPT, operates entirely in Spain. SPT's business value in U.S. dollars is $10 million. From the U.S. dollar perspective, SPT's FX business exposure to the euro is 1. What is the FX business exposure to the euro of the overall multinational company, GGT?

To answer the question, view the overall multinational company as a portfolio of its business operations. The portfolio weights are based on the business values. The total value of all of GGT's businesses is $35 million + 5 million + 10 million = $50 million. So the portfolio weight for UST is $35 million/$50 million = 0.70; the weight for IRT is $5 million/$50 million = 0.10; and the weight for SPT is $10 million/$50 million = 0.20. Using the portfolio weights and the FX business exposures, GGT's overall FX business exposure to the euro is 0.70(–0.20) + 0.10(2.50) + 0.20(1) = 0.31.

The U.S. multinational ISB Co. consists of three businesses that sell industrial materials in three countries: the United States, Belgium (in the Eurozone), and Germany (in the Eurozone). The U.S. operation has a business value of $50 million with no FX business exposure to the euro. The Belgian business produces in the United States and sells in Belgium; the business value in U.S. dollars is $20 million, and the FX business exposure to the euro is 2. The German business consists of two subsidiaries; one is a U.S. company that produces components and ships them to the other, in Germany, for assembly and distribution. The total business value in U.S. dollars of both companies of the German business is $30 million, and the German business has an FX business exposure to the euro of 1.50. What is the ISB's FX business exposure to the euro?

Answer: 0.50(0) + 0.20(2) + 0.30(1.50) = 0.85.

FX Equity Exposure

A firm's *FX equity exposure* to a foreign currency is the elasticity of the equity value to changes in the spot FX price of the currency, viewed from the perspective of the firm's home currency. We use the "S" (for "stock") for equity notation, so $S^\$$ denotes the equity value in U.S. dollars. A U.S. firm's FX equity exposure to the euro is denoted $\xi_{S\epsilon}^\$$ and is computed as $\%\Delta S^\$/x^{\$/\epsilon}$, the percentage change in the equity value in U.S. dollars, given the percentage change in the euro.

Three elements determine a firm's FX equity exposure to a currency: (a) the firm's FX business exposure to the currency; (b) the *net financial leverage ratio*, which is the ratio of net debt to business value; and (c) the relative amount of net debt denominated in the exposure currency. We'll look at the effects of foreign currency net debt in the next chapter. For this chapter, we focus on the case where net debt is entirely in the home currency. FX changes have no impact on the home currency value of net debt denominated in the home currency.

Assume the U.S. firm XYZ Co. has (a) an FX business exposure to the euro, $\xi_{Be}^\$$, of **1.20**; (b) a business value in U.S. dollars of $2,000; and (c) net debt, $ND^\$$, of $600. Thus, the equity value is initially $S^\$ = \$2,000 - 600 = \$1,400$, as shown in the top panel of Exhibit 2.2.

Assume a "what if" 5% depreciation of the euro. Due to the FX business exposure of 1.20, this spot FX change will causes a 6% drop in the

Exhibit 2.2. XYZ Company Value Balance Sheet $600 Net Debt

Initial		
	Value	*Net Debt & Equity*
		$ 600 Net Debt
	$2,000 $V_B^\$$	1,400 $S^\$$
	$2,000	$2,000
"What if" the Euro Depreciates by 5%?		
	Value	*Net Debt & Equity*
		$ 600 Net Debt
	$1,880 $V_B^\$$	1,280 $S^\$$
	$1,880	$1,880

business value, to 0.94($2,000) = $1,880. Because XYZ's $600 in net debt is denominated entirely in U.S. dollars, the spot FX change has no impact on the net debt. So XYZ's "what if" equity value is $1,880 – 600 = $1,280. See the bottom panel of Exhibit 2.2.

The percentage change in XYZ's equity value is $1,280/$1,400 – 1 = –0.0857, or an 8.57% drop. In short, a 5% depreciation of the euro results in an 8.57% drop in the equity value, implying that XYZ's FX equity exposure to the euro, $\xi_{S\epsilon}^{\$}$, is –0.0857/–0.05 = **1.71**.

XYZ's FX equity exposure to the euro, 1.71, is higher than its FX business exposure, 1.20, due to the impact of the financial leverage. To see this point, consider the same XYZ Company with the same business value of $2,000 and a higher net financial leverage ratio, 0.40 instead of 0.30. So the initial net debt is $800 and initial equity value of $1,200, as shown in the top panel of Exhibit 2.3. Because the net debt stays at $800 when the spot FX rate changes, XYZ's "what if" equity value is $1,880 – 800 = $1,080. See the bottom panel of Exhibit 2.3. The percentage change in XYZ's equity value is $1,080/$1,200 – 1 = –0.10, or a 10% drop. So a 5% depreciation of the euro results in a 10% drop in equity value, implying an FX equity exposure to the euro of –0.10/–0.05 = 2. This example shows that a higher net financial leverage ratio implies a higher FX equity exposure for a given FX business exposure.

Now we'll create a scenario where the net debt is negative. In this case, we'll see that the FX equity exposure is lower than the FX business

Exhibit 2.3. XYZ Company Value Balance Sheet $800 Net Debt

Initial		
	Value	*Net Debt & Equity*
		$ 800 Net Debt
	$2,000 $V_B^{\$}$	1,200 $S^{\$}$
	$2,000	$2,000
"What if" the Euro Depreciates by 5%?		
	Value	*Net Debt & Equity*
		$ 800 Net Debt
	$1,880 $V_B^{\$}$	1,080 $S^{\$}$
	$1,880	$1,880

Exhibit 2.4. *XYZ Company Value Balance Sheet* –$800 *Net Debt*

Initial		
	Value	_Net Debt & Equity_
		–$ 800 Net Debt
	$2,000 $V_B^\$$	2,800 $S^\$$
	$2,000	$2,000
"What if" the Euro Depreciates by 5%?		
	Value	_Net Debt & Equity_
		–$ 800 Net Debt
	$1,880 $V_B^\$$	2,680 $S^\$$
	$1,880	$1,880

exposure. Consider the same XYZ operation as before, except with $ND^\$/V_B^\$ = -0.40$. Now the initial net debt is –$800 and equity value is $2,800, as shown in the top panel of Exhibit 2.4. Because the net debt stays at –$800 when the spot FX rate changes, XYZ's "what if" equity value is $1,880 – (–800) = $2,680. See the bottom panel of Exhibit 2.4. The percentage change in equity value is $2,680/$2,800 – 1 = –0.043, or a 4.3% drop. So a 5% depreciation of the euro results in a 4.3% drop in the equity value, implying an FX equity exposure to the euro is –0.043/–0.05 = 0.86.

A formula for FX equity exposure as a function of FX business exposure and the net financial leverage ratio, $ND^\$/V_B^\$$, is shown in equation (2.2):[3]

FX Equity Exposure

$$\xi_{S\epsilon}^\$ = \xi_{B\epsilon}^\$ / (1 - ND^\$/V_B^\$) \qquad (2.2)$$

We demonstrate equation (2.2) using the XYZ examples. If XYZ's net debt is $600 and equity value is $1,400, $ND^\$/V_B^\$ = \$600/\$2,000 = 0.30$. Using equation (2.2), we get $\xi_{S\epsilon}^\$ = (1.20 - 0)/(1 - 0.30) = 1.71$, as seen earlier. In the second scenario, where net debt is $800 and equity value is $1,200, $ND^\$/V_B^\$ = \$800/\$2,000 = 0.40$. Using equation (2.2), we get $\xi_{S\epsilon}^\$ = 1.20/(1 - 0.40) = 2$. In the third scenario, where the net debt is –$800 and the equity value is $2,800, $ND^\$/V_B^\$ = -\$800/\$2,000 = -0.40$. Using equation (2.2), we get $\xi_{S\epsilon}^\$ = 1.20/(1 - (-0.40)) = 0.86$.

The U.S. firm ABC Co. has $V_B^\$ = \$5,000$, $ND^\$ = \$2,000$, and thus $S^\$ = \$3,000$. All of ABC's net debt is U.S. dollar-denominated. ABC's FX business exposure to the euro is 0.80. (a) Find the new value of ABC's equity, and the FX equity exposure directly by the "what if" approach, given a 10% depreciation of the euro. (b) Verify the FX equity exposure using equation (2.2).

Answers: (a) ABC's business value will change by 0.80(–10%), or –8%, to $4,600, when the euro depreciates by 10%. The net debt stays at $2,000. The "what if" equity value is $4,600 – 2,000 = $2,600. The change in equity value is by $2,600/$3,000 – 1 = –0.133, or –13.3%. The FX equity exposure is –0.133/–0.10 = 1.33. (b) Because $ND^\$/V_B^\$ = 0.40$, the FX equity exposure is consistent with equation (2.2): $\xi_{S\epsilon}^\$ = 0.80/(1 – 0.40) = 1.33$.

The U.S. firm DEF Co. has $V_B^\$ = \$5,000$, $ND^\$ = \$3,000$, and thus $S^\$ = \$2,000$. All of DEF's net debt is U.S. dollar-denominated. DEF's FX business exposure to the euro is 0.80. (a) Find the new value of DEF's equity, and the FX equity exposure directly by the "what if" approach, given a 10% depreciation of the euro. (b) Verify the FX equity exposure using equation (2.2).

Answers: (a) DEF's business value will change by 0.80(–10%), or –8%, to $4,600, when the euro depreciates by 10%. The net debt stays at $3,000. The "what if" equity value is $4,600 – 3,000 = $1,600. The equity value changes by $1,600/$2,000 – 1 = –0.20, or –20%. The FX equity exposure is –0.20/–0.10 = 2. (b) Because $ND^\$/V_B^\$ = 0.60$, the FX equity exposure is consistent with equation (2.2): $\xi_{S\epsilon}^\$ = 0.80/(1 – 0.60) = 2$.

The U.S. firm GHI Co. has $V_B^\$ = \$5,000$, $ND^\$ = -\$2,000$, and so $S^\$ = \$7,000$. All of GHI's net debt is U.S. dollar-denominated. GHI's FX business exposure to the euro is 0.80. (a) Find the new value of GHI's equity, and the FX equity exposure directly by the "what if" approach, given a 10% depreciation in the euro. (b) Verify the FX equity exposure using equation (2.2).

Answers: (a) GHI's business value will change by 0.80(–10%), or –8%, to $4,600, when the euro depreciates by 10%. The net debt stays at –$2,000.

Thus, the "what if" equity value is $4,600 − (−2,000) = $6,600. So GHI's equity value changes by $6,600/$7,000 − 1 = −0.057, or −5.7%. The FX equity exposure is −0.057/−0.10 = 0.57. (b) Because $ND^\$/V_B^\$ =$ −0.40, the FX equity exposure is consistent with equation (2.2): $\xi_{SE}^\$ =$ 0.80/(1 − (−0.40)) = 0.57.

Financial leverage also magnifies a <u>negative</u> FX business exposure. For example, assume the U.S. firm ZYX Co. has an FX business exposure of −1.20 to the euro, a business value of $2,000, and a net debt of $600. Thus, the equity value is currently $2,000 − 600 = $1,400, as shown in the top panel of Exhibit 2.5. Assume a 5% depreciation in the euro. Owing to the FX business exposure of −1.20, this spot FX change implies a <u>rise</u> in the business value by 6%, to 1.06($2,000) = $2,120. If ZYX's $600 in net debt is denominated entirely in U.S. dollars, the net debt does not change, so ZYX's "what if" equity value is $2,120 − 600 = $1,520. See the bottom panel of Exhibit 2.5. The percentage change in ZYX's equity value is $1,520/$1,400 − 1 = 0.0857, or 8.57%. In short, a 5% depreciation in the euro results in an 8.57% <u>rise</u> in the equity value, implying that ZYX's FX equity exposure to the euro is 0.0857/−0.05 = −1.71. We confirm with equation (2.2): −1.20/(1 − 0.30) = −1.71. In this case, the firm's FX business exposure is −1.20, but the FX equity exposure is higher (in absolute value), −1.71, due to the firm's net financial leverage.

Exhibit 2.5. ZYX Company Value Balance Sheet FX Operating Exposure = −1.20; $600 Net Debt

Initial		
	Value	_Net Debt & Equity_
		$ 600 Net Debt
	$2,000 $V_B^\$$	1,400 $S^\$$
	$2,000	$2,000
"What if" the Euro Depreciates by 5%?		
	Value	_Net Debt & Equity_
		$ 600 Net Debt
	$2,120 $V_B^\$$	1,520 $S^\$$
	$2,120	$2,120

Regression Estimates of FX Equity Exposure

FX equity exposure is sometimes empirically estimated with actual stock returns. For Gillette, Merck, and General Electric, we see below the estimated FX equity exposures to the yen, the British pound, and the euro, which were computed by regressing monthly stock returns on monthly percentage spot FX changes, using data for 1999 to May 2004.

	Yen	Pound	Euro
Gillette	0.207	0.364	0.463
Merck	–0.018	0.500	–0.007
General Electric	0.785	–0.197	–0.364

Source: Author's estimates using monthly data for 1999–2004.

FX equity exposure estimates like these should be taken with a grain of salt. A firm's FX exposure to a currency applies to a given operating and financial structure at a given time, but time series observations may span a period when a firm's operating structure, capital structure, or financial risk management strategy are changing. Another issue is that FX changes may affect equity returns by affecting the discount rate for cash flows to equity. Still, FX equity return exposures estimated this way might be useful. You may want to use returns for periods longer than 1 month, because empirical research suggests that equity prices do not respond to FX changes as quickly as they should in an efficient market. This is possibly due to investors' inability to rapidly grasp the complex implications of FX changes. Similarly, estimated FX equity exposures tend to be higher the longer the horizon for the returns used in the estimation process.

Exhibit 2.6 shows the empirical FX equity exposure estimates to a major currency index (MCI) for 70 selected U.S. companies. These estimates were calculated with roughly 30 years of quarterly equity rate of return observations from 1981 through 2010. The 35 companies shown on the left in Exhibit 2.6 have a negative estimated FX equity exposure to the MCI, while those on the right have a positive estimated FX equity exposure to the MCI.

The FX exposure estimates in Exhibit 2.6 tend to have smaller magnitudes than the ones in the chapter's hypothetical examples. This is likely

Exhibit 2.6. Regression Estimates of FX Equity Exposure to Major Currency Index (MCI): Selected U.S. Stocks

Family Dollar Stores Inc	−1.42	Mcdonalds Corp	0.28
Astronics Corp	−1.30	Coca Cola Co	0.38
Genesco Inc	−1.14	Becton Dickinson & Co	0.51
American Biltrite Rubr Inc	−1.08	Tesoro Petroleum Corp	0.52
Bowmar Instrument Corp	−1.04	Alberto Culver Co	0.54
Spectrum Control Inc	−1.02	Nike Inc	0.54
Goldfield Corp	−0.98	Kellogg Co	0.55
La Barge Inc	−0.96	Air Products & Chemicals	0.56
Graham Manufacturing	−0.96	Schlumberger Ltd	0.57
Advanced Micro Devices	−0.94	Alabama Gas Corp	0.57
Continental Materials	−0.92	Murphy Oil Corp	0.62
Haverty Furniture Cos Inc	−0.90	American Greetings Corp	0.64
Home Depot Inc	−0.89	Eastman Kodak Co	0.65
Lowes Companies Inc	−0.85	Amerada Hess Corp	0.68
Arden Mayfair Inc	−0.82	Ingersoll Rand Co	0.70
Zayre Corp	−0.72	Lubrizol Corp	0.71
Todd Shipyards Corp	−0.71	Texas Instruments Inc	0.73
American Airls Inc	−0.68	Textron Inc	0.74
Lockheed Aircraft Corp	−0.64	Aluminum Company Amer	0.75
Vicon Industries Inc	−0.64	Phillips Petroleum Co	0.76
Dayton Hudson Corp	−0.63	Archer Daniels Midland Co	0.78
Hasbro Industries Inc	−0.61	National Semiconductor	0.79
Alaska Airls Inc	−0.58	Deere & Co	0.81
Southwest Airlines Co	−0.51	Nucor Corp	0.83
K R M Petroleum Corp	−0.51	Newmont Mining Corp	0.83
Boothe Computer Corp	−0.47	International Paper Co	0.89
Alpha Industries Inc	−0.47	Ashland Oil Inc	0.95
Kroger Company	−0.47	Unit Drilling & Expl Co	0.96
Limited Stores Inc	−0.47	Caterpillar Tractor Inc	0.99
International Rectifier	−0.46	Boise Cascade Corp	1.16
Winnebago Industries Inc	−0.46	Dow Chemical Co	1.21
Leggett & Platt Inc	−0.45	Halliburton Company	1.24
Northrop Corp	−0.43	Rite Aid Corp	1.26
Hershey Foods Corp	−0.43	Coeur D Alene Mines Corp	1.51
Gap Inc	−0.42	Hecla Mining Co	2.24

Source: Alain Krapl, with quarterly data from 1980 to 2010.

due, at least in part, to the use of a currency index instead of an individual currency. Companies might have a large FX equity exposure to a given currency, but a smaller FX exposure to a currency index. In addition, many of the companies are large firms, and so many are likely to have implemented risk management programs to deal with FX business exposures.

You can observe some interesting trends in the data in Exhibit 2.6. For example, airline companies (American, Alaska, and Southwest) tend to have negative FX exposure estimates. The negative FX equity exposure estimates for the aircraft producers—Lockheed and Northrop—make sense when we note that aircraft revenues are generated in U.S. dollars, but some inputs are likely priced in foreign currencies. Retailing and apparel companies also tend to have negative FX exposure estimates. Some domestic "food" companies, especially supermarket chains, tend to have negative FX exposure estimates, while multinational "food" companies like McDonalds and Coca Cola have positive FX equity exposure estimates. Other companies with positive FX equity exposure estimates include those in industries such as mining (Newmont, Coeur d'Alene, and Hecla), paper (Boise Cascade and International Paper), petroleum (Ashland, Amerada Hess, Tesoro, and Phillips), chemicals (Dow and DuPont), heavy machinery (Halliburton, Schlumberger, Deere, Textron, and Caterpillar), and industrial metals (Alcoa and Nucor).

FX Translation Exposure

Accounting rules for the preparation of consolidated financial statements require a multinational parent to make a one-time choice of the *functional currency* for each overseas affiliate (branch, subsidiary, division, and so forth). The functional currency is the currency of the primary economic environment in which the entity generates and expends cash. For most affiliates, especially in developed economies, the functional currency is the currency of the entity's country.

When the functional currency is the foreign affiliate's local currency, the accounting treatment for FX rate changes is by the so-called *modified closing rate method*. Under this method, all the affiliate's assets and liabilities are translated from their local currency to the parent's currency at the current spot FX rate, whereas the affiliate's equity is translated at a historical spot FX rate. This way, the translated values of the affiliate's balance sheet will <u>not</u> equal out, and the resulting difference represents an (unrealized) *FX translation* gain or loss. FX translation gains and losses are booked in a special account in the parent's consolidated equity, called the *Cumulative Translation Adjustment (CTA)*, which is part of the broader equity account, *Accumulated Other Comprehensive Income (AOCI)*.

An example, shown in Exhibit 2.7a, considers the U.S. parent, GGT Co., of the wholly owned Spanish subsidiary, SPT. The functional currency of SPT is the euro. The total book value of SPT's assets in euros is €8 million. Assume further that SPT has €2 million in euro-denominated debt. SPT's equity thus has a book value of €6 million. Assume the current spot FX rate is 1 $/€. SPT's assets of €8 million and liabilities of €2 million are translated into U.S. dollars at the current spot rate, as $8 million and $2 million, respectively. SPT's equity of €6 million is translated at its historical spot FX rate, which we assume to be 1.25 $/€. So SPT's equity is always translated as $7.50 million. SPT's CTA at time 0 is thus $8 million − 2 million − 7.5 million = −$1.50 million.

The *net investment* item in bold font in Exhibit 2.7a is the net book value in U.S. dollars of GGT's two equity entries for SPT: $7.50 million − 1.50 million = $6 million. GGT's net investment in SPT is also equal to the net of SPT's translated assets minus its translated liabilities, $8 million − 2 million = $6 million.

If the spot FX rate drops to 0.80 $/€ at the next accounting time (time 1), the new translation for SPT is as shown in Exhibit 2.7b. SPT's book value of assets of €8 million is translated as $6.40 million, which is a book loss of $1.60 million during the period, and SPT's book value of liabilities of €2 million is translated as $1.60 million, which is a

Exhibit 2.7a. SPT's Translated Balance Sheet <u>Time 0</u> (in $)

<u>Assets</u>		<u>Liabilities & Equity</u>	
		Debt	*$2 million*
		Equity:	
		Common	*7.50 million*
		CTA (AOCI)	*−1.50 million*
		Net Investment	**$6 million**
Assets Total	*$8 million*	*Total*	*$8 million*

Exhibit 2.7b. SPT's Translated Balance Sheet <u>*Time 1*</u> *(in $)*

Assets		Liabilities & Equity	
		Debt	$1.60 million
		Equity:	
		Common	7.50 million
		CTA (AOCI)	−2.70 million
		Net Investment	**$4.80 million**
Assets Total	$6.40 million	Total	$6.40 million

book gain of $0.40 million. So there is a net FX translation loss of $1.20 million during the period. The accounting entries will show that SPT's translated equity is still $7.50 million and that the new CTA amount for SPT is $6.40 million − 1.60 million − 7.50 million = −$2.70 million. The new book value of GGT's net investment in SPT is now $7.50 million − 2.70 million = $4.80 million. The same answer is found by $6.40 million − 1.60 million = $4.80 million, a drop of $1.20 million from the net investment book value of $6 million. The $1.20 million FX translation loss for the period is reflected as the change in the CTA (AOCI) account.

FX translation exposure is the impact of FX translation gains and losses on a parent's balance sheet and is always "1" when translation is at the current spot FX rate. For example, we saw that the book value of GGT's net investment in SPT drops by 20%, from $6 million to $4.80 million, when the euro depreciates by 20%, from 1 $/€ to 0.80 $/€.

Consider the U.S. multinational, ISB, which wholly owns the German company, GSG. The functional currency of GSG is the euro. GSG has total assets with a book value of €10 million, euro-denominated debt of €3 million, and so the equity book value is €7 million. Assume a current spot FX rate of 1.25 $/€ and a historical spot FX rate for GSG's equity of 1 $/€. (a) What is the CTA for GSG? (b) What is the book value of ISB's net investment in GSG? (c) If the spot FX rate rises to 1.50 $/€, find the new CTA, the new book value of ISB's the net investment in GSG, and the FX translation gain/loss. (d) Show that the

FX translation exposure of the book value of ISB's net investment in GSG is 1.

Answers:

a. GSG's assets of €10 million and liabilities of €3 million are translated into U.S. dollars at the current spot rate, as $12.5 million and $3.75 million, respectively. GSG's equity of €7 million is translated at its historical spot FX rate, as $7 million. GSG's CTA at time 0 is thus $12.5 million − 3.75 million − 7 million = $1.75 million.

b. The net book value in U.S. dollars of GSG's two equity entries is $7 million + 1.75 million = $8.75 million, which is the book value of ISB's net investment in GSG, also equal to GSG's translated assets minus its translated liabilities, $12.5 million − 3.75 million = $8.75 million.

c. GSG's assets of €10 million and liabilities of €3 million are translated at the current spot rate, as $15 million and $4.5 million, respectively. GSG's equity of €7 million is translated at its historical spot FX rate, as $7 million. GSG's CTA at time 1 is $15 million − 4.5 million − 7 million = $3.5 million. The net book value in U.S. dollars of GSG's two equity entries is $7 million + 3.5 million = $10.5 million, which is the new book value of ISB's net investment in GSG, and also equal to the net of GSG's translated assets minus its translated liabilities, $15 million − 4.5 million = $10.5 million. There is an FX translation gain on ISB's net investment from time 0 to time 1 of $10.5 million − 8.75 million = $1.75 million. This gain is the same as the change in the CTA account, $3.50 million − 1.75 million = $1.75 million.

d. The FX translation gain of $1.75 million is a 20% increase in the book value of ISB's net investment in GSG, given the time 0 level of $8.75 million. Because the euro appreciates by 20% in the FX change from 1.25 $/€ to 1.50 $/€, the FX translation exposure is 1.

FX translation gains and losses are not included in a parent's current reported earnings when a foreign currency is the functional currency of the affiliate. Basically, the FX translation gains and losses are reserved in the CTA (AOCI) account until the affiliate gets liquidated (if ever), at which time the accumulated FX translation gain or loss up to that point will get included in computation of the parent's current earnings.

In some cases, usually in an emerging market affiliate, a U.S. parent elects to make the functional currency the U.S. dollar. A typical example of this is an affiliate in a less developed country, like a *maquiladora* in Mexico, which is a cheap labor part of the production process. If a foreign entity's functional currency is the U.S. dollar, any asset or liability that is carried on the entity's local currency books at historical cost is translated into U.S. dollars at the historical FX rate at the time the item was recorded, while any asset or liability that is carried on the entity's local currency books at fair value is translated at the current spot FX rate. Under this accounting method, which is the called the *temporal method*, there is FX accounting exposure only for the fair value accounts, and the gains and losses must be included in the parent's current reported earnings. The economic reasoning behind this treatment is that the U.S. dollar is the primary economic environment in which the entity generates and expends cash, so the impact of FX changes figure directly into the entity's short-run profitability.

Hedging FX Exposure

Although FX translation exposure affects the book value of a parent's equity, FX translation exposure does not necessarily reflect FX business exposure. Often, there will be some overlap between FX translation exposure and FX business exposure, but sometimes a firm can have FX translation exposure without having *any* FX business exposure, and vice versa. Academic advice on FX translation exposure is that companies should ignore it, because it is only about accounting book values and not real variables, like cash flow and business value. If a company uses financial instruments to hedge the FX translation exposure on its balance sheet that does not overlap with FX business exposure, a "real" FX exposure is created where one did not exist before.

Despite the academic advice, many firms do hedge FX translation exposure. A recent study found that 47% of 622 companies from 25 countries hedge FX translation exposure.[4] The primary reason is that FX translation exposure creates volatility in a firm's equity book value, which in turn creates volatility in the firm's "debt ratio." The debt ratio, which is the ratio of debt to book value of total capital, is an important factor in a company's credit rating and is often a factor in a firm's debt covenants. On the other hand, many firms do not mind the volatility in equity book value, and thus do not hedge FX translation exposure.[5]

In the theoretical world of perfect financial markets, financial hedging of FX operating/business exposure is "irrelevant" in that it does not affect the *current* intrinsic value of the firm's equity. Academics recognize that in the real world however, hedging FX operating exposure will typically reduce the costs of financial distress, including the cost of the inability to carry out strategic plans. Moreover, Wall Street wants stability in reported earnings and growth rates, and thus stabilizing the cash flow stream has a desirable impact on the real-world stock price. So the typical academic advice is that financial hedging of FX operating and business exposure is a good idea.

Still, some firms choose <u>not</u> to hedge FX operating and business exposure. Managers justify this decision in different ways: (a) Some think that the impact of FX changes will even out over time in the long run. These managers are not concerned about the costs of financial distress. (b) Others do not want to regret hedging, when it turns out that with 20–20 hindsight, not hedging would have led to a better outcome. (c) Still others think that some shareholders *want* FX exposure and thus do not want hedging; and any shareholders who do not want FX exposure are free to use their own financial hedging. (d) Some are not willing to live with the accounting rules for financial hedging, which we will explain in the next chapter. (e) If the hedging involves financial derivatives, like forward FX contracts, some managers may not hedge because derivatives are often viewed negatively by people who do not understand the useful role of derivatives in hedging.

But many firms <u>do</u> hedge FX operating and business exposure. Some hedge because, in reality, a firm's shareholders often cannot hedge FX exposure on their own even if they want to, as the firm's FX exposures are too complex for them to understand. And providing shareholders with information on FX operating exposures would be expensive and might reveal strategic information to competitors. Other firms simply agree with the academic advice that in the imperfect markets of the real world, financial hedging will reduce the costs of financial distress.[6]

MERCK

Merck's corporate strategy at one time did not allow the company to weather the impact of FX changes on its foreign revenues. It needed a minimum consistent cash flow stream in U.S. dollars to support its research and development program, which was concentrated in the United States, to stay competitive with other pharmaceutical firms. So Merck wanted to hedge its FX operating exposure. It concluded that operational hedging by producing overseas was not viable, given the need to centralize R&D efforts in the United States. Moreover, it could not pass through FX changes to foreign customers due to regulatory controls on pharmaceutical prices. So Merck decided to use hedge its FX operating exposure with derivatives.[7]

Some firms use financial hedging when operational strategies are not viable. For a mining company that cannot change the location of its operations, for example, there may be no way to do any operational hedging. Other firms use financial hedging after all reasonable strategies for operational management of FX exposure have been implemented. Some firms use financial hedging of FX operating and business exposure as an alternative to operational strategies, sometimes in cases where operational hedging is too permanent and financial hedging is more flexible. Still other firms use financial hedging as an intermediate-term measure while more strategic operational solutions to FX operating and business exposure are being developed.[8]

Summary Action Points

- A firm's FX business exposure to a currency measures how FX movements affect the firm's business value, and is based on the firm's FX operating exposure.
- Two factors affecting a firm's FX equity exposure are the firm's FX business exposure and the firm's net financial leverage.
- The book value of a parent's net investment into a foreign affiliate is subject to an accounting treatment that results in FX translation exposure to a currency. FX translation exposure is fundamentally different from FX equity exposure, which is based on real cash flows, and business values, rather than book values.

- There are pros and cons of hedging FX exposure. Academics tend to recommend that companies should ignore FX translation exposure, but should hedge FX operating and business exposure in order to reduce the likelihood and costs of financial distress.

Glossary

Accumulated Other Comprehensive Income (AOCI): An equity account used to reserve valuation changes that are not included in current earnings.

Business Value: The value of an operation if it has no net debt, also known as unlevered value.

Cumulative Translation Adjustment (CTA): A subaccount of the AOCI account that reflects FX translation gains/losses.

Enterprise Value: The market capitalization of the firm's equity plus the firm's total debt minus the firm's cash and marketable securities, or equivalently, equity market cap plus net debt; the same as levered value.

FX Business Exposure: The variability in a firm's business value caused by uncertain FX rate changes.

FX Equity Exposure: The variability in the intrinsic value of a firm's equity caused by uncertain FX rate changes.

FX Translation Exposure: The impact of FX changes on the reported home currency values of the book value of a firm's net investment in a foreign affiliate.

Functional Currency: The currency in which a foreign entity's books are kept, chosen by the parent under accounting rules.

Intrinsic Business Value: The intrinsic value of an operation if with no net debt; the present value of the operation's future operating cash flows.

Maquiladora: A foreign affiliate in a less developed country that uses cheap labor to assemble products for a developed market with parts imported from the foreign market.

Modified Closing Rate Method: Under this method, all of the affiliate's assets and liabilities are translated at the current spot FX rate and owners' equity is translated with historical rates. The resulting difference is booked in a special equity account called the *Cumulative Translation Adjustment (CTA)*.

Net Debt: A firm's total debt minus cash and marketable securities.

Net Financial Leverage: The ratio of net debt to business value.

Temporal Method: Any asset or liability that is carried on the affiliate's local currency books at fair value is translated at the current spot FX rate. Any asset or liability of the foreign affiliate that is carried on the affiliate's local currency books at historical cost is translated into U.S. dollars at the historical FX rate at the time the item was recorded. Used when the home currency is the functional currency.

Translation: The conversion of accounting items from one currency into another.

Discussion Questions

1. Explain the difference between business value and enterprise value.
2. Suppose an overseas subsidiary of a U.S. multinational reinvests all cash flows in its own growth, rather than repatriating any to the parent. Does the parent have FX business exposure to the foreign currency? Discuss.
3. Explain how an overseas subsidiary may *not* cause its multinational parent to have any FX business exposure, but would cause the parent to have FX translation exposure. (Hint: Recall the Vulcan Materials scenario box in the previous chapter.)
4. What are some of the reasons corporations might be able to do a better job at managing FX operating and business exposure than their investors?
5. Give some examples of cases where financial hedging is useful instead of operational hedging or in addition to operational hedging.

Problems

1. CDG Co. expects a future operating cash flow of $200,000 initially and a constant perpetual growth rate of 4% per annum. The discount rate is 8%. Find CDG's intrinsic business value.

2. CDG Co. in the previous problem has estimated its FX business exposure to the euro is 0.60. What would be CDG's new intrinsic business value if the euro depreciates by 20%?

3. BNG Company has 100 million shares outstanding. The share price is $10. The company has $50 million in cash and $150 million in debt. Find BNG's enterprise value.

4. GNB Company has 100 million shares outstanding. The share price is $10. The company has $150 million in cash and $50 million in debt. Find GNB's enterprise value.

5. GTZ Company is a U.S. multinational consisting of businesses that sell industrial materials in three countries, the United States, Portugal (in the Eurozone), and France (in the Eurozone). Assume that the U.S. subsidiary, UTZ, has a business value of $40 million and an FX business exposure to the euro of 0.20, due to competitor from the Eurozone operating in the United States. The business that sells in Portugal, PTZ, is an export company that produces entirely in the United States. PTZ's business value is $10 million and FX business exposure to the euro is 2. The business that sells in France, FTZ, consists of two operations; the first produces raw product in the United States, which is shipped FTZ-France for finishing and distribution. FTZ's total business value is $30 million and FX business exposure to the euro is 1.40. What is the FX business exposure to the euro of the overall multinational company, GTZ?

6. The U.S. firm ABC Co. has $V_B^\$ = \$5,000$, $ND^\$ = \$1,000$, and thus $S^\$ = \$4,000$. All of ABC's net debt is U.S. dollar-denominated. ABC has an FX business exposure to the euro of 1.25. (a) Use the "what if" approach to find the new value of ABC's equity, and the FX equity exposure to the euro, given a 20% depreciation in the euro. (b) Verify the FX equity exposure using equation (2.2).

7. The U.S. firm ABC Co. has $V_B^\$ = \$5,000$, $ND^\$ = \$1,500$, and thus $S^\$ = \$3,500$. All of ABC's net debt is U.S. dollar-denominated. ABC has an FX business exposure to the euro of 1.25. (a) Use the "what if" approach to find the new value of ABC's equity, and the FX equity exposure to the euro, given a 20% depreciation in the euro. (b) Verify the FX equity exposure using equation (2.2).

8. The U.S. firm ABC Co. has $V_B^{\$} = \$5,000$, $ND^{\$} = -\$1,000$, and thus $S^{\$} = \$6,000$. All of ABC's net debt is U.S. dollar-denominated. ABC has an FX business exposure to the euro of 1.25. (a) Use the "what if" approach to find the new value of ABC's equity, and the FX equity exposure to the euro, given a 20% depreciation in the euro. (b) Verify the FX equity exposure using equation (2.2).

9. The U.S. firm ABC Co. has $V_B^{\$} = \$5,000$, $ND^{\$} = -\$1,000$, and thus $S^{\$} = \$6,000$. All of ABC's net debt is U.S. dollar-denominated. ABC has an FX business exposure to the euro of -1.25. (a) Use the "what if" approach to find the new value of ABC's equity, and the FX equity exposure to the euro, given a 20% depreciation in the euro. (b) Verify the FX equity exposure using equation (2.2).

10. Extend the GGT/SPT FX translation example in the text, assuming the euro appreciates by 10% between times 1 and 2, from 0.80 $/€ to 0.88 $/€. (a) What is GGT's net investment in SPT at time 2? (b) Find the FX translation gain/loss between times 1 and 2. (c) Show the FX translation exposure is 1.

11. GXC Corporation is a U.S. manufacturer. GXC's sales are entirely in the Eurozone. GXC buys a plant in the Eurozone, and sells the production capacity in the United States, in order to produce the instruments closer to the market. Assume the expected cash flow (in U.S. dollars) does not change. Circle a, b, c, or d: From the U.S. dollar perspective: (a) GXC's FX operating exposure is higher and FX translation exposure is higher; (b) GXC's FX operating exposure is lower and FX translation exposure is lower; (c) GXC's FX operating exposure is higher and FX translation exposure is lower; (d) GXC's FX operating exposure is lower and FX translation exposure is higher.

12. TBR is a U.S. firm that expects future operating cash flow, in U.S. dollars, of $2 million initially and a constant perpetual growth rate of 5% per annum. Assume the discount rate is 10%. Assume the FX business exposure to the euro is 3. (a) Find TBR's intrinsic business value. (b) What would be TBR's new intrinsic business value if the euro depreciates by 10%? (c) Assume that the time-0 total book value of all of TBR's assets (in the United States and Europe) is $25 million. In U.S. dollars, the book value of TBR's net investment

in Eurozone assets is $10 million. The functional currency is the euro. If the FX price of the euro drops by 10%, what is TBR's FX translation gain or loss?

Answers to Problems

1. $200,000/(0.08 − 0.04) = $5 million.

2. 0.88($5 million) = $4.40 million.

3. Equity market cap is $1 billion. The net debt is $100 million. The enterprise value is $1 billion + $100 million = $1.1 billion.

4. Equity market cap is $1 billion. The net debt is −$100 million. The enterprise value is $1 billion − $100 million = $900 million.

5. 0.50(0.20) + 0.125(2) + 0.375(1.40) = 0.875.

6. (a) ABC's business value falls by 1.25(20%), or 25%, to $3,750, when the euro depreciates by 20%. The net debt stays at $1,000. The new equity value is $3,750 − 1,000 = $2,750. The equity value changes by $2,750/$4,000 − 1 = −0.3125, or −31.25%. The FX equity exposure is −0.3125/−0.20 = 1.5625. (b) Because $ND^\$/V_B^\$ = 0.20$, the FX equity exposure is consistent with equation (2.2): $\xi_{SE}^\$ = 1.25/(1 − 0.20) =$ 1.562.

7. (a) ABC's business value falls by 1.25(20%), or 25%, to $3,750, when the euro depreciates by 20%. The net debt stays at $1,500. The new equity value is $3,750 − 1,500 = $2,250. The equity value changes by $2,250/$3,500 − 1 = −0.357, or −35.7%. The FX equity exposure is −0.357/−0.20 = 1.786. (b) Because $ND^\$/V_B^\$ = 0.30$, the FX equity exposure is consistent with equation (2.2): $\xi_{SE}^\$ = 1.25/(1 − 0.30) = 1.786$.

8. (a) ABC's business value falls by 1.25(20%), or 25%, to $3,750, when the euro depreciates by 20%. The net debt stays at −$1,000. The new equity value is $3,750 − (−1,000) = $4,750. The equity value changes by $4,750/$6,000 − 1 = −0.208, or −20.8%. The FX equity exposure is −0.208/−0.20 = 1.04. (b) Because $ND^\$/V_B^\$ = −0.20$, the FX equity exposure reconciles with equation (2.2): $\xi_{SE}^\$ = 1.25/(1 − (−0.20)) = 1.04$.

9. (a) ABC's business value rises by 1.25(20%), or 25%, to $6,250, when the euro depreciates by 20%. The net debt stays at −$1,000. The new equity value is $6,250 − (−1,000) = $7,250. The equity value changes by

$7,250/$6,000 − 1 = 0.208, or 20.8%. The FX equity exposure is 0.208/ −0.20 = −1.04. (b) Because $ND^\$/V_B^\$ = -0.20$, the FX equity exposure reconciles with equation (2.2): $\xi_{S\epsilon}^\$ = -1.25/(1 - (-0.20)) = -1.04$.

10. (a) If the euro appreciates to 0.88 $/€ at time 2, SPT's book value of assets of €8 million is translated as $7.04 million, liabilities as $1.76 million, but equity again as $7.50 million. So SPT's new CTA is −$2.22 million. (b) The new book value of GGT's net investment is $7.50 million − 2.22 million = $7.04 million − 1.76 million = $5.28 million, a gain of $0.48 million from the time-1 level of $4.80 million. The $0.48 million gain is the change in the CTA (AOCI) account, that is, an FX translation gain for the period. (c) The FX translation gain of $0.48 million is 10% of the time-1 net investment in SPT. Because the spot FX price of the euro rises by 10%, we see that the FX translation exposure is 0.10/0.10 = 1.

11. (d).

12. (a) $2 million/(0.10 − 0.05) = $40 million.

    (b) $40 million(1 − 0.30) = $28 million.

    (c) $10 million(−0.10) = −$1 million.

CHAPTER 3

Foreign Currency Debt

A recent study of manufacturing firms from 16 countries found that the average firm hedges 20–30% of its FX operating exposure by operational methods, such as operational hedging and FX pass-through. The study also found that the average firm mitigates its FX operating and business exposure a further 40% through financial hedging strategies, mainly with foreign currency debt.[1]

This chapter shows how foreign currency debt works to hedge the effects of FX rate changes on a firm with a positive (long) FX business exposure to the foreign currency. As the FX price of the foreign currency changes, the value of the foreign currency debt, when measured in the firm's home currency, changes in the same direction as the firm's business value. So the foreign currency debt dampens the impact of FX fluctuations on the firm's equity value.

But debt in any currency also involves the risk connected with *financial leverage*, which can magnify FX business exposure in the manner we saw in the previous chapter. So we need to keep the financial leverage effect in mind when analyzing the use of foreign currency debt in the financial hedging of FX business exposure. The chapter also covers some accounting and tax issues of foreign currency debt that managers should know about.

Foreign Currency Debt

How do spot FX rate changes affect the value of a firm's debt? The answer depends on the currency denomination of the debt. For debt denominated in the firm's home currency, spot FX changes do not affect the debt value. But for debt denominated in a foreign currency, FX changes do affect the value of the debt when viewed in the home currency, and in a pure FX conversion manner.

For example, assume a U.S. firm currently has £625,000 in British pound debt, and the spot FX rate is 1.60 $/£. Thus the value of the debt in U.S. dollars is currently £625,000(1.60 $/£) = $1 million. Assume next that the British pound appreciates by 20%, to 1.92 $/£. The value of the firm's £-debt in U.S. dollars increases to £625,000(1.92 $/£) = $1.20 million. So we see that the value of the £-debt in U.S. dollars increases by 20% when the British pound appreciates by 20%. By itself, the $200,000 increase in the U.S. dollar value of the £-debt is a loss to the shareholders.

An example of a foreign currency debt issue is the McDonalds yen bonds floated in 2000 for ¥15 billion (about $125 million); see Exhibit 3.1. Note that although the 10-year bond was denominated in yen, McDonalds could have exchanged the bond issue proceeds from yen into another currency in the spot FX market. In other words, the liability does not have to be denominated in the currency of the country where the proceeds of the issue will be put to use.

U.S. firms significantly increased their foreign currency debt from around $1 billion in 1982 to about $62 billion in 1998. Between 1993 and 2005, U.S. firms issued an estimated $200 billion worth of foreign currency bonds denominated in euros (or German marks or French francs), British pounds, Japanese yen, and Swiss francs. The financial hedging of FX operating and business exposure appears to be the main reason for having debt denominated in a foreign currency. One survey found that over

Exhibit 3.1. McDonalds 10-Year Global Bonds

London, March 2, 2000 (Bloomberg)
 Amount: 15 billion yen
 Type: Global
 Coupon: 2 percent, payable semi-annually
 Issue Price: 99.927
 Reoffer Price: 99.927
 Reoffer Yield: 2.008 percent, semi-annually
 Spread: 22 basis points more than governments
 Maturity: March 9, 2010

85% of U.S. Chief Financial Officers say that financial hedging is a reason for foreign currency debt.[2] By hedging FX exposure, foreign currency debt can reduce financial distress costs relative to those faced by a firm that has only home currency debt.[3]

We focus in this chapter on the use of foreign currency debt in the financial hedging of FX business exposure, but there are other motivations for foreign currency debt. Some firms may want to have foreign currency debt when they think the currency is overvalued, hoping to capture a gain when the currency realigns with the intrinsic FX value. Of course, the issuer would need to trade-off the anticipated speculative FX gain against two downsides. The first is the risk that the foreign currency might appreciate instead of depreciate. Second, there may be undesirable accounting implications, which we cover later in the chapter. While some firms might speculate on foreign currency movements in this way, many firms would not consider this strategy.

However, researchers have reported that many companies issue foreign currency debt if the interest rate is low, under the apparent belief that the uncovered interest rate parity (UIRP) condition does not hold. If the UIRP condition holds, the lower interest rate currency would be expected to appreciate. If corporate managers do not expect this appreciation, the managers basically believe that the currency with the low interest rate is overvalued, given the UIRP approach to intrinsic FX value. This strategy is a less obvious way of issuing overvalued foreign currency debt.[4]

For example, we see in Exhibit 3.1 that the interest rate on the McDonalds yen bond issue is low, 2%, compared to the interest rate on 10-year U.S. dollar corporate bonds of around 6.50% at the time. Does this mean McDonalds got a cut-rate deal by issuing bonds in yen rather than in U.S. dollars? The answer would be "no" if the UIRP condition holds, because the yen would be expected to appreciate at a rate that offsets the interest rate differential. Thus, McDonalds would pay a low interest rate, but the value of the yen debt would be expected to rise in U.S. dollars, which would be a loss that offsets the interest rate differential. But if McDonalds' managers expected the yen to change at a lower rate than expected under the UIRP condition, they would have been implicitly taking advantage of a perceived opportunity to issue bonds denominated in an overvalued foreign currency.

Foreign Currency Debt and FX Equity Exposure

As mentioned in the previous chapter, a firm's *FX equity exposure* is the elasticity of the firm's equity value to spot FX changes, viewed from the perspective of the firm's home currency. A U.S. firm's FX equity exposure to the euro is denoted $\xi_{S\epsilon}^{\$}$ and is computed as $\%\Delta S^{\$}/x^{\$/\epsilon}$, the percentage change in the equity value in U.S. dollars, given the percentage FX change in the euro. We showed that when a firm's net debt is entirely in the home currency, a firm's FX equity exposure to a currency depends on the firm's FX business exposure to the currency and the net financial leverage. Now we analyze the relative amount of net debt denominated in the exposure currency.

For example, assume the U.S. firm XYZ has (a) FX business exposure to the euro of $\xi_{Be}^{\$} = 1.20$; (b) a business value in U.S. dollars of $V_B^{\$} = \$2,000$; and (c) a net debt value in U.S. dollars of $ND^{\$} = \$600$, half of which is denominated in euros. Thus, the equity value is currently $S^{\$} = \$2,000 - 600 = \$1,400$, as shown in the top panel of Exhibit 3.2. Assume a 5% depreciation of the euro. Due to the FX business exposure of 1.20, the business value drops by 6%, to 0.94($2,000$) = $1,880. From the U.S. dollar perspective, the value of the euro-denominated net debt drops by 5%, from $300 to $285, while the value of the U.S. dollar net debt stays at $300. The "what if" equity value is $1,880 − 285 − 300 = $1,295, as shown in the

Exhibit 3.2. XYZ Company Value Balance Sheet $300 Euro Net Debt

	Initial	
	Value	*Net Debt & Equity*
		$ 300 €-Net Debt
		300 $-Net Debt
	$2,000 $V_B^{\$}$	1,400 $S^{\$}$
	$2,000	$2,000
	"What if" the Euro Depreciates by 5%?	
	Value	*Net Debt & Equity*
		$ 285 €-Net Debt
		300 $-Net Debt
	$1,880 $V_B^{\$}$	1,295 $S^{\$}$
	$1,880	$1,880

bottom panel of Exhibit 3.2. The percentage change in the equity value would be $1,295/$1,400 − 1 = −0.075, or −7.5%. XYZ's FX equity exposure to the euro is thus −0.075/−0.05 = **1.50**. So if XYZ has the euro-denominated debt, its FX equity exposure of 1.50 is lower than that found in the previous chapter in the example where all $600 of the net debt is denominated in U.S. dollars, 1.71.

Figure 3.1 shows XYZ's FX equity exposure for the two cases where the ratio of net debt to business value is 30% and the FX business exposure is 1.20. For the case when 50% of XYZ's net debt is denominated in euros, the FX equity exposure is lower, 1.50, than for the case of no euro-denominated net debt, 1.71.

To show this effect in an equation, let $ND_\epsilon^{\$}$ denote the value, measured in U.S. dollars, of the firm's euro-denominated net debt. $ND^{\$}$ denotes the value of <u>all</u> of the firm's net debt, measured in U.S. dollars, regardless of currency denomination. The relationship for FX equity exposure as a function of FX business exposure and capital structure is shown in equation (3.1).

FX Equity Exposure and Foreign Currency Net Debt

$$\xi_{S\epsilon}^{\$} = (\xi_{B\epsilon}^{\$} - ND_\epsilon^{\$}/V_B^{\$})/(1 - ND^{\$}/V_B^{\$}) \qquad (3.1)$$

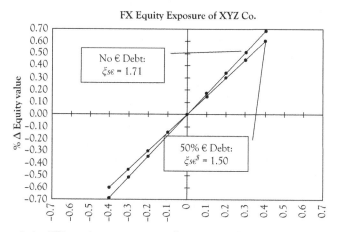

Figure 3.1. FX equity exposure and currency denomination of debt.

We demonstrate equation (3.1) using the XYZ example above. Because half of XYZ's \$600 in net debt is denominated in euros, $ND_\epsilon^\$/V_B^\$ = \$300/\$2,000 = 0.15$ and $ND^\$/V_B^\$ = \$600/\$2,000 = 0.30$; the FX equity exposure of 1.50 (found earlier) is also consistent with equation (3.1): $\xi_{S\epsilon}^\$ = (1.20 - 0.15)/(1 - 0.30) = 1.50$.

Equation (3.1) is a special case of equation (2.2) where all debt is in U.S. dollars and thus $ND_\epsilon^\$/V_B^\$ = 0$. From equation (3.1), we have that $\xi_{S\epsilon}^\$ = (1.20 - 0)/(1 - 0.30) = 1.71$, as we already found.

The U.S. firm ABC Co. has $V_B^\$ = \$5,000$, $ND^\$ = \$3,000$, and thus $S^\$ = \$2,000$. \$2,000 of ABC's \$3,000 net debt is euro-denominated and the rest is U.S. dollar-denominated. ABC's FX business exposure to the euro is 1.60. (a) Find the new value of ABC's equity, and the FX equity exposure, using the "what if" method, given a 10% depreciation of the euro. (b) Verify the FX equity exposure using equation (3.1).

Answers: (a) ABC's business value falls by 1.60(10%), or 16%, to \$4,200, when the euro depreciates by 10%. The value of the euro-denominated net debt (in U.S. dollars) drops by 10%, to \$1,800, while the value of the other net debt stays at \$1,000. The "what if" equity value is \$4,200 − 1,800 − 1,000 = \$1,400. The equity value changes by \$1,400/\$2,000 − 1 = −0.30, or −30%. The FX equity exposure is −0.30/−0.10 = 3. (b) Because $ND_\epsilon^\$/V_B^\$ = \$2,000/\$5,000 = 0.40$ and $ND^\$/V_B^\$ = \$3,000/\$5,000 = 0.60$, the FX equity exposure is consistent with equation (3.1): $\xi_{S\epsilon}^\$ = (1.60 - 0.40)/(1 - 0.60) = 3$.

Applied Materials' Yen Debt

The U.S. semiconductor firm Applied Materials (AMAT) reported roughly \$50 million worth of long-term Japanese yen debt on its consolidated financial statement at fiscal year-end (October) 1998. AMAT uses yen-debt as a hedge of the FX business exposure to the yen from its Japanese operations.

Between October 1998 and 1999, the spot FX rate changed from 134 ¥/\$ to 107 ¥/\$, a yen appreciation of 26%. Assuming that the value of AMAT's ¥-debt remained constant in yen during that time, the value of AMAT's ¥-debt in U.S. dollars would be 26% higher in 1999 than a year earlier. Thus the value of AMAT's ¥-debt in U.S. dollars would have been $50 million (1.26) = $63 million in 1999. By itself, the $13 million additional value of the ¥-debt would have represented a loss of $13 million. However, because the debt served as a hedge of FX business exposure, the yen appreciation would have caused an offsetting gain in the Japanese operation's business value, measured in U.S. dollars.

Foreign Currency Debt and Hedge Accounting

We have seen that if the euro depreciates by 10%, the U.S. dollar value of euro-denominated debt also drops by 10%. We have so far been thinking about this kind of change in debt value in an economic sense. The exact same treatment is also seen on a firm's reported balance sheet: The book value of euro-denominated debt will be written down by 10% when the euro depreciates by 10%. The drop in the debt book value, measured in U.S. dollars, is a gain that results in an increase in the book value of the firm's equity.

An important question is whether the gains/losses of changes in the book value of foreign currency debt are considered in the computation of a firm's current earnings or not. Other things the same, managers would prefer for these gains and losses to not be included in current earnings, but accounting rules for foreign currency debt generally require that the gains/ losses be included in current earnings. However, an exception to the rule is granted if the foreign currency debt qualifies as a hedge under the rules for *hedge accounting*.

The most common way for foreign currency debt to qualify for hedge accounting is as a *net investment hedge*. The idea is that if the foreign currency debt hedges the FX translation changes of the book value of a firm's net investment in a foreign affiliate, the firm may elect to have the changes in the book value of the debt receive the same accounting treatment as the FX translation changes themselves. In this treatment, the changes in the book value of foreign currency debt by-pass current earnings and go directly to the cumulative translation adjustment (CTA) account in the equity section of the balance sheet. If the debt level, measured in the home currency, is equal to the net investment in the foreign affiliate, then the CTA account does not change, because the changes in the debt's book value will exactly offset the translation changes in the book value of the net investment in the foreign affiliate.

Foreign currency debt automatically qualifies as a net investment hedge for an amount up to the book value of the net investment in the foreign affiliate. The excess of a firm's foreign currency debt *over* the net investment book value does *not* qualify for hedge accounting. The gains/losses on any foreign currency debt that does not qualify for hedge accounting must be reported in current earnings. These gains/losses go to the equity section of the balance sheet via Retained Earnings.

As an example, consider the U.S. multinational GGT Co., which has a business value of $50 million and an FX business exposure to the euro of 0.30. We'll assume that GGT has $15 million in net debt denominated in euros. Let's assume that the rest of GGT's capital is equity, so that GGT's equity value is $50 million – 15 million = $35 million. (Thus, GGT's FX equity exposure to the euro is (0.30 – 0.30)/(1 – 0.30) = 0.) However, GGT's only foreign investment is its operation in Spain, SPT, and the book value of GGT's net investment in SPT is only $10 million. Any amount of €-debt up to the net investment in SPT, $10 million, automatically qualifies as a net investment hedge, even if SPT is not the source of GGT's FX business exposure, but any €-debt in excess of $10 million cannot receive hedge accounting treatment as a net investment hedge. Because GGT has $15 million in €-debt, GGT may elect for $10 million to receive hedge accounting treatment, but not the remaining €-debt, $15 million – 10 million = $5 million.

The accounting treatment of the changes in the book value of $10 million of €-debt that receives hedge accounting is the same as the FX translation changes on the $10 million book value of the net investment in SPT. Both changes go to directly the CTA account, bypassing current earnings. But because the changes on the debt offset the FX translation changes on the net investment in SPT, the CTA account does not change. The changes in the book value of the $5 million of excess €-debt that does <u>not</u> qualify as a net investment hedge <u>do</u> figure into the reported earnings each period. For example, if the euro appreciates by 10% over a quarter, the book value of the $5 million "excess" €-debt rises by $0.50 million. This $0.50 million increase is regarded as a loss that needs to be included in the calculation of the reported earnings for the quarter.

In principle, GGT might be able to get a higher amount of €-debt to qualify for hedge accounting as a *cash flow hedge*, perhaps because the business that exports to Italy has revenues denominated in euros. But the accounting rules for cash flow hedges require that the cash flow be "highly predictable." In addition, there is a heavy documentation burden for U.S. firms in qualifying a financial position as a cash flow hedge. Therefore, many U.S. managers ignore this option.

What if GGT only has $5 million in €-net debt to hedge the FX business exposure, and $10 million in U.S. dollar debt? In this case, there will be no impact of FX changes on reported earnings, because all of the $5 million in €-net debt automatically qualifies for hedge accounting as a net investment hedge. However, there will be some FX translation exposure in the book value of the firm's equity. The reason is due to the FX translation changes on the $10 million book value of the net investment in SPT, but only $5 million in €-net debt. And there will be FX equity exposure, of $(0.30 - 0.10)/(1 - 0.30) = 0.286$.

Altria, Inc. Note to Financial Statements (2002)

"Altria Group, Inc. designates certain foreign currency denominated debt as net investment hedges of foreign operations. During the years ended December 31, 2002 and 2001, losses of $163 million, net of income taxes of $88 million, and losses of $18 million, net of income taxes of $10 million, respectively, which represented effective hedges of net investments, were reported as a component of accumulated other comprehensive losses within currency translation adjustments."

Source: Altria Annual Report, Notes to Financial Statements, 2002.

A firm that has a negative FX business exposure to a foreign currency has a more challenging accounting problem. In principle, the firm can hedge the FX exposure with a foreign currency cash ("negative net debt") position, but the accounting rules would not allow the position to qualify as a net investment hedge. So, unless the company is willing and able to get the position qualified as a cash flow hedge, the company has two choices. The first is to hedge and tolerate the effect on current earnings of the FX changes on the hedge position. The second is to not hedge. A company with an indirect FX business exposure to a foreign currency may face a similar situation. If the company has no cash flows in that currency or foreign assets in that country, the company must either accept the effects of hedging on current earnings or not hedge.

ABC Co. is a U.S. owner of the Eurozone subsidiary, TZL Plc. TZL's functional currency is the euro. ABC's time-0 reported and value balance sheets are shown below. For simplicity, the book values and the economic values are the same at time 0. The book value of ABC's net investment in TZL is $2,000 at time 0, and is shown on ABC's reported balance sheet as a net asset (rather than showing the subsidiary's assets and liabilities separately). ABC's €-debt does not qualify as a cash flow hedge. ABC's FX business exposure to the euro is 0.50. Assume that the euro appreciates by 10%. (a) What will ABC's time-1 reported and value balance sheets look like? (b) Ignoring the impact of the FX change on operating cash flow, what will be the impact on ABC's reported current earnings?

ABC Time-0 Balance Sheets (in $s)

Reported	Assets	Liabilities & Equity	
	$ 2,000 Net Inv TZL	$ 4,000 €-Debt	
		$ 1,000 AOCI	
		$ 3,000 Other Equity	
	$ 6,000 Other	$ 4,000 Equity	
	$ 8,000	$ 8,000	
Value	Value	Liabilities & Equity	
		$ 4,000 €-Debt $(ND_\epsilon^\$)$	
	$ 8,000 $V_B^\$$	$ 4,000 $S^\$$	
	$ 8,000	$ 8,000	

Answers: (a) ABC's business value will increase by 0.50(10%), or 5%, so the time-1 business value is $8,400. The book value of the net investment in TZL increases by 10%, so the time-1 book value is $2,200. In U.S. dollars, the book value of the $4,000 in €-debt increases by 10% to $4,400, a $400 loss. Because $2,000 of the €-debt qualifies as a net investment hedge, $200 of the $400 loss on the €-debt offsets the FX translation gain on the TZL net investment book value, so the AOCI does not change. (b) Current reported earnings will be lower by $200, because only half ($2,000) of the €-debt qualifies as a hedge, and thus the loss on the nonqualifying portion goes to the current earnings. So Accumulated Retained Earnings (here part of Other Equity) drops.

ABC Time-1 Balance Sheets (in $)

Reported	Assets	Liabilities & Equity
	$ 2,200 Net Inv TZL	$ 4,400 €-Debt
		$ 1,000 AOCI
		$ 2,800 Other Equity
	$ 6,000 Other	$ 3,800 Equity
	$ 8,200	$ 8,200
Value	Value	Liabilities & Equity
		$ 4,400 €-Debt
	$ 8,400 $V_B^\$$	$ 4,000 $S^\$$
	$ 8,400	$ 8,400

FX Equity Exposure = 0

If a firm's debt and equity are correctly valued in the financial market, the traditional "trade-off theory" of capital structure says that a firm's optimal debt level is one that maximizes the difference between the tax shield benefits of the debt interest and the costs of financial distress. Both of these variables get larger as a firm increases its net financial leverage. At relatively low debt levels, the tax shield benefits outweigh the financial distress costs, but at relatively high debt levels, the situation is reversed. The trick is to find the optimal debt level, where the net difference between the tax benefits and the financial distress costs is maximized. And if a firm's debt and equity are *not* correctly valued in the market, this misvaluation is an additional factor that, in principle, managers should consider for a firm's optimal capital structure.

In this section, we bring foreign currency net debt into the theoretical discussion. Ignoring misvaluation and tax issues, the optimal foreign currency debt level is the one that minimizes financial distress costs. Therefore, the idea would be to achieve an FX equity exposure of 0. You can see from equation (3.1) that setting the ratio of euro net debt to business value equal to the FX business exposure $(ND_\epsilon^\$/V_B^\$ = \xi_{B\epsilon}^\$)$ will make the FX equity exposure 0. Thus, in some cases, it is possible to completely hedge FX business exposure solely with foreign currency net debt.

If a company has an FX business exposure to the euro of 0.20, for example, and it has €-net debt in the amount of 20% of the business value, the company has zero FX equity exposure to the euro. Note that the book value of the business is irrelevant in finding the level of €-debt that eliminates FX equity exposure. The drivers are the firm's business value and the FX business exposure.

The U.S. firm ABC Co. has $V_B^\$ = \$5,000$, $ND^\$ = \$3,000$, and thus $S^\$ = \$2,000$. Assume the FX business exposure to the euro is 0.30. How much of ABC's net debt should be euro-denominated in order to eliminate the firm's FX equity exposure to the euro?

Answer: Setting $ND_\epsilon^\$/V_B^\$ = \xi_{B\epsilon}^\$$ $ND_\epsilon^\$ = \xi_{B\epsilon}^\$ V_B^\$ = 0.30(\$5,000) = \$1,500$.

We need to acknowledge that, in reality, managers can at best come up with a crude estimate of their company's FX business exposure to a currency. Still, it is useful for managers to understand the ideas we cover when we assume a given FX business exposure.

FX business exposure to a currency may be relatively low, like 0.20 for a company with a relatively small proportion of its business in an overseas market. But other companies have higher FX business exposures. A company with an FX business exposure to a foreign currency of 0.80 could in principle eliminate its FX equity exposure to the currency by having net debt denominated in the exposure currency in the amount of 80% of the firm's business value. Then again, it may be unreasonable for a company to have net financial leverage as high as 0.80. We will address this problem further in the next chapter with currency swaps.

Vulcan Materials

Vulcan Materials considered denominating some of its debt in British pounds because the multinational had a large UK subsidiary. The reason was to hedge the FX business exposure to the pound that the parent perceived was posed by its British subsidiary. But a regression analysis revealed the FX business exposure to the pound was approximately equal to 0 (see Chapter 1), suggesting that the UK subsidiary did not actually expose its U.S. parent to FX changes in the British pound. Had Vulcan issued the sterling denominated debt, the firm would actually have created a negative FX equity exposure to the pound.[5]

If a company's FX business exposure to a currency is negative, positive net debt denominated in that currency does not hedge the FX exposure and in fact will exacerbate it. For example, assume a firm has a natural short FX business exposure to the yen of -1.25. Assume all of the firm's net debt is denominated in yen, and the net financial leverage ratio is 0.25. The firm's FX equity exposure to the yen, from equation (3.1), is $(-1.25 - 0.25)/(1 - 0.25) = -2$. Thus, a classic importer, with a negative FX business exposure to a currency, cannot use positive net debt denominated in the exposure currency to manage its FX exposure problem.

In principle, one way for a firm to manage a negative FX business exposure is with negative net debt denominated in the exposure currency. For example, let the business value be $4,000 and the FX business exposure to the yen be -1.25. From equation (3.1), the ratio of ¥-net debt to business value needs to be -1.25, so the ¥-net debt should be $-1.25(\$4,000) = -\$5,000$. And $-\$5,000 in net debt is the same as $5,000 in cash. This company would have $9,000 in total value: $4,000 in business value and $5,000 in ¥-cash. When the yen appreciates by 10%, the U.S. dollar value of the ¥-cash rises by 10%, to $5,500, while business value drops by 12.5%, from $4,000 to $3,500. So equity value is unchanged. Of course, there is some limit to the cash level, particularly if the cash is denominated in foreign currency. We'll address this issue also with currency swaps in the next chapter.

The U.S. firm BFG Import Co. has $V_B^\$ = \$5,000$ and an FX business exposure to the euro of –1.60. BFG has \$3,000 in euro-denominated cash and no other net debt. (a) Find BFG's FX equity exposure to the euro. (b) Find the amount of euro cash (in U.S. dollars) that would make the FX equity exposure to the euro equal to 0?

Answers: (a) $[-1.60 - (-0.60)]/[1 - (-0.60)] = -0.625$. (b) The ratio of €-net debt to business value needs to be –1.60 to make the FX equity exposure to the euro equal to 0. So the €-net debt needs to be –\$8,000. When the euro rises by 10%, the U.S. dollar value of the euro cash assets rises by 10% to \$8,800, and the business value drops by 16% to \$4,200. Thus the equity value is unchanged.

Foreign Currency Debt: FX Hedging and Financial Leverage

Equation (3.1) shows how two effects of foreign currency net debt come into play. First, the FX hedging effect of net debt denominated in the exposure currency is seen in the numerator. The negative sign on the $ND_\epsilon^\$/V_B^\$$ term implies that if a firm with positive FX business exposure uses a positive level of €-net debt, other things the same, the FX equity exposure is lower than using non-€-net debt. Second, the financial leverage effect of <u>all</u> net debt denominated in the exposure currency or otherwise, is seen in the denominator. Higher net financial leverage causes a higher FX equity exposure, opposite to the direction of the FX hedging effect.

The ultimate influence of foreign currency debt on a firm's FX equity exposure depends on the firm's FX business exposure to the currency. If the FX business exposure to a currency is higher than 1, the FX equity exposure is always *higher* than FX business exposure. In addition, we get the somewhat surprising result that the more net debt denominated in that currency in lieu of equity, the **higher** the FX equity exposure.

To illustrate, say AXZ Co. is initially an all-equity company with $V_B^\$ = S^\$ = \$2,000$, and AXZ's FX business exposure to the euro is 1.20. Since AXZ has no net debt, its FX equity exposure is initially equal to its FX business exposure. Next, say AXZ wants to try to hedge its FX business exposure to the euro by having some euro-denominated debt. Assume that at time 0, AXZ recapitalizes by issuing the debt with a value in U.S. dollars of \$500

Exhibit 3.3. AXZ Co. Value Balance Sheet
$500 Euro Net Debt

Initial		
	Value	Net Debt & Equity
		$ 500 €-Net Debt
	$2,000 $V_B^\$$	1,500 $S^\$$
	$2,000	$2,000
"What if" the Euro Depreciates by 5%?		
	Valued	Net Debt & Equity
		$ 475 €-Net Debt
	$1,880 $V_B^\$$	1,405 $S^\$$
	$1,880	$1,880

and uses the proceeds to repurchase shares, making the new equity value $1,500. So the net financial leverage ratio, $ND^\$/V_B^\$$, is $5,000/$2,000 = 0.25, and the new ratio of €-net debt to business value, $ND_€^\$/V_B^\$$, is also $500/$2,000 = 0.25. If the euro depreciates by 5%, AXZ's business value drops by 6%, to $1,880. The value of the €-net debt in U.S. dollars drops by 5%, from $500 to $475. The "what if" time-1 equity value is thus $1,880 – 475 = $1,405. So the percentage change in equity value equals $1,405/ $1,500 – 1 = –0.0633, or a 6.33% drop. AXZ's FX equity exposure to the euro is thus equal to –0.0633/–0.05 = 1.267. Because $ND_€^\$/V_B^\$ = 0.25$, and $ND^\$/V_B^\$ = 0.25$, the FX equity exposure to the euro of 1.267 is consistent with equation (3.1): $\xi_{S€}^\$ = (1.20 – 0.25)/(1 – 0.25) = 1.267$. Thus, we see that by increasing the €-net debt and replacing equity, AXZ raises its FX equity exposure to the euro from 1.20 to 1.267. The reason is that the FX business exposure > 1. This scenario is summarized in Exhibit 3.3.

The U.S. firm ABC Co. has $V_B^\$ = \$5,000$, $ND^\$ = \$3,000$, and thus $S^\$ = \$2,000$. ABC's FX business exposure to the euro is 1.60. (a) If all of ABC's net debt is euro-denominated, what is ABC's FX equity exposure to the euro? (b) What is the FX equity exposure to the euro if ABC has $4,000 in euro-denominated debt and only $1,000 in equity value?

Answers: (a) $\xi_{S€}^\$ = (\xi_{B€}^\$ – ND_€^\$/V_B^\$)/(1 – ND^\$/V_B^\$) = (1.60 – 0.60)/ (1 – 0.60) = 2.50$; (b) $\xi_{S€}^\$ = (1.60 – 0.80)/(1 – 0.80) = 4$.

Other Issues With Foreign Currency Debt

We dwelled on the target of zero FX equity exposure as the means to min-imize a firm's costs of financial distress. But as we said earlier, some man-agers may want to also consider FX misvaluation in the foreign currency debt decision. Let us say that the business value is $10,000 and the FX business exposure to the euro is 0.30, so that $3,000 of net debt in euros would make the FX equity exposure equal to 0. If the euro is undervalued, the firm may want to have less than $3,000 in net debt in euros. By the same token, the more undervalued the euro, the less net debt in euros that the firm would want to have. If the euro is overvalued, the firm may want to have more than $3,000 in net debt in euros. The more overvalued the euro, the more net debt in euros that the firm would want to have. How-ever, there is no formula for this trade-off at present, and so managers must use their own judgment on this matter.

Another real-world issue that managers need to consider in the foreign currency debt decision has to do with the accounting rules. Even with a correctly valued spot FX rate, managers may face a trade-off. For example, consider GGT's euro-denominated debt decision in the example above, where the FX business exposure is 0.30, the business value is $50 million, and so $15 million of net debt in euros would make the FX equity expo-sure equal to 0. Because the book value of the net investment is only $10 million, GGT's managers face a trade-off. If GGT chooses to hedge with only $10 million in euro-denominated debt, the company has no FX accounting exposure, but has FX equity exposure. That is, FX changes in the euro will not affect reported earnings or the book value of GGT's equity period by period, but will affect the firm's equity value.

Instead, if GGT chooses to hedge with $15 million in euro-denominated debt, the company has no FX equity exposure, but has FX accounting expo-sure in the form of higher volatility in reported earnings. Also, the gains/losses that go through current earnings are reflected in book equity in the Accumulated Retained Earnings (ARE) account. So there will be a <u>negative</u> FX exposure of the book value of GGT's equity. GGT's managers would have to use their judgment about how much €-debt to have, trading off the financial distress costs of nonzero FX equity exposure with the accounting drawbacks of a zero FX equity exposure. Many managers are much concerned with earnings volatility, and may tend to _not_ use more foreign-currency debt than the amount that qualifies for hedge accounting.[6]

Regardless of whether debt is issued by a subsidiary or the parent, the impact on hedging FX business exposure and the accounting implications are the same. Other factors may influence the choice, however: For example, multinational managers sometimes find a foreign subsidiary can issue parent-guaranteed debt denominated in the local currency at a lower interest rate than the parent would have to pay. In this case, a parent can have the subsidiary issue debt instead of the parent. Another reason to have a subsidiary issue its own debt locally is to manage "political risk exposure." That is, being indebted to local country lenders may reduce the probability and magnitude of incurring "political problems" with the local government. Finally, corporate taxes may also have an impact on the decision as to which entity should issue the debt.

Many countries, including the United States, are on a so-called _worldwide tax system_. In such a tax system, taxes are paid to a parent's home government on the foreign income of a subsidiary, but credit is given for foreign taxes paid by the subsidiary. Therefore, if the foreign tax rate is _higher_ than the parent's home tax rate, there will be more than enough credit for foreign taxes paid to ensure that the parent will not have to pay any tax to its home country government on the foreign income of the subsidiary. On the other hand, if the foreign tax rate is _lower_ than the parent's home tax rate, the credit for the foreign taxes paid will not be as much as what would be owed to the parent's government on the foreign income of the subsidiary. The net result is summarized as follows:

If the foreign tax rate > the home tax rate, the effective tax rate for foreign income is the foreign tax rate, and the effective tax rate for home country income is the home tax rate.

If the foreign tax rate < the home tax rate, the home tax rate is the effective tax rate for _both_ foreign income and home country income.

Therefore, all else the same, if the foreign tax rate is higher than the home country tax rate, a U.S. company's debt should be issued by the foreign subsidiary rather than the parent, because the tax benefits of the debt's interest payments will be greater due to the higher effective tax rate. On the other hand, if the foreign tax rate is lower than the home country tax rate, it does not matter which entity issues the debt, because the effective tax rate is the same in either case.

In some of our earlier examples, the financing of a foreign subsidiary consists of equity owned by the subsidiary's parent and possibly some external debt. Frequently, foreign subsidiaries are also financed with internal debt, that is, a loan from the parent. If there were no taxes and no restrictions on repatriation of income, a loan from a parent would be equivalent to equity. But sometimes a country's rules on a subsidiary's dividend payments to a parent are more restrictive than the rules on payment of interest. So the internal loan approach can be a way around the restrictions on repatriation of foreign income back to the parent.

Even if there are no restrictions on the repatriation of a foreign subsidiary's income, tax differences can be a driver of a parent's decision on how to structure its internal financing of a foreign subsidiary. Again, assume the parent is domiciled in a country on a worldwide tax system. If the foreign tax rate is higher than the parent's home tax rate, the parent should structure the internal financing with as much debt as possible. This way, the tax payments to the foreign country are minimized. The interest on the debt received by the parent is taxed at the parent country's lower tax rate. On the other hand, if the foreign tax rate is lower than the parent's home tax rate, the parent should structure the internal financing with as much equity as possible. The reason is that home country taxes on the foreign income can often be deferred into the future if not repatriated as dividends.

Summary Action Points

- Sometimes a firm can use foreign currency net debt to hedge FX business exposure to a foreign currency. Having foreign currency net debt involves a financial leverage effect in addition to an FX hedging effect.
- When FX business exposure is positive and less than 1, the financial leverage effect is less pronounced, and foreign currency net debt is often an effective way to hedge FX business exposure. When FX business exposure is greater than 1, the financial leverage effect

dominates the FX hedging effect, which may create problems when managers try to use foreign currency debt for hedging.

- The impact of FX changes on the book value of foreign currency net debt can make a firm's reported earnings more volatile, unless the foreign currency debt qualifies for hedge accounting.
- Some of the factors that managers need to consider in finding the optimal level of foreign currency debt for a given firm are financial distress costs, misvaluation of the currency, accounting implications, and taxes.

Glossary

Cash Flow Hedge: Financial instruments may, in some cases, be regarded as a hedge of foreign currency cash flows, and thus qualify for hedge accounting.

Financial Hedging of FX Exposure: Hedging FX risk using financial instruments instead of using operational strategies.

Hedge Accounting: An accounting treatment allowing the gains/losses on financial instruments to not affect current earnings when changes in the value of underlying asset being hedged do not affect current earnings.

Net Investment Hedge: Financial instruments that hedge the book value of a firm's net investment in a foreign affiliate, which automatically qualify for hedge accounting treatment.

Worldwide Tax System: For a multinational company headquartered in a country on a worldwide tax system, taxes are paid to a parent's home government on the foreign income of a subsidiary, but credit is given for foreign taxes paid by the subsidiary.

Discussion Questions

1. Why is borrowing in yen at 2% not necessarily advantageous to borrowing in U.S. dollars at 6%?
2. Would foreign currency debt be an effective hedge for a company with an FX business exposure higher than 1? Explain.
3. When would using foreign currency debt as a hedge cause higher volatility in a firm's current earnings? Discuss.

4. Under what circumstances would it be advantageous for a foreign subsidiary to issue parent-guaranteed debt instead of the parent?

5. What is the impact on FX equity exposure and FX accounting exposure if a foreign subsidiary issues parent-guaranteed debt instead of the parent?

6. Explain why, in the absence of taxes, an internal loan from a parent to a subsidiary is the same as parent equity in the subsidiary.

Problems

1. AGC Company issues €20 million of euro-denominated debt when the spot FX rate is 1.25 $/€. (a) What is the value of the debt in U.S. dollars? (b) What is the value of the debt in U.S. dollars if the euro depreciates by 10%?

2. Assume a U.S. firm's FX business exposure to the euro is 1.60. The firm's net debt is entirely denominated in euros. (a) The ratio of net debt to business value is 40%. Find the firm's FX equity exposure to the euro. (b) The ratio of net debt to business value is 70%. Find the firm's FX equity exposure to the euro.

3. Assume a U.S. company has an FX business exposure to the British pound of 0.40. The company wants no FX equity exposure to the pound. What amount of net debt should the firm denominate in British pounds if the firm's business value is $2.50 million?

4. Assume ABC Co. currently has $V_B^{\$} = \$10$ million, $ND^{\$} = \$4$ million, and thus $S^{\$} = \$6$ million. Assume the FX business exposure to the euro is 1.25. Assume that $3 million of the firm's net debt is denominated in euros and the rest is in U.S. dollars. Assume the euro depreciates by 10%. (a) Find the new equity value and the FX equity exposure to the euro using the "what if" method. (b) Verify the FX equity exposure using equation (3.1).

5. Assume a U.S. firm's business value is $20,000 and the FX business exposure to the yen is −0.35. (a) If the firm has $5,000 in yen cash and no other net debt, find the firm's FX equity exposure to the yen. (b) Find the level of yen cash that would make the FX equity exposure to the yen equal to 0.

For 6-9: TYR is a U.S. company with business value of $500 million. TYR has $25 million in cash denominated in U.S. dollars. TYR has U.S. dollar-denominated debt of $100 million and euro-denominated debt of €20 million (note amount given in euros). Assume today's spot FX rate is 1.25 $/€. TYR has estimated its FX business exposure to the euro is 0.60.

6. What is TYR's new business value if the euro depreciates by 20%?
7. What is the new value in U.S. dollars of TYR's €-debt if the euro depreciates by 20%?
8. What is TYR's new equity value if the euro depreciates by 20%?
9. What is TYR's FX equity exposure to the euro at time 0?

For 10-13: RYT Company is a U.S. firm with a business value of $28.2 million. RYT has $2 million in cash denominated in U.S. dollars, U.S. dollar-denominated debt of $6 million, and €3 million in euro-denominated debt. Assume today's spot FX rate is 1.40 $/€. RYT's FX business exposure to the euro is 0.60. Use the "what if" method with a euro depreciation of 25%.

10. Find RYT's "what if" business value.
11. Find the "what if" value in U.S. dollars of RYT's euro-denominated debt.
12. Find RYT's "what if" equity value.
13. What is RYT's FX equity exposure to the euro at time 0?

14. ABC Co. is a U.S. firm that owns the Eurozone subsidiary TDL, and the functional currency is the euro. ABC has no other Eurozone subsidiaries. TDL has no debt and has a book value of total assets of €1,000. The spot FX rate is 1.35 $/€. ABC has $3,000 of its own euro-denominated debt, not on TDL's balance sheet. (a) What is ABC's net investment in TDL? For (b), (c), and (d), assume the euro appreciates by 10%. (b) What is the new level of TDL's assets shown on ABC's consolidated balance sheet? (c) What is the change in ABC's Cumulative Translation Adjustment (CTA) account? (d) Ignoring the impact of the FX change on operating cash flow, what will be the impact on ABC's reported current earnings?

15. TZL is a Eurozone subsidiary of the U.S. multinational DTD Company, with the euro as its functional currency. DTD's net investment in TZL is $2,000. DTD's FX business exposure to the euro is 0.40. DTD's reported (book) and value balance sheets are shown below. Assume the euro depreciates by 10%. (a) What will DTD's new book and value balance sheets look like? (b) Ignoring the impact on operating cash flow, what will be the impact of the FX change on reported DTD's current earnings?

DTD Company Time-0 Balance Sheets (in $s)

Reported (Book)	Assets	Liabilities & Equity	
	$ 2,000 Net Inv TZL	$ 1,000 €-Debt	
		$ 1,000 AOCI	
		$ 6,000 Other Equity	
	$ 6,000 Other	$ 7,000 Equity	
	$ 8,000	$ 8,000	
Value	Value	Liabilities & Equity	
		$ 1,000 €-Debt $(ND_\epsilon^\$)$	
	$ 8,000 $V_B^\$$	$ 7,000 $S^\$$	
	$ 8,000	$ 8,000	

For 16-19: TBR Co. is a U.S. company. Assume that at time 0: (1) The book value of TBR's net investment in Eurozone assets is $10 million. (2) The book value of all of TBR's other assets (in the United States and elsewhere) is $25 million. (3) TBR's business value is $40 million. (4) TBR has $15 million in euro-denominated net debt and no other net debt. (5) TBR's FX business exposure to the euro is 2.50. (6) The spot FX rate is 1.30 $/€.

16. What is TBR's FX equity exposure to the euro?
17. If the euro depreciates by 10%, what is TBR's new equity value?
18. TBR cannot qualify any €-debt as a cash flow hedge, but TBR does qualify the maximum amount of €-debt as a net investment hedge. Assume the euro depreciates by 10%. (a) What is the change in the book value of TBR's equity? (b) Is the level of current earnings affected by the FX change?

19. TBR's CFO is considering issuing $5 million more of euro-denominated debt and using the proceeds of the debt issue to reduce outstanding equity by open market repurchase of equity shares. Will the restructuring reduce TBR's FX equity exposure to the euro? Explain. Find the new FX equity exposure to the euro.

Answers to Problems

1. (a) $25 million; (b) $22.5 million.
2. (a) $(1.60 - 0.40)/(1 - 0.40) = 2$; (b) $(1.60 - 0.70)/(1 - 0.70) = 3$.
3. $0.40(\$2.5 \text{ million}) = \$1 \text{ million}$.
4. (a) The business value drops by 12.5%, to $8.75 million. The value of the euro-debt in U.S. dollars drops by 10%, to $2.70 million, while the value of the other debt stays the same, $1 million. The "what if" equity value is $8.75 million $-$ 2.70 million $-$ 1 million = $5.05 million. The percentage change in equity value is $5.05 million/$6 million $-$ 1 = -0.158, or -15.8%. So the firm's FX equity exposure is $-0.158/ -0.10 = 1.58$. (b) Because $ND_\epsilon^\$/V_B^\$ = 0.30$ and $ND^\$/V_B^\$ = 0.40$, the FX equity exposure of 1.58 is consistent with equation (3.1): $\xi_{S\epsilon}^\$ = (1.25 - 0.30)/(1 - 0.40) = 1.58$.
5. (a) From equation (3.1), the FX equity exposure is $(-0.35 - (-0.25))/ (1 - (-0.25)) = -0.08$. (b) The ratio of net debt to business value needs to be -0.35, and thus the net debt in yen needs to be $-\$7,000$, or $7,000 in yen cash. When the yen appreciates by 10%, the U.S. dollar value of the yen cash rises by 10% to $7,700, and the business value drops by 3.5% to $19,300. Thus the equity value is not changed.
6. $0.88(\$500 \text{ million}) = \$440 \text{ million}$.
7. $20 million.
8. $440 million + 25 million $-$ 100 million $-$ 20 million = $345 million.
9. $345/$400 $-$ 1 = -0.1375; FX equity exposure = $-0.1375/-0.20 = 0.6875$. Or, $(0.60 - 0.05)/(1 - 0.20) = 0.6875$.
10. $0.85(\$28.2 \text{ million}) = \$23.97 \text{ million}$.
11. $3.15 million.
12. $23.97 million + 2 million $-$ 6 million $-$ 3.15 million = $16.82 million.

13. $16.82/$20 − 1 = −0.159; FX equity exposure = −0.159/−0.25 = 0.636. Or, (0.60 − 4.2/28.2)/(1 − 8.2/28.2) = 0.636.

14. (a) $1,350; (b) $1,485; (c) No net change, because there is (more than) enough debt to hedge the FX translation exposure of the foreign asset; (d) $165 loss, from the $1,650 of euro-denominated debt that does not follow hedge accounting.

15. (a) Business value drops by 0.40(10%), to $7,680. The book value of the net investment in TZL drops by 10%, to $1,800. In U.S. dollars, the $1,000 in €-debt drops by 10%, to $900, both in book value and economic value. The FX translation loss of $200 on TZL goes to the AOCI account, but is offset (partially) by the $100 gain on the €-debt, because the debt qualifies as a net investment hedge. (b) Reported earnings do not change, because all the €-debt qualifies for hedge accounting.

DTD Company Time-1 Balance Sheets (in $s)

Reported	Assets	Liabilities & Equity	
	$ 1,800 Net Inv TZL	$ 900 €-Debt	
		$ 6,000 AOCI	
		$ 6,000 Other Equity	
	$ 6,000 Other	$ 6,900 Equity	
	$ 7,800	$ 7,800	
Value	Value	Liabilities & Equity	
		$ 900 €-Debt ($ND_{\epsilon}^{\$}$)	
	$ 8,000 $V_B^{\$}$	$ 6,780 $S^{\$}$	
	$ 7,680	$ 7,680	

16. (2.5 − 0.375)/(1 − 0.375) = 3.4.

17. Business value changes by 2.5(−10%) = −25%. So new business value = 0.75($40 million) = $30 million; New value of net debt = 0.90 × ($15 million) = $13.5 million; $30 million − 13.5 million = $16.5 million. Or, old equity value was $40 million − 15 million = $25 million; New equity value = 0.66($25 million) = $16.5 million.

18. (a) Old book equity = \$35 million – \$15 million = \$20 million. New book equity = \$34 million – 13.5 million = \$20.5 million, an increase of 0.50 million; (b) Yes; the rise in the equity book value will be reflected in current earnings, because this change represents a drop in value of the debt that does not qualify for hedge accounting.

19. No; it will increase, due to the increase in financial leverage, because TBR's FX business exposure > 1. New FX equity exposure = (2.50 – 0.50)/(1 – 0.50) = 4.

CHAPTER 4

Currency Swaps

The advent of swaps, as much as anything else, helped transform the world's segmented capital markets into a single, truly integrated, international capital market.
—John F. Marshall and Kenneth R. Kapner (1993)

A *currency swap* is a contract to exchange two streams of future cash flows in different currencies. Currency swaps were designed to circumvent capital controls imposed by governments and to make borrowing more efficient in global markets. We will see that currency swaps are used to convert debt denominated in one currency into synthetic debt denominated in another currency. Synthetic debt created in this way sometimes allows a segment of the capital market to be tapped that would otherwise not be accessible with debt actually denominated in that currency. By themselves, currency swaps are useful in managing FX business exposure in situations where foreign currency net debt is not practical.

World Bank-IBM Swap

The first currency swap seems to be a 1981 transaction between the World Bank and IBM. Its details are instructive. The World Bank wanted to raise additional capital by issuing new debt and to denominate the debt payments in Swiss francs because of a low interest rate in that currency. The U.S. market, though, was more receptive to World Bank bonds than was the Swiss market, because the World Bank had already saturated the Swiss market for its bonds, and U.S. investors regarded World Bank bonds to have much less credit risk than Swiss investors did. But the U.S. investors wanted bonds denominated in U.S. dollars.

At the same time, IBM had previously financed by issuing some Swiss franc debt, but had since developed the view that the Swiss franc was undervalued, and thus was likely to appreciate abnormally relative to the U.S. dollar. IBM thus wanted to replace its Swiss franc debt with U.S. dollar debt. But issuing new U.S. dollar bonds and using the proceeds to repurchase the Swiss franc bonds would be relatively expensive in terms of transaction costs.

A major global bank saw that both parties could benefit by making a private deal, which it termed a currency swap. The swap let IBM receive Swiss franc cash flows from the World Bank, and the World Bank received U.S. dollars from IBM. The World Bank could then go ahead and borrow from U.S. investors at the favorable U.S. market interest rate, planning to use its U.S. dollar receipts from the currency swap to make the U.S. dollar bond payments. This way, the Swiss franc swap payments to IBM represented the new effective liability for the World Bank. Similarly, IBM could use the Swiss francs received from the World Bank to meet its existing Swiss franc debt obligations, while its U.S. dollar payments to the World Bank represented its new effective debt in U.S. dollars. Figure 4.1 shows the basic structure of the World Bank–IBM currency swap.

IBM's motivation was clear. IBM had issued Swiss franc bonds but subsequently wanted to change that debt into a U.S. dollar debt, as it feared an abnormal appreciation of the Swiss franc. IBM used the currency swap as an expeditious way to convert the debt, without having to retire its Swiss franc debt and reissue new U.S. dollar debt. This was money saving and time saving. The World Bank, on the other hand, used the currency swap in a capital raising strategy. You might ask why the World Bank didn't simply issue Swiss franc bonds in the first place, if it wanted its debt

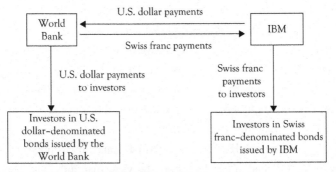

Figure 4.1. World Bank–IBM Currency Swap.

to be denominated in Swiss francs. The answer is that the World Bank was able to get a lower effective Swiss franc interest rate than it could by issuing Swiss franc bonds directly. The World Bank took advantage of the financing opportunity in the U.S. market, and achieved its preferred liability denomination of Swiss francs through the swap deal.

We describe the positions in currency swaps like positions in forward FX contracts. IBM had a long Swiss franc position and a short U.S. dollar position in the swap because it received Swiss francs and paid U.S. dollars. The World Bank had a short Swiss franc position and a long U.S. dollar position in the swap because it paid Swiss francs and received U.S. dollars.

Fixed-for-Fixed Currency Swaps

The basic "plain vanilla" currency swap is a *fixed-for-fixed* swap. In this case, the cash flows are based on straight bonds in two currencies, where a *straight bond* has no features other than promised coupon interest and principal repayment. The swap stipulates the tenor (time until maturity), the two coupon interest rates, and the *notional principal*.

An example is a 5-year, 6% U.S. dollars for 4% Swiss francs currency swap, with notional principal of $1,000. This swap's payments are based on two 5-year straight bonds, one denominated in U.S. dollars and the other in Swiss francs, which make annual coupon interest payments. The coupon rate of the 5-year U.S. dollar bond is 6%, and the coupon rate of the 5-year Swiss franc bond is 4%. Given a principal of $1,000 for the U.S. dollar bond, the coupon payments are 0.06($1,000) = $60 per year. At maturity, at the same time as the final coupon payment, the $1,000 principal must also be repaid. Now consider the equivalent amount of principal in Swiss francs. Given an assumed time-0 spot FX rate of 1.60 Sf/$, $1,000(1.60 Sf/$) = Sf 1,600. Thus, the Swiss franc bond makes coupon payments of 0.04(Sf 1,600) = Sf 64 per year and then also repays the principal of Sf 1,600 at the same time as the last coupon payment.

Any two counterparties can agree to exchange the cash flows based "notionally" on these two bonds, whether the counterparties actually own the bonds or not. Counterparty U would agree to receive, from counterparty S, the Swiss franc cash flows of Sf 64 annually for 5 years, plus Sf 1,600 at maturity. Counterparty S would agree to receive, from counterparty U, the U.S.

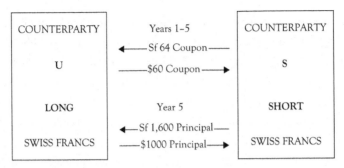

Figure 4.2. 5-year fixed-for-fixed currency swap
4% Swiss francs for 6% U.S. dollars
Notional principal $1,000 = Sf 1,600

dollar cash flows of $60 annually for 5 years, plus $1,000 at maturity. The two counterparties have agreed to a currency swap; counterparty U has the long position on Swiss francs and counterparty S has the short position on Swiss francs. Figure 4.2 shows this currency swap.

If the coupon rates on the two underlying bonds are the same as the market yields for the two bonds, the swap is termed an *at-market swap*. In our Swiss franc–U.S. dollar swap example, if the current market yield on 5-year bonds is 4% in U.S. dollars and 6% in Swiss francs, the principal of each bond is equal to the present value of its future cash flows. Thus, the present values of the swapped cash flows are equivalent at time 0. A future cash flow stream worth Sf 1,600 today is swapped for one worth $1,000 today, which is fair at the assumed current spot FX rate of 1.60 Sf/$. In an at-market swap, no time-0 funds transfer is necessary, because the present values of the underlying notional bonds are equivalent, given the current spot FX rate. Many currency swaps originate as at-market swaps.

Another popular currency swap arrangement is a fixed-for-floating swap. An exchange of fixed-coupon payments in one currency for floating-rate payments in another currency is sometimes called a *cross-currency swap*. An exchange of fixed-coupon bond payments in a currency for floating-rate payments in the same currency is called an *interest rate swap*. These swaps are beyond our scope here.

Example swap rates for at-market swaps for September 2, 2000, taken from www.cfoweb.com before that site closed to the public, are shown in Exhibit 4.1. DKK is the Danish krone, and SEK is the Swedish krona. Given

Exhibit 4.1. *Example Currency Swap Rates September 2, 2000*

	USD	EUR	JPY	CHF	DKK	SEK
2Y	6.84	5.41	0.70	3.89	5.94	5.12
3Y	6.85	5.48	0.93	3.93	5.94	5.39
4Y	6.86	5.54	1.17	3.97	5.94	5.60
5Y	6.87	5.60	1.41	4.00	5.96	5.72
7Y	6.90	5.70	1.81	4.10	5.98	5.88
10Y	6.96	5.79	2.20	4.23	6.01	6.01

Source: www.cfoweb.com

the swap rates in Exhibit 4.1, if you wanted a short yen position in an at-market 5-year swap, you would pay yen at the coupon rate of 1.41% on the swap's notional yen principal, and receive U.S. dollars at the rate of 6.87% on the equivalent notional principal in U.S. dollars, at the current spot FX rate.

You enter into a 5-year fixed-for-fixed currency swap to receive cash flows in British pounds and to pay cash flows in U.S. dollars. The swap's notional principal of $1 million. What are the cash flows of the swap, if the 5-year coupon interest rates are 5.50% for U.S. dollars and 9.00% for British pounds, and if the spot FX rate is currently 1.50 $/£?

Answer: You pay 0.055($1 million) = $55,000 per year for 5 years, plus a payment of $1 million at the end of year 5. The cash flows you receive are based on a sterling denominated bond with a principal amount equal to the sterling equivalent of $1 million, given the spot FX rate of 1.50 $/£. Thus, the principal on the sterling bond is $1 million/(1.50 $/£) = £666,667. At a coupon interest rate of 9%, you'd receive 0.09(£666,667) = £60,000 per year for 5 years, and a principal component of £666,667 at the end of year 5.

Parallel Loans and Back-to-Back Loans

Currency swaps evolved from *parallel loans*, devised years ago to get around cross border capital controls. At one time, for example, it was illegal by British law for a British company to use capital from the United Kingdom for overseas investment. The law was intended to prompt the use of British capital for domestic investment and thus to help create jobs at home. There was no law, however, to prevent a British company, like British Petroleum (BP), from lending British pounds to the local UK subsidiary of a U.S. multinational, say DuPont. And DuPont could lend the equivalent amount in U.S. dollars to the U.S. subsidiary of BP. This arrangement is known as a *parallel loan*.

While DuPont's UK subsidiary made pound denominated interest and principal payments to BP, BP's U.S. subsidiary would make U.S. dollar interest and principal payments to DuPont. BP's U.S. subsidiary would receive the financing it needed, circumventing Britain's capital export controls. Moreover, DuPont could effectively repatriate earnings of its UK subsidiary to the United States without paying repatriation taxes to the British government. Thus, parallel loans not only got around capital controls, but also helped avoid foreign tax on the repatriated returns of overseas investments.

It isn't much of a leap to see that even if companies in different countries do not need new capital, they can arrange *hypothetical* loans to each other's subsidiaries and thus accomplish the exchange of future cash flow streams. Suppose Toyota's U.S. subsidiary is generating U.S. dollars, and Goodyear's Japanese subsidiary is generating yen. Toyota's U.S. subsidiary puts a U.S. dollar loan on its balance sheet, payable to Goodyear, and then in the future makes U.S. dollar interest and principal payments to Goodyear. At the same time, Goodyear's Japanese subsidiary puts a yen loan on its balance sheet, payable to Toyota, and then makes future yen interest and principal payments to Toyota. No principal amounts are actually exchanged. This type of an arrangement is called a *back-to-back loan*.

Exhibit 4.2 shows hypothetical balance sheets representing both parallel loan and back-to-back loan arrangements, using DuPont and BP as the representative companies. The spot FX rate is assumed to be 2 $/£. BP's U.S. subsidiary owes $3,000 to DuPont, and DuPont's UK subsidiary owes the equivalent amount in pounds, £1,500, to BP.

Although parallel loans and back-to-back loans are ways to avoid cross border capital controls and repatriation taxes, they have some drawbacks.

Exhibit 4.2. Parallel Loans or Back-to-Back Loans Balance Sheets for Parents and Subsidiaries

UK Subsidiary of DuPont (£s)		DuPont ($s)
Assets	_Debt & Equity_	_Assets_
£2,500	£1,500 Debt to BP	$3,000 Loan to BP's U.S. Sub
_____	1,000 Equity DuPont	2,000 Equity Investment in own UK Sub
£2,500	£2,500	4,000 Other Assets
		$9,000 Total
U.S. Subsidiary of BP ($s)		**BP (£s)**
Assets	_Debt & Equity_	_Assets_
$4,000	$3,000 Debt to DuPont	£1,500 Loan to DuPont's UK Sub
_____	1,000 Equity BP	500 Equity Investment in own U.S. Sub
$4,000	$4,000	£4,000 Other Assets
		£6,000 Total
Spot FX rate = 2 $/£		

First, parallel and back-to-back loans are shown on reported balance sheets, so they result in higher debt ratios, a key factor in credit ratings. Second, different legal provisions in different countries make it very difficult to link the loans legally. If one party defaults on its loan, the laws in the other country would still require the other party to pay off the loan on its side of the agreement. Third, each side had to make full payment of the cash flow; that is, there is no difference check settlement.

Enter global financial intermediaries to serve as brokers. The various companies would no longer have to search for suitable partners. The global banks took the key step of structuring the deals as legal swaps of cash flow streams instead of mutual loans, and thus to solve all three drawbacks: (a) Swap positions were off balance sheet, and not figured into debt ratio computations. (b) The cash flows could legally be viewed as offsetting legs of a single transaction, which solved the legal problems. In the process, global banks began to serve as swaps dealers, meaning that swap counterparties dealt only with banks. A bankruptcy by one company would be the bank's problem, not the other company's problem. (c) Structuring currency swaps as instruments whose periodic exchanges can be settled with one way net difference checks relieved the counterparties from having to exchange of the full amounts of funds at each exchange time. This feature in turn reduced the counterparty risk of default.

Swap-Driven Financing

A currency swap can sometimes help companies reduce the cost of borrowing because of "inefficiencies" in cross-border capital markets. Companies that really want to have a foreign currency debt may sometimes find it advantageous to issue home currency debt, and then swap to create the foreign currency debt synthetically.

For example, say the spot FX rate is 1.25 $/€, and General Electric (GE) wants to borrow €200 million, equivalent to $250 million, and Siemens wants to borrow $250 million, both at fixed coupon rates. Assume that GE can borrow euros at 8.25% and U.S. dollars at 7.5%, while Siemens can borrow euros at 8% and U.S. dollars at 7.75%. For their preferred liability denominations without a currency swap, GE would pay 8.25% to borrow euros, and the Siemens would pay 7.75% to borrow U.S. dollars. If GE borrows U.S. dollars at 7.5%, and Siemens borrows euros at 8%, however, and the two companies engage in a currency swap of 7.5% U.S. dollars for 8% euros, each ends up with lower effective financing costs in their preferred currencies. The 7.5% incoming U.S. dollars from the swap would cover GE's actual 7.5% U.S. dollar liability, and GE would effectively be paying euro interest at the rate of 8%, lower than the 8.25% it would have to pay on actual euro borrowing. Siemens's 8% euro liability would be covered by the currency swap receipts, and the net effective liability would be 7.5% on U.S. dollars, again a lower rate than the 7.75% it would have to pay on actual U.S. dollar borrowing.

When an organization issues securities to raise capital and simultaneously originates a swap as an integral part of the deal, we call this *swap-driven financing*. A recent study of 13 Asia-Pacific countries finds that the motivation for borrowers to raise foreign currency debt and swap the proceeds into local currency, rather than borrowing the local currency directly, was to overcome market limitations and arbitrage cost differentials.[1]

In the GE–Siemens example, GE issues synthetic euro debt through an actual issue of U.S. dollar debt, and a short euro position in a currency swap. Siemens creates *synthetic U.S. dollar debt*, via a long swap position in euros combined with actual euro debt.

Synthetic Euro Debt (General Electric)

1. GE has actual U.S. dollar debt.
2. GE takes short currency swap position on euros.

Synthetic U.S. Dollar Debt (Siemens)

1. Siemens has actual euro debt.
2. Siemens takes long currency swap position on euros.

U.S. companies that want foreign currency-denominated debt, say for purposes of hedging FX business exposure, have sometimes found foreign investors reluctant to accept the risk of a corporate takeover, and so face a high financing cost in the foreign debt market. It is less expensive to issue synthetic foreign currency debt by combining a swap position with actual U.S. dollar debt issued to U.S. investors. Another example is found in Disney's synthetic yen financing, described in the box.

Disney's Synthetic Yen Financing

In the 1990s, a French utility company with an AAA credit rating wanted to borrow in European Currency Units (ECUs), a basket of European currencies that was a precursor to the euro, but had already borrowed too much from the European market in the sense that its cost of borrowing would be slightly higher than the typical AAA credit.

Disney had a positive FX business exposure to the Japanese yen and wanted therefore to borrow in yen to hedge. But as a company with a single-A credit rating, Disney was not welcome in the Japanese bond market by the Japanese central bank. Hence, Disney could only borrow from a Japanese bank rather than issue yen-denominated bonds, and at an interest rate higher than a typical company with a single-A credit rating would borrow in Japan.

On the other hand, the French utility's credit rating was welcome in Japan and would get a fair rate, and Disney was very welcome in

Europe and would get a fair rate there. So, each company had a comparative advantage in the other market. This is an interesting point. Even though the French utility could get a better rate than Disney in each market (because it was an AAA-rated company), Disney had the comparative advantage in Europe.

So it was beneficial to both companies to let the French utility borrow in Japan, and let Disney borrow in Europe, and then swap and share the saving between themselves (and throw a bone to the swap bank who bore the risk of swapping with a single-A firm.)[2]

Difference Check Settlement of Swap Components

Although the idea behind a swap is to exchange cash flow streams, the settlement of swap cash flows is often accomplished using difference checks. Let's look again at the 5-year fixed-for-fixed currency swap of 6% U.S. dollars for 4% Swiss francs for a notional principal of $1,000. At the time-0 spot FX rate of 1.60 Sf/$, the currency swap is effectively an exchange of $60 for Sf 64 each year for 5 years, and then a final exchange of $1,000 for Sf 1,600 at year 5. The long Swiss franc position has contracted to pay the $60 and receive Sf 64 each year for 5 years, and to pay $1,000 and receive Sf 1,600 at year 5.

In fact, each swap cash flow is typically settled by a difference check based on the actual spot FX rate at the time of the cash flow. If the spot FX rate has moved to 2 Sf/$ as of the time of the first interest component cash flow, the Sf 64 time-1 payment would be worth Sf 64/(2 Sf/$) = $32. The long Swiss franc position is scheduled to pay $60, but the U.S. dollar value of the Sf 64 to be received is now $32. The scheduled payment may thus be settled simply by a difference payment of $60 − 32 = $28, from the counterparty that is long Swiss francs to the counterparty that is short Swiss francs.

A difference check in a currency swap works in a fashion similar to a forward FX contract. The forward FX rate is replaced by an *FX conversion rate* for a component swap payment. There are generally two different FX conversion rates in a fixed-for-fixed swap: one for the interest components, and the other for the principal component.

The FX conversion rate for the interest components is the spot FX rate times the ratio of the coupon interest rates. The FX conversion rate for the interest components, $C_I^{Sf/\$}$, is shown in equation (4.1a):

FX Conversion Rate: Swap _Interest_ Component

$$C_I^{Sf/\$} = X_0^{Sf/\$}(r^{Sf}/r^{\$})$$ (4.1a)

The FX conversion rate for the principal component, $C_P^{Sf/\$}$, is simply the spot FX rate at the time the swap originated, as shown in equation (4.1b):

FX Conversion Rate: Swap _Principal_ Component

$$C_P^{Sf/\$} = X_0^{Sf/\$}$$ (4.1b)

In the U.S. dollar/Swiss franc swap example, the FX conversion rate for the interest components is $C_I^{Sf/\$}$ = (1.60 Sf/$)(0.04/0.06) = 1.0667 Sf/$. The numerator coupon interest rate should be consistent with the numerator currency of the FX rate. The FX conversion rate for the principal payment is simply the spot FX rate at time 0, so $C_P^{Sf/\$}$ = 1.60 Sf/$.

The difference check for a time-N component, from the point of view of the long foreign currency position, may be computed using equation (4.2). In equation (4.2), $D_{Sf}^{\$}$ denotes the difference check amount in the pricing currency, which is assumed to be U.S. dollars. $C^{\$/Sf}$ is the FX conversion rate for the particular component, expressed in direct terms from the point of view of the pricing currency, the U.S. dollar. Z^{Sf} is the foreign currency component, which here is assumed to be in Swiss francs.

Difference Check Settlement of Swap Component

$$D_{Sf}^{\$} = Z^{Sf}[X_N^{\$/Sf} - C^{\$/Sf}]$$ (4.2)

In the U.S. dollar/Swiss franc fixed-for-fixed currency swap example, Z^{Sf} for the interest component is Sf 64, and the FX conversion rate is 1.0667 Sf/$. Thus, if the spot FX rate at the time of settling an interest component is 2 Sf/$, equation (4.2) indicates the long Swiss franc position should receive a difference check settlement of Sf 64[1/(2 Sf/$) – 1/(1.0667 Sf/$)] = Sf 64[0.50 $/Sf – 0.9375 $/Sf] = –$28, where the negative sign implies that the long Swiss franc position must pay $28 to the counterparty that is short Swiss francs.

The difference check settlement for the principal component uses the spot FX rate at the time the swap originated as the FX conversion rate in equation (4.2). The Z^{Sf} for the principal is the swap's notional principal in foreign currency. Assume the spot FX rate at the time of principal component settlement is 2.50 Sf/$. The counterparty short Swiss francs owes Sf 1,600, which is equivalent to Sf 1,600/(2.50 Sf/$) = $640. Because the long position in Swiss francs owes a notional principal of $1,000, the counterparty long Swiss francs must send a difference check for $360 to settle the principal component at maturity. According to equation (4.2), the swap's long position in Swiss francs is entitled to (Sf 1,600)[1/(2.50 Sf/$) − 1/(1.60 Sf/$)] = Sf1,600[0.40 $/Sf − 0.625 $/Sf] = −$360. Because the sign is negative, the long position in Swiss francs settles with a difference check for $360 sent to the short position in Swiss francs.

Consider a 6-year fixed-for-fixed currency swap of 5% U.S. dollars for 7% Japanese yen on notional principal of $1 million. Assume that the spot FX rate when the swap originates is 140 ¥/$. (a) Find the difference check settlement on the interest component if the spot FX rate is 160 ¥/$ at time 1. (b) Find the difference check settlement on the principal component at time 6 if the spot FX rate then is 160 ¥/$.

Answers: The notional principal in yen is $1 million(140 ¥/$) = ¥140 million. (a) The U.S. dollar interest component is 0.05($1 million) = $50,000, and the yen interest component is 0.07(¥140 million) = ¥9.80 million. The FX conversion rate for the interest components is thus ¥9.80 million/$50,000 = 196 ¥/$. At 160 ¥/$, the time-1 interest component settles (from the viewpoint of the long position on yen) at ¥9.8 million × [1/(160 ¥/$) − 1/(196 ¥/$)] = $11,250. Thus, the long yen position receives $11,250 from the short yen position to settle the interest component at time 1. (b) At time 6, the settlement of the principal component (from the viewpoint of the long position on yen) is equal to ¥140 million × [1/(160 ¥/$) − 1/(140 ¥/$)] = −$125,000. The short yen position receives $125,000 (or equivalently $125,000(160 ¥/$) = ¥20 million) from the long yen position to settle the principal component at time 6.

Mark-to-Market Value of a Currency Swap

Like other financial instruments, a currency swap position's mark-to-market (MTM) value fluctuates with market conditions, namely, the spot FX rate and the interest rates in the two currencies. To find the MTM value of a currency swap position, subtract the present value of the future outflows from the present value of the future inflows, using the current spot FX rate to compare the present values in a common currency. Look at the long Swiss franc position of a fixed-for-fixed currency swap as a combination of owning a coupon bond in Swiss francs and owing a coupon bond in U.S. dollars. Thus, the MTM value of the long Swiss franc position, denoted $M_{Sf}^{\$}$, may be viewed as the swap's one-sided value of the notional Swiss franc bond, $B_{Sf}^{\$}$, minus the one-sided value of the notional U.S. dollar bond, $B_{\$}^{\$}$, as shown in equation (4.3). The MTM value of an at market swap is zero when the swap originates.

MTM Value of Currency Swap Position Long Swiss Francs

$$M_{Sf}^{\$} = B_{Sf}^{\$} - B_{\$}^{\$} \qquad (4.3)$$

Consider again a 5-year, 6% U.S. dollar for 4% Swiss franc currency swap, with $1,000 in notional principal, that originated as an at-market swap when the spot FX rate was 1.60 Sf/$. What would be the MTM value just after the second interest settlement of the long Swiss franc position? To answer this question, you would need to know, at the time immediately after the second interest component, the spot FX rate and the market yields of both currencies for a horizon equal to the remaining life of the swap. In this case, the swap has 3 years left, as we are saying that the second interest component has just been settled.

To focus only on the influence of the spot FX rate change, we assume that after the time-2 interest component settlement, the market yields on 3-year coupon bonds are 6% in U.S. dollars and 4% in Swiss francs, the same as the original coupon rates of the swap. Thus, with 3 years left, the present value of the U.S. dollar payments of $60 for 3 more years, plus the principal payment of $1,000, given the 6% market yield, is $1,000 (= $60/1.06 + $60/1.06^2 + $1,060/1.06^3). This is the one-sided value of the U.S. dollar bond, $B_{\$}^{\$}$, at time 2. Similarly, the present value of the payments of Sf 64 for 3 years plus the Sf 1,600 principal payment at the 4% market yield is Sf 1,600 (= Sf 64/1.04 + Sf 64/1.04^2 + Sf (64 + 1,600)/1.04^3). If the spot FX rate is 1.60 Sf/$ at time 2, the one-sided value in U.S. dollars of the Swiss franc bond, $B_{Sf}^{\$}$, is $1,000.

Thus, at a spot FX rate at time 2 of 1.60 Sf/$, the long Swiss franc swap position's MTM value is $M_{Sf}^{\$} = B_{Sf}^{\$} - B_{\$}^{\$} = \$1,000 - \$1,000 = 0$, because the present values of the two sides of the underlying cash flows, $1,000 and Sf 1,600, balance each other at that spot FX rate. If the spot FX rate at time 2 is 1.25 Sf/$, however, the Sf 1,600 present value of the future Swiss franc cash flows would be equivalent to a U.S. dollar value of Sf 1,600/ (1.25 Sf/$) = $1,280. Thus, the long Swiss franc position owns a future cash flow stream of Swiss francs (equivalent to a 3-year Swiss franc 4% coupon bond) that has a one-sided value in U.S. dollars of $B_{Sf}^{\$} =$ $1,280, but owes a cash flow stream in U.S. dollars with a present value of $B_{\$}^{\$} = \$1,000$. The MTM value of the swap, from the viewpoint of the long Swiss franc position, is thus $1,280 – 1,000 = $280. The Swiss franc appreciated from the time the swap was originated, from 1.60 Sf/$ to 1.25 Sf/$, and the long Swiss franc position thus gained $280 in value. Now, if the long Swiss franc party wants to liquidate in the open market, essentially finding a third party to assume the position, the third party would have to pay $280 in order to take over the long swap position.

The MTM value for the short Swiss franc position is the negative of the MTM value for the long Swiss franc position. In our example, the MTM value of the short Swiss franc position is –$280. If the short Swiss franc party wants to liquidate in the open market, essentially finding a third party to assume the position, the short position would have to pay the third party $280 in order to get out from under the short swap position.

Consider the U.S. dollar-Swiss franc example in the text. Assume the spot FX rate at time 2 is 2 Sf/$, but all else remains the same. (a) Find the MTM value of the long Swiss franc swap position after the second interest component payment. (b) Find the MTM value of the short Swiss franc position.

Answers: (a) After the second interest component settlement, the present value of the remaining Swiss franc cash flows is Sf 1,600, which is equiv-alent to Sf 1,600/(2 Sf/$) = $800. Thus, the MTM value of the swap

from the viewpoint of the long position on Swiss francs is $800 − 1,000 =
−$200. The long Swiss francs counterparty would have to pay $200 to
turn the swap position over to a third party, given the assumed spot FX
rate of 2 Sf/$ and the time-2 U.S. dollar and Swiss franc interest rates. In
this case, the Swiss franc has depreciated since the swap originated, and
the swap's long position on Swiss francs lost $200 in value because of the
depreciation. (b) The short Swiss franc position's MTM value is $200.

Currency Swaps and FX Equity Exposure

Currency swaps will have an impact on a firm's FX equity exposure just
like foreign currency debt does. When a firm combines a currency swap
position with actual debt to engineer synthetic debt in a different currency,
we regard the synthetic debt as actual debt for purposes of applying equation (3.1) to compute FX equity exposure. Recall that equation (3.1) is
$\xi_{S\epsilon}{}^{\$} = [\xi_{B\epsilon}{}^{\$} - ND_{\epsilon}{}^{\$}/V_{B}{}^{\$}]/[1 - ND^{\$}/V_{B}{}^{\$}]$.

In other cases, a firm may use a currency swap on its own and not in
order to create synthetic debt. We call these *naked currency swap positions*.
We can adapt equation (3.1) into equation (4.4) when a firm has naked
currency swap positions.

FX Equity Exposure with Currency Swaps

$$\xi_{S\epsilon}{}^{\$} = [\xi_{B\epsilon}{}^{\$} - NL_{\epsilon}{}^{\$}/V_{B}{}^{\$}]/[1 - ND^{\$}/V_{B}{}^{\$}] \qquad (4.4)$$

Equation (4.4) is identical to equation (3.1) except that the term $NL_{\epsilon}{}^{\$}$
replaces $ND_{\epsilon}{}^{\$}$. $NL_{\epsilon}{}^{\$}$ represents the net value of all euro <u>liabilities</u>, including both actual euro net debt and the net of all one-sided notional values of
euro financial derivative positions. To determine $NL_{\epsilon}{}^{\$}$, the one-sided
notional values of short euro derivative positions would be added to any
actual euro net debt, while the one-sided values of long euro derivative
positions would be subtracted.

For example, if a U.S. firm has actual euro net debt with a value in U.S.
dollars of $20 million and a <u>short</u> euro position in a currency swap with a
$B_{\epsilon}{}^{\$}$ value (in U.S. dollars) of $15 million, then $NL_{\epsilon}{}^{\$}$ = $20 million +
15 million = $35 million. If a firm has actual euro net debt with a value
in U.S. dollars of $20 million and a <u>long</u> euro position in a currency swap

with a $B_\epsilon^\$$ of \$15 million, then $NL_\epsilon^\$$ = \$20 million − 15 million = \$5 million. The ratio of net euro liabilities to business value, $NL_\epsilon^\$/V_B^\$$, is in the numerator of equation (4.4). But the net financial leverage ratio in the denominator, $ND^\$/V_B^\$$, should be the ratio of the *actual* net debt to business value.

Assume XYZ Co. has a business value of \$2,000, \$200 of actual euro net debt, \$200 of actual non-euro net debt, and thus an equity value of \$1,600. In addition, assume XYZ has a naked short currency swap position on euros with notional principal of \$1,000. Assume the swap currently has an MTM value of zero. Assume that XYZ has an FX business exposure to the euro of 2. Find XYZ's FX equity exposure using equation (4.4).

Because the currency swap has no MTM value at time 0, the value in U.S. dollars of the short euro side of the swap is \$1,000. Thus, $NL_\epsilon^\$/V_B^\$$ = (\$200 + 1,000)/\$2,000 = \$1,200/\$2,000 = 0.60. With equation (4.4) we have that $\xi_{S\epsilon}^\$$ = [2 − 0.60]/[1 − 0.20] = **1.75**.

To double check the FX equity exposure, let's do a "what if" analysis. If the euro depreciates by 5%, the firm's business value falls by 10% to \$1,800, by virtue of the FX business exposure of 2. The value of the actual euro net debt (in U.S. dollars) falls to \$190, while the value of the actual U.S. dollar net debt stays at \$200. The equity value would be \$1,410, without considering the swap. The euro side of the swap position will have a new value in U.S. dollars of $B_\epsilon^\$$ = \$950, if the euro depreciates by 5%. The currency swap position is short euros, so there is an MTM gain of \$1,000 − 950 = \$50. With this gain, the "what if" value of XYZ's equity is \$1,410 + 50 = \$1,460. So the FX equity exposure computed by the "what if" method is (\$1,460/\$1,600 − 1)/(−0.05) = 1.75, which reconciles with the one found using equation (4.4).

It might help you to visualize what is going on in the example to see the two value balance sheets, before and after the FX rate change, in Exhibit 4.3. The one-sided values of the currency swap are shown above the dashed line, as off-balance sheet. The one-sided value of the long U.S. dollar side is shown on the asset side, while the one-sided value of the short euro side is shown on the liability side. We put the MTM value of the swap below the dashed line onto the value balance sheet, with net MTM gains shown as an asset and net MTM losses as a liability. There is no MTM value on the time-0 balance sheet, because the swap originated as an at-market swap.

Exhibit 4.3. XYZ Company Value Balance Sheets
Short Euro Currency Swap Position
$300 Euro Net Debt

Initial		
	Value	*Liabilities & Equity*
(Off)	$ 1,000 (Long $, $B_\$^\$$)	$ 1,000 (Short €, $B_€^\$$)
		$ 200 $ND_€^\$$
		$ 200 $ND_\$^\$$
	$ 2,000 $V_B^\$$	$ 1,600 $S^\$$
	$ 2,000	$ 2,000

"What if" the Euro Depreciates by 5%?

	Value	*Liabilities & Equity*
(Off)	$ 1,000 (Long $, $B_\$^\$$)	$ 950 (Short €, $B_€^\$$)
	$ 50 (Gain on Swap, $M_€^\$$)	$ 190 $ND_€^\$$
		$ 200 $ND_\$^\$$
	$ 1,800 $V_B^\$$	$ 1,460 $S^\$$
	$ 1,850	$ 1,850

Assume the U.S. firm ABC Co. has $V_B^\$$ = $5,000, $ND^\$$ = $3,000, and thus $S^\$$ = $2,000. Assume FX business exposure to the euro = 1.40. Say $2,000 of the firm's net debt is euro-denominated, and the rest is U.S. dollar-denominated. ABC also has a <u>long</u> euro position in a currency swap with notional principal of $1,000. The swap is currently an at-market swap. (a) Find ABC's FX equity exposure using equation (4.4). (b) Assume the euro depreciates by 10%. Find ABC's "what if" equity value, and verify the FX equity exposure.

Answers: (a) $NL_€^\$$ = $2,000 − 1,000 = $1,000, so $NL_€^\$/V_B^\$$ = $1,000/ $5,000 = 0.20. $ND^\$/V_B^\$$ = $3,000/$5,000 = 0.60. Thus with equation (4.4) we have that $\xi_{S€}^\$$ = [1.40 − 0.20]/[1 − 0.60] = 3. (b) If the euro depreciates by 10%, the business value drops by 14%, to $4,300, by virtue of the FX business exposure of 1.40. The value of the actual euro net debt (in U.S. dollars) falls to $1,800, while the value of the actual U.S. dollar net debt stays at $1,000. Before considering the currency swap position, the "what if" equity value would be $4,300 − 1,800 − 1,000 = $1,500. The euro side of the currency swap position would have a new value in U.S. dollars of $900, if the euro drops by 10%. Because the currency swap position is long euros, there is an MTM loss on the currency swap position: $900 − 1,000 = −$100. With this loss, the new value of ABC's equity is $1,500 − 100 = $1,400. The FX equity exposure found directly is ($1,400/ $2,000 − 1)/(−0.10) = 3, which reconciles with the FX equity exposure found using equation (4.4).

Managing FX Exposure with Currency Swaps

A firm may have a long FX business exposure that is too large to hedge with actual foreign currency debt. The firm may then want to consider supplementing actual foreign currency debt with a naked short currency swap position. To see how a currency swap works to hedge FX business exposure in this case, let us return to the XYZ Co. example and assume now that XYZ takes a $3,800 (notional principal) short euro position in a currency swap. Before any FX change, XYZ's business value is $2,000, and the on-balance sheet capital structure consists of $200 of euro net debt, $200 of non-euro net debt, and $1,600 of equity. In addition, there is now the off-balance sheet short euro currency swap position of $3,800. If the euro depreciates by 5%, the firm's business value falls by 10% to $1,800, by virtue of its FX business exposure of 2. The U.S. dollar value of the actual euro net debt falls to $190, while the value of the U.S. dollar net debt stays the same at $200. Before considering the currency swap position, the new equity value would be $1,410, as before.

The currency swap position is short euros, so the position will have a gain of 5% of the value (in U.S. dollars) of the euro side of the swap, when the euro depreciates by 5%. The MTM gain on the currency swap position is thus 0.05($3,800) = $190. With this gain, the new value of XYZ's equity is $1,410 + 190 = $1,600, exactly the equity value prior to FX change. In this scenario, the $3,800 short currency swap position combines with the actual euro net debt to completely hedge the firm's FX business exposure to the euro, so the firm's FX equity exposure to the euro is zero.

The key is to make the *total* amount of euro net liabilities, $NL_\epsilon^\$$ including both the actual euro net debt and the off-balance sheet short euro position of the currency swap, equal to the FX business exposure times the business value, $\xi_{B\epsilon}^\$ V_B^\$$. In this case, $\xi_{B\epsilon}^\$ = 2$ and $V_B^\$ = \$2,000$, so the total euro net liability level in U.S. dollar terms should be $NL_\epsilon^\$ = \xi_{B\epsilon}^\$ V_B^\$ = 2(\$2,000) = \$4,000$. Because XYZ already had $\$200$ in actual euro net debt, the hedge is completed by the $\$3,800$ short currency swap position on euros.

Assume the U.S. firm ABC Co. currently has $V_B^\$ = \$5,000$, $ND^\$ = \$3,000$, and thus $S^\$ = \$2,000$. Assume an FX business exposure to the euro of 1.60. Let us say $\$2,000$ of the firm's net debt is euro-denominated, and the rest is U.S. dollar-denominated. (a) Determine the notional principal of a currency swap position that will eliminate ABC's FX equity exposure. (b) Assume the euro depreciates by 10%. Show that the equity value stays at $\$2,000$.

Answers: (a) The total amount of euro net liabilities should be $NL_\epsilon^\$ = \xi_{B\epsilon}^\$ V_B^\$ = 1.60(\$5,000) = \$8,000$. Because the firm already has $\$2,000$ in actual euro net debt, the (at-market) currency swap should have a notional principal of $\$6,000$. (b) Due to the FX business exposure of 1.60, the business value falls by 16%, from $\$5,000$ to $\$4,200$, when the euro depreciates by 10%. The U.S. dollar value of the actual euro net debt drops by 10% to $\$1,800$, while the value of the other actual net debt stays at $\$1,000$. The new equity value would be $\$4,200 - 1,800 - 1,000 = \$1,400$ before considering the currency swap gain/loss. The swap has a gain of $\$600$, because the swap position is short on $\$6,000$ worth of euros, and the euro depreciates by 10%. Thus, this $\$600$ gain on the swap position would bring the firm's equity value back to $\$2,000$.

Altria Group, Inc.

"Altria Group, Inc. uses foreign currency swaps to mitigate its exposure to changes in exchange rates related to foreign currency denominated debt. These swaps typically convert fixed-rate foreign currency denominated debt to fixed-rate debt denominated in the functional currency of the borrowing entity. A substantial portion of the foreign currency swap agreements are accounted for as cash flow hedges. The unrealized gain (loss) relating to foreign currency swap agreements that do not qualify for hedge accounting treatment was insignificant as of December 31, 2002 and 2001. At December 31, 2002 and 2001, the notional amounts of foreign currency swap agreements aggregated to $2.5 billion and $2.3 billion, respectively. Aggregate maturities of foreign currency swap agreements at December 31, 2002 (in millions) were as follows: 2003 ($142); 2004 ($189); 2006 ($968); and 2008 ($1,165)."

Source: Altria Annual Report, Notes to Financial Statements, 2002 http://www.altria.com/annualreport2002/ar2002_07_07_1400.asp

A firm with a negative FX business exposure can manage this exposure with a *long* position on the foreign currency in a currency swap. The notional principal should be equal to the absolute value of $\xi_{B\epsilon}{}^{\$}V_B{}^{\$}$. For example, assume that the UK firm FBN Ltd. has a business value of £100 million and its FX business exposure to the U.S. dollar is −1.25. Then FBN could hedge its FX exposure, eliminating the FX equity exposure, via a long currency swap position on U.S. dollars with a notional principal of £125 million.

Assume that the U.S. firm DEF Co. has $V_B{}^{\$}$ = $5 million, $ND^{\$}$ = $2 million, and thus $S^{\$}$ = $3 million. Assume DEF's FX business exposure to the euro is −1.60. All of the firm's actual net debt is U.S. dollar-denominated. Determine the currency swap position that will eliminate DEF's FX equity exposure.

Answers: The total amount of euro-denominated net liabilities should be $NL_\epsilon{}^{\$} = \xi_{B\epsilon}{}^{\$}V_B{}^{\$}$ = (−1.60)($5 million) = −$8 million. To have a negative net liability in euros of $8 million, the firm should take a naked <u>long</u> currency swap position on euros with a notional principal of $8 million. The value balance sheets for DEF below illustrate how the FX equity exposure is zero, because the equity value is $3 million at both time 0 and time 1.

DEF Co. Value Balance Sheets

Initial

	Value	Liabilities & Equity
(Off)	$ 8 million (Long €, $B_\epsilon^{\$}$)	$ 8 million (Short $, $B_{\$}^{\$}$)
		$ 2 million $ND_{\$}^{\$}$
	$ 5 million $V_B^{\$}$	$ 3 million $S^{\$}$
	$ 5 million	$ 5 million

"What if" the Euro Depreciates by 10%?

	Value	Liabilities & Equity
(Off)	$ 7.20 million (Long €, $B_\epsilon^{\$}$)	$ 8 million (Short $, $B_{\$}^{\$}$)
		$ 0.80 million (MTM Loss, $-M_\epsilon^{\$}$)
		$ 2 million $ND_{\$}^{\$}$
	$ 5.80 million $V_B^{\$}$	$ 3 million $S^{\$}$
	$ 5.80 million	$ 5.80 million

Off-Market Swaps

Any two parties can agree to exchange cash flow streams that do *not* have the same present value, given the current spot FX rate. In this case, the recipient of the cash flow stream with the higher present value must make a time-0 balancing payment to the party receiving the cash flow stream with the lower present value. This swap is called *off-market swap*. Assume that the time-0 spot FX rate is 1.60 $/£. You want to make the future payments on a 5-year, 5.50% coupon U.S. dollar par bond, and receive payments on a 5-year, 10% coupon sterling bond. Assume the market yield to maturity on 5-year, 10% coupon sterling bonds is 9%, not 10%. What time-0 payment would make this work?

For a notional principal of $1,000, the sterling notional principal is £625, because the time-0 spot FX rate is assumed to be 1.60 $/£. The 10% sterling coupon rate means that you'll receive 0.10(£625) = £62.50 per year for 5 years, in addition to the principal repayment of £625 at year 5. Thus, the present value of the underlying sterling bond payments is £62.50/$1.09 + 62.50/1.09^2 + 62.50/1.09^3 + 62.50/1.09^4 + 62.50/1.09^5 + 625/1.09^5$ = £649.30, which is equivalent to a U.S. dollar value of £649.30 (1.60 $/£) = $1,039. The present value of the U.S. dollar payments is $1,000, while the present value of the sterling receipts is equivalent to $1,039. Thus, you should make a time-0 payment of $1,039 – 1,000 = $39.

Extend the text example. What is the time-0 swap payment, if you have the long sterling position, and if you want a coupon payment of 8%, all else the same?

Answer: You'll receive $0.08(£625) = £50$ per year for 5 years, and the principal repayment of £625 at year 5. The present value of the sterling payments is $£50/1.09 + 50/1.09^2 + 50/1.09^3 + 50/1.09^4 + 50/1.09^5 + 625/1.09^5 = £601$. Now the present value of the sterling receipts is equivalent to a U.S. dollar value of $£601(1.60 \text{ $/£}) = \$962$. Thus, because you are willing to accept future receipts at a below-market coupon rate, you should receive a time-0 payment of $\$1,000 - 962 = \$38$.

Summary Action Points

- A fixed for fixed currency swap is essentially an exchange of fixed-coupon bond payments in one currency for those of another currency.
- One important use of currency swaps is in creating synthetic debt in another currency by covering the FX risk of debt issued in markets offering opportunities for favorable financing costs.
- Another important use of a currency swap is the hedging of FX business exposure that is either negative or too large to be managed with foreign currency net debt.
- The mark-to-market value of a currency swap is found by valuing the underlying financial instruments represented in the swap.

Glossary

At-Market Swap: A swap with a present value of zero and thus that involves no time-0 cash flow to initiate a position.

Back-to-Back Loan: A precursor to currency swaps, where the subsidiary in country A of a parent in country B makes loan payments to a parent company in country A, and vice versa, even though the loan proceeds cancel out and thus are not exchanged.

Cross-Currency Swap: An exchange of fixed-coupon payments in one currency for floating-rate payments in another currency.

Currency Swap: A contract to exchange two streams of future cash flows in different currencies.

FX Conversion Rate: The rate to use as the contract FX rate when finding the difference check payment of a currency swap.

Fixed-for-Fixed Currency Swap: An exchange of cash flows calculated as the exchange of fixed-coupon bond payments in one currency for those in another currency.

Fixed-for-Floating Currency Swap: Also called a cross-currency swap. An exchange of cash flows calculated as the exchange of fixed-coupon bond payments in one currency for floating-rate payments in another currency.

Interest Rate Swap: An exchange of fixed-coupon bond payments in a currency for floating-rate payments in the same currency.

Naked Currency Swap Position: Use of a currency swap on its own and not in order to create synthetic debt.

Notional Principal: The presumable amount of bond principal upon which a swap's payment amounts are based.

Off-Market Swap: A swap with present value of not zero that involves an immediate cash flow to initiate a position.

Par Bond: A coupon bond whose market value is equal to its face value, and whose yield to maturity is thus exactly equal to the coupon rate.

Parallel Loan: A precursor to currency swaps; a loan by a parent company in country A to the local subsidiary of a parent firm in country B, and vice versa.

Straight Bond: Also called bullet bonds or coupon bonds; a bond that makes interest and principal payments at a set coupon rate in a single currency and has no call provisions or other features.

Swap-Driven Financing: The use of swaps as a planned part of a capital raising strategy.

Synthetic Foreign Currency Debt: Actual home currency debt combined with a short foreign currency swap position.

Synthetic Home Currency Debt: Actual foreign currency debt combined with a long foreign currency swap position.

Problems

1. You enter into a 3-year annual-pay, fixed-for-fixed currency swap, so that the cash flow stream you are receiving is in Japanese yen and the cash flow stream you are paying is in U.S. dollars. The swap has a notional principal of $1 million. What are the cash flows on which the currency swap is based, if the swap is an at-market swap and the 3-year par coupon rates are 5% for U.S. dollars and 2% for yen, and if the spot FX rate is currently 112.50 ¥/$?

2. Consider the same swap as in #1, a 3-year annual-pay, fixed-for-fixed currency swap of 5% U.S. dollars for 2% Japanese yen. The notional principal is $1 million. The spot FX rate was 112.50 ¥/$ when the swap originates. (a) What is the FX conversion rate for the interest component settlements? (b) Find the difference check settlement in U.S. dollars if the yen depreciates to 120 ¥/$ at time 1 (the time of the first payment), and state which counterparty gets the check.

3. What would be the settlement of principal at maturity of the swap in the previous problem if the spot FX rate at that time is 120 ¥/$?

4. Consider a 6-year annual-pay, fixed-for-fixed currency swap of 5% U.S. dollars for 8% British pounds on notional principal of $1 million. The spot FX rate is 1.60 $/£ when the swap originates. Find the two final difference checks, interest and principal, if the spot FX rate is 1.80 $/£ at that time. State the direction of each check.

5. Consider a 6-year annual-pay, fixed-for-fixed currency swap of 5% U.S. dollars for 2% yen on notional principal of $1 million. The swap originated when the spot FX rate was 110 ¥/$. Assume a spot FX rate of 120 ¥/$ at time 3, and that the market yields on 3-year coupon bonds are 2% in yen and 5% in U.S. dollars at time 3. Find the MTM value, after 3 annual interest component payments, of a long yen position.

6. Assume the U.S. firm DZD Co. currently has $V_B^\$ = \$5$ million, $ND^\$ = \$3$ million, and thus $S^\$ = \$2$ million. Assume an FX business exposure to the euro of 1.60. Let us say that $2 million of the firm's actual net debt is euro-denominated and the rest is U.S. dollar-denominated. DZD also has a naked short currency swap position on euros with a notional principal of $2 million. Find DZD's FX equity exposure to

the euro using a "what if" 10% depreciation of the euro, and reconcile the answer using equation (4.4).

7. The U.S. firm ABC Co. currently has $V_B^\$ = \$10$ million, $ND^\$ = \$4$ million, and thus $S^\$ = \$6$ million. Assume an FX business exposure to the euro of 1.25. Assume that $3 million of the firm's actual net debt is euro-denominated and the rest is U.S. dollar-denominated. (a) Determine the notional principal of a currency swap position that will eliminate ABC's FX equity exposure to the euro. (b) Assume the euro appreciates by 10%. Show how the equity value stays at $6 million.

8. The U.S. firm ABC Co. currently has $V_B^\$ = \$10$ million, $ND^\$ = \$4$ million, and thus $S^\$ = \$6$ million. Assume an FX business exposure to the euro of -1.25. Assume that all of the net debt is U.S. dollar-denominated. (a) Determine the notional principal of a currency swap position that will eliminate ABC's FX equity exposure to the euro. (b) Assume the euro appreciates by 10%. Show how the equity value stays at $6 million.

For 9–13: TBR is a U.S. firm. Assume that at time 0: (1) TBR has a business value of $40 million; (2) TBR's FX business exposure to the euro is 2.50; (3) TBR has $15 million in euro-denominated net debt and no other net debt.

The market yield on 5-year par U.S. dollar straight coupon bonds is 4%. The market yield on 5-year par euro straight coupon bonds is 5.50%. The spot FX rate is presently 1.30 $/€. TBR takes a short euro position in a 5-year at-market, annual-pay currency swap with a notional principal of $52 million.

9. What is TBR's FX equity exposure to the euro?

10. Provide the payment structure on the currency swap.

11. If the euro depreciates by 10% as of a year from now, what is the amount in U.S. dollars of the difference check settlement of the interest component? Does TBR pay or receive?

12. Assume that the euro depreciates by 10% as of a year from now, and that the market yield on a 4-year par coupon U.S. dollar bond is 4% and a 4-year par coupon euro bond is 5.5%. What is the MTM value of TBR's swap position in U.S. dollars immediately

after the difference check settlement of the coupon interest component?

13. What notional swap principal would eliminate TBR's FX equity exposure to the euro?

Answers to Problems

1. You would receive ¥2.25 million per year for 3 years and a principal payment of ¥112.50 million at year 3. You would pay $50,000 per year for 3 years and then a payment of $1 million.

2. (a) The FX conversion rate is 45 ¥/$. (b) The short position on yen gets $31,250.

3. The net payment to the short position on yen is $62,500.

4. The long position on pounds receives $40,000 to settle the interest component. The principal on the swap at maturity is settled with a difference check of $125,000 to the long position on pounds.

5. The swap has an MTM value in U.S. dollars of –$83,333.

6. DZD's business value falls by 16% to $4.20 million. The U.S. dollar value of the actual euro net debt drops by 10% to $1.80 million, while the U.S. dollar value of the other actual net debt stays at $1 million. The new equity value is $4.20 million – 1.80 million – 1 million = $1.40 million before considering the currency swap MTM gain or loss. The swap has a gain of $200,000, because the swap position is short on $2 million worth of euros, and the euro depreciates by 10%. Thus the "what if" equity value is $1.60 million. The firm's FX equity exposure to the euro is ($1.60 million/$2 million – 1)/(–0.10) = 2. Using equation (4.4), the total amount of euro-denominated net liabilities is $4 million, and the ratio of euro net liabilities to business value is $4 million/$5 million = 0.80. The FX equity exposure to the euro is [1.60 – 0.80]/[1 – 0.60] = 2.

7. (a) The total amount of ABC's euro net liabilities should be 1.25 × ($10 million) = $12.5 million. Because the firm already has $3 million in actual euro net debt, the short euro swap position should have a notional principal of $9.50 million. (b) The business value rises by 12.5% to $11.25 million. The U.S. dollar value of the actual euro net debt rises by 10% to $3.30 million, while the value of the other net

debt stays at $1 million. The firm's new equity value would be $11.25 million – 3.30 million – 1 million = $6.95 million before considering the swap gain or loss. The swap has a loss of $950,000, because the swap position is short $9.50 million worth of euros, and the euro appreciates by 10%. Thus the equity value remains at $6 million.

8. (a) The total amount of ABC's euro net liabilities should be –1.25 ($10 million) = –$12.5 million. The long euro swap position should have a notional principal of $12.50 million. (b) The business value drops by 12.5% to $8.75 million. The U.S. dollar value of the U.S. dollar net debt stays at $4 million. The firm's new equity value would be $8.75 million – 4 million = $4.75 million before considering the swap gain or loss. The swap has a gain of $1.25, because the swap position is long $12.50 million worth of euros, and the euro appreciates by 10%. Thus the equity value remains at $6 million.

9. $(2.50 – 67/40)/(1 – 0.375) = 1.32$.

10. TBR receives 0.04($52 million) = $2.08 million per year and $52 million at the end of 5 years. TBR pays 0.055(€40) = €2.20 million per year and €40 million at the end of 5 years.

11. The contract FX rate for an interest component is $2.08/€2.20 = 0.945 $/€. The difference check to the long euro position is €2.20 million (1.17 $/€ – 0.945 $/€) = $495,000. Because TBR is short euros, TBR pays the difference check.

12. The long U.S. dollar side is still worth $52 million; the short euro side is worth $46.8 million, so the MTM value of TBR's swap contract is $5.2 million.

13. TBR needs total euro liabilities of 2.50($40 million) = $100 million. There is $15 million of actual net debt in euros. So the answer is $85 million.

CASE

Adventure & Recreation Technologies, Inc.

Sitting behind his desk, Ben Nunnally told Anna Martin, "At last week's corporate board meeting, there was a discussion on the economic situation in Europe. One board member said that he had read that two major banks were predicting a substantially lower euro by year's end (from the spot FX rate of 1.333 $/€ in February 2013, to 1.20 $/€ by the end of 2013). Another asked me how I thought a depreciation of the euro might affect the company's future cash flows and stock value." The meeting between Nunnally and Martin was taking place in early March 2013 in Nunnally's office at Adventure & Recreation Technologies, Inc. (ART), in Boise, Idaho.

Nunnally, who had been the company's chief financial officer and treasurer even before the company went public in the 1980s, added, "I told them that because roughly 20% of the company's FY 2012 revenues were in euros, both future cash flows and stock value would likely drop; the amount of the drop would naturally depend on how far the euro depreciates. How is that for sounding informed while stating the obvious?" Nunnally also told Martin, "I promised to study the question and provide a more thorough answer at the next board meeting, and that's where you come in."

Martin had been an assistant treasurer with the company for 5 years. Nunnally asked Martin to take a thorough look at ART's FX exposure to the euro and report back. Martin had taken a course in International

Corporate Finance at Michigan State University, and had enjoyed the course more that she had thought she would. She told Nunnally that she would get back to him as soon as possible with an analysis.

Adventure & Recreation Technologies, Inc.

Adventure & Recreation Technologies (ART) was founded in 1973 by out-doorsman Rick Zuber to produce plastic watercraft, mainly canoes and kayaks. In the 1980s, ART bought Divemaster Company from its founders, Mauricio "Mo" Rodriguez and the legendary Navy "frogman" Carmelo Giaccotto. Divemaster manufactures the most technologically advanced scuba diving equipment in the world, having developed the dive computer that had become the industry standard. Divemaster's headquarters are in the United States, but the company's renowned research center, where the dive computer was developed, is in Italy. A significant portion of Divemaster's sales and production are also in Europe. In 2006, ART acquired a marine sonar business, Houston Marine Electronics (HME). ART's strategy across its three business segments is to use sophisticated research and cutting-edge technology to create the world's best-known brands of outdoor recreational products.

ART's consolidated revenue for FY 2012 was around $300 million, with roughly $150 million from Divemaster, $100 million from HME, and $50 million from the watercraft business. ART's sales of marine electronics and watercraft products in Europe were small, but $60 million of Divemaster's revenues were in euros. ART's overall operating cash flow in FY 2012 was about $40 million. In the previous 5 years, ART substantially reduced its long-term debt, to $10 million by the end of FY 2012. In February 2013, ART held $60 million in cash, for a net debt position of −$50 million. The securities held in the cash account were mainly denominated in U.S. dollars.

ART's shares trade on the Nasdaq. In February 2013, ART's share price fluctuated around $22, and total equity market capitalization was about $250 million. Historically, the share price rose from about $10 in 2000 to about $25 in 2007, but then plunged to a low of $6 in March 2009 before gradually rising to around $22 by March 2013.

ART's FX Operating Exposure to the Euro

Martin looked first at the $60 million in euro revenues from Divemaster's sales in Europe. She understood the conversion impact of FX changes: If Divemaster were to generate the same revenues in euros in FY 2013 as in FY 2012, and if the euro were to depreciate by 10%, the FY 2013 euro revenues would convert to a U.S. dollar amount that would be 10% lower than $60 million, or only $54 million.

Martin called the Divemaster CFO, Alain Krapl, to see if he had any additional insights. Krapl told her that he thought there was more to the FX exposure story. He told her that it seemed to him that in the past, when the euro appreciated, Divemaster's equipment sales in Europe tended to rise, and so the revenues *in euros* rose. By the same token, when the euro depreciated, Divemaster's equipment sales in Europe tended to drop, and so the revenues in euros dropped. Krapl said that he thought the FX rate was reflecting the fortunes of the European economy. He added, "I think that Divemaster's euro revenues have tended to change by roughly 20% of the FX rate change. So, if the euro were to appreciate (depreciate) by 10%, my best guess is that the Eurozone revenues would rise (drop) by 2% in euros." Combining the conversion and economic effects, Martin expected that in U.S. dollars, Divemaster's revenues in the Eurozone would drop by roughly 12%, to $52.8 million, if the euro were to depreciate by 10% in FY 2013.

Martin next looked at operating costs. The euro FX rate had a negligible effect on the operating costs of both the watercraft and marine electronics businesses, so Martin focused on Divemaster. She knew that the direct cost of sales for diving equipment was approximately 40% of revenues. Divemaster's production was concentrated in two locations, Malaysia and Italy. The output from the Malaysian facility was distributed in the United States and the rest of the world, excluding Europe. The equipment produced in Italy was sold exclusively in the Eurozone. So, from the U.S. dollar perspective, if the European portion of diving equipment revenues were to drop by 12% in FY 2013, the direct cost of those sales would also drop by 12%.

The indirect operating costs for Divemaster's Eurozone sales, mainly sales and marketing expenses, were €12 million in FY 2012. At the spot FX rate in early March 2013 of 1.333 $/€, €12 million was equivalent to

$16 million. The sales and marketing budget did not depend on sales volume, so in U.S. dollars, the indirect costs of the Eurozone sales would drop (rise) by 10% if the euro depreciated (appreciated) by 10%. In addition, Divemaster's research was conducted entirely at the large facility in Italy. The FY 2012 research budget was €12 million. Because the research budget did not depend on sales volume, the research expenses would change by the same percentage as the euro, when the research expenses were measured in U.S. dollars.

Martin's "what if" analysis resulted in an estimate of 0.28 for ART's FX operating exposure to the euro. The interpretation of the estimate is that for a 10% drop in the euro, ART's operating cash flow would likely drop by 2.80%. Martin was a bit surprised to find the relatively low estimate of ART's FX operating exposure to the euro, given the sizable revenues in euros, but after she thought about it, she realized that the Divemaster's substantial research program in Italy, the costs of which are fixed in euros, serves as an operational hedge. (Q1)

ART's FX Equity Exposure to the Euro

Martin turned her attention to an analysis of how an unexpected change in the euro might affect ART's equity value. ART's total equity market capitalization was $250 million in late February 2013. Because ART's net debt position was –$50 million, Martin reasoned that the market's estimate of ART's business value was $200 million. Martin believed that ART's shares were close to correctly valued at that time.

Martin recalled that the professor for her international finance course at Michigan State University had stressed that many economists believed that spot FX rates follow a "random walk." This idea implies that if the euro depreciates by 10%, from 1.333 $/€ to 1.20 $/€, the best guess for the subsequent future spot FX rate would then be 1.20 $/€. With the random walk approach, if the euro were to depreciate by 10%, and ART's operating cash flow was lower in 2013 than in 2012 by 2.80%, the expectation of all of ART's future operating cash flows would be 2.80% lower, and so ART's business value would likewise drop by 2.80%. That is, the FX business exposure is the same as the firm's FX operating exposure.

Martin computed an estimate of 0.224 for ART's FX equity exposure to the euro. (Q2)

Martin next did a different sort of analysis of ART's FX equity exposure to the euro. The idea had been introduced in her international finance course. Using 5 years of recent data, she estimated ART's FX equity exposure statistically, using a simple Excel regression of ART's monthly stock returns (dependent variable) on percentage changes in the FX rate for the euro (independent variable). The result was an extremely high estimate of FX equity exposure, 1.40. The interpretation of the estimate is that a 10% drop in the euro would be associated with an unexpected equity return of −14%. This finding was significantly different than the FX equity exposure estimate of 0.224 she had obtained through her "what if" analysis. Martin added the finding to her report, anticipating some discussion. (Q3)

Financial Hedging

Martin finished the analysis and forwarded her report to Nunnally, and the two met again. Nunnally thanked Martin, saying that she had done an excellent job with her analysis. Nunnally pointed out that even though the "what if" analysis suggested a relatively small FX exposure to the euro, any reduction in cash flow volatility and stock value volatility would be beneficial for ART. He asked Martin for her thoughts on what, if anything, ART might do about the FX exposure to the euro.

Martin responded that she did not think a forward FX position was the way to go, because the need was to hedge the ongoing FX exposure in both cash flows and business value. She suggested having euro-denominated debt, and threw out the number $56 million, based on her "what if" estimate of FX business exposure. (Q4)

Nunnally told Martin, "I agree with that a forward FX position does not work in this situation, whereas euro debt would be appropriate, in principle. However, $56 million in euro debt seems like a lot. I cannot argue with your 'what if' analysis of the near-term FX operating exposure, but I am less confident in the long-term FX business exposure estimate based on the random walk idea. On the other hand, the recent banks forecasts that the euro is likely to drop over the next year suggests the euro may be overvalued… that would support a higher level of financial hedging." (Q5)

Nunnally added that a secondary benefit of the euro debt would be to reduce some of the volatility of the <u>book value</u> of ART's equity. Because the book value of ART's net investment in the Eurozone facility in Italy was about $45 million, ART had ongoing volatility in the book value of its equity due to FX translation gains and losses. "Some analysts like to look at ratios like return on book equity, so it may be beneficial to stabilize those as much as possible," Nunnally said. (Q6)

"However," Nunnally told Martin, "I am opposed to putting debt back onto ART's balance sheet, given all we have done over the past several years to reduce the company's debt level. But we could accomplish the same objective with a currency swap. Both the economic and accounting implications of a currency swap are the same as euro debt, but the transaction is off-balance sheet."

Switching to the statistical analysis, Nunnally told Martin, "Your statistical estimates are really high compared to the estimates of the 'what if' analysis." Nunnally had looked at recent charts for both ART's stock price and the euro. Both had plummeted during the global financial crisis of 2008, and both had bounced back in the recovery. He told Martin, "Your regression picked up a strong connection between our stock return and the euro, but I don't think the analysis is really measuring FX equity exposure in the sense of being the response of our stock value to a change in the euro. Instead, I think both our share price and the euro moved together in response to the changes in the overall economic conditions. But this connection, and the tough time the company went through during the financial crisis of 2008, has made me wonder about the following tactic. Why not financially hedge euro movements as a way of indirectly hedging economic conditions?" (Q7)

Questions

1. Show how Martin arrived at her "what if" estimate of 0.28 for ART's FX operating exposure to the euro.
2. Verify Martin's "what if" estimate of 0.224 for ART's FX equity exposure to the euro.
3. With data in the Appendix, use Excel to verify Martin's statistical estimate of 1.40 for ART's FX equity exposure to the euro. Unlever

the FX equity exposure estimate to find an estimate of ART's FX operating exposure to the euro.

4. Show how Martin arrived at her estimate that $56 million in euro debt would eliminate ART's FX equity exposure to the euro, given the "what if" estimate of FX business exposure.

5. If the forecast were for the euro to appreciate, how might this affect the financial hedging decision?

6. Discuss the issue of the volatility of ART's equity book value and the volatility of periodic reported earnings, if ART does not hedge with euro debt, versus if ART hedges with $56 million of euro debt.

7. Describe and discuss the pros and cons of using a currency swap position to hedge ART's exposure to economic conditions. What are the accounting implications?

Appendix

Date	ART Return	FX $/€	FX Return
11/30/2006		1.286	
12/29/2006	0.004	1.320	0.026
1/31/2007	−0.003	1.300	−0.015
2/28/2007	−0.015	1.307	0.005
3/30/2007	0.011	1.324	0.013
4/30/2007	0.030	1.350	0.020
5/31/2007	0.001	1.352	0.002
6/29/2007	0.062	1.342	−0.008
7/31/2007	0.149	1.371	0.021
8/31/2007	−0.185	1.363	−0.006
9/28/2007	0.145	1.388	0.019
10/31/2007	0.011	1.423	0.025
11/30/2007	0.064	1.467	0.031
12/31/2007	−0.035	1.456	−0.007

(Continued)

(Continued)

Date	ART Return	FX $/€	FX Return
1/31/2008	−0.176	1.470	0.010
2/29/2008	−0.002	1.472	0.001
3/31/2008	−0.077	1.549	0.052
4/30/2008	−0.064	1.576	0.018
5/30/2008	−0.002	1.556	−0.013
6/30/2008	−0.023	1.557	0.001
7/31/2008	0.008	1.578	0.013
8/29/2008	0.016	1.499	−0.050
9/30/2008	−0.212	1.439	−0.040
10/31/2008	−0.337	1.335	−0.073
11/28/2008	−0.172	1.271	−0.048
12/31/2008	−0.195	1.344	0.058
1/30/2009	0.362	1.335	−0.007
2/27/2009	−0.364	1.282	−0.040
3/31/2009	0.046	1.303	0.016
4/30/2009	0.255	1.321	0.014
5/29/2009	−0.022	1.363	0.032
6/30/2009	−0.111	1.402	0.028
7/31/2009	0.187	1.407	0.004
8/31/2009	0.491	1.426	0.013
9/30/2009	−0.077	1.455	0.021
10/30/2009	−0.028	1.481	0.018
11/30/2009	0.086	1.490	0.006
12/31/2009	0.028	1.460	−0.020
1/29/2010	0.086	1.428	−0.022
2/26/2010	0.015	1.368	−0.042
3/31/2010	0.054	1.358	−0.007
4/30/2010	0.120	1.344	−0.010
5/28/2010	0.131	1.262	−0.062
6/30/2010	−0.218	1.222	−0.032
7/30/2010	0.132	1.276	0.044

(Continued)

(*Continued*)

Date	ART Return	FX $/€	FX Return
8/31/2010	−0.218	1.291	0.012
9/30/2010	0.288	1.303	0.009
10/29/2010	0.114	1.390	0.067
11/30/2010	−0.093	1.369	−0.015
12/31/2010	−0.033	1.322	−0.035
1/31/2011	0.216	1.335	0.010
2/28/2011	0.014	1.365	0.022
3/31/2011	−0.016	1.400	0.026
4/29/2011	0.092	1.444	0.031
5/31/2011	−0.039	1.434	−0.007
6/30/2011	0.073	1.438	0.003
7/29/2011	0.041	1.431	−0.005
8/31/2011	−0.113	1.435	0.003
9/30/2011	−0.028	1.380	−0.038
10/31/2011	0.209	1.370	−0.008
11/30/2011	−0.113	1.359	−0.008
12/30/2011	−0.069	1.319	−0.030

PART II

International Cost of Capital and Capital Budgeting

CHAPTER 5

Global Risk and Return

Because the future value of an investment is usually uncertain, an investor needs to think in terms of an *expected* rate of return. The investor has a target expected rate of return that will compensate for the risk specific to the investment. That target expected rate of return is sometimes called the investor's *required rate of return* for the investment. Given the risk taken, the investor makes a good investment if he expects a higher rate of return than the required rate of return.

Finance theory thinks in terms of an investment's aggregate required rate of return, meaning the "market's" required rate of return for the investment, which is sometimes called the investment's *opportunity cost of capital*, or more often simply the cost of capital. Another synonym is the *equilibrium expected rate of return*, which is the expected rate of return only if the investment is correctly priced.

Finance theorists for many years have searched for the best model of how an investment's cost of capital should be related to the investment's risk. The most popular of the various risk–return trade-off models is the Capital Asset Pricing Model (CAPM), which you likely learned in other finance courses.

In this chapter, we introduce you to a version of the CAPM called the *global CAPM*, which is a model of risk and return in internationally integrated financial markets. Given the significant extent of international financial market integration and investors' international diversification, an international risk–return model is theoretically superior to the traditional CAPM, which is usually thought of as a local (or domestic) risk–return model. In the global CAPM, the risk–return trade-off for all investments in the integrated international financial market may be viewed from the perspective of any given currency. Moreover, there is a consistency connection between an investment's risk and required return measured in different currencies.

This chapter also shows how to use the global CAPM to make a risk adjustment to the traditional uncovered interest rate parity (UIRP) condition. This adjustment may help a manager better estimate a currency's expected rate of intrinsic FX change that is consistent with financial market conditions.

Traditional CAPM Review

The traditional CAPM is a standard risk–return model that practitioners have found to be very useful. In a 2012 survey of 19 highly regarded U.S. companies, all but one reported using the CAPM to estimate cost of capital.[1] The CAPM is more controversial in academic circles, but has a substantial number of supporters and remains the primary risk–return model of finance textbooks.[2] A 2009 survey of finance professors found that 75% recommend the CAPM approach to the cost of capital.[3]

You should recall that in the traditional CAPM, asset i's *equilibrium* expected rate of return, or cost of capital, is $k_i = r_f + \beta_i(MRP)$. In this equation, the equilibrium expected rate of return on asset i, k_i, is not the *actual* expected asset return, but is the *minimum* expected rate of return that market investors in the aggregate need to earn to compensate for the asset's risk. On the right-hand side, r_f is the risk-free rate of interest, β_i is the *beta* of asset i relative to the market portfolio; and *MRP* is the required *market risk premium*.

Standard practice in U.S. applications has been to use a U.S. Treasury yield for the risk-free rate. Historically, there has been disagreement on whether the rate should be a short-term or long-term rate. Recent survey evidence shows that managers strongly prefer using a long-term rate.[4] We'll say more about risk-free rates in the next chapter.

An asset's beta is its sensitivity to unexpected returns on the market index. If an asset has a beta of 1.20 and the market index's rate of return is 10% higher than expected, then the asset's rate of return will tend to be (on average) 1.20(10%) = 12% higher than expected. By definition, the beta of the market index, relative to itself, is 1. We'll say more about betas shortly in this chapter.

The required market risk premium, *MRP*, is equal to $k_M - r_f$, the aggregate required rate of return on the market index minus the risk-free rate. That is, *MRP* is the minimum rate of return over the risk-free rate that investors require as compensation for the risk in the diversified portfolio of risky assets that comprise the market index. In other words, *MRP* is the equilibrium market risk premium, meaning the expected market risk premium if the market index is correctly valued.

The *MRP* depends on both the volatility (risk) in the overall market and the average investor's degree of risk aversion. Thus, the *MRP* tends to change as market volatility changes and as investors' tolerance for risk fluctuates with economic conditions. Years ago, it was standard to use a range of 7–9% for the U.S. *MRP*. More recent estimates for the U.S. *MRP* tend to be in the range of 4–6%.[5] Perhaps investors have lowered the required rate of return on their portfolios, because they have used international diversification to reduce their portfolios' risk.

Given the modern estimate range of 4–6%, a reasonable way to estimate the U.S. *MRP* these days may be as follows: Use 5% in a "normal" economic period. If the market is relatively low due to heightened risk aversion ("fear"), maybe 6% would be a better *MRP* estimate to use. And if the market is in an aggressive stage with higher tolerance for risk ("greed"), perhaps the 4% estimate should be used. Obviously, estimating the *MRP* is more art than science, and opinions vary.

There is a reason we express the *MRP* as $k_M - r_f$, and not the way you often see it, $E(R_M) - r_f$. The reason is that if the market index is misvalued at a point in time, the required and expected rate of return on the market index are not equal to each other at that time. If the *MRP* is 5%, but the market is undervalued, the difference between the expected rate of return on the market index and the risk-free rate is higher than 5%. Likewise, if the market is overvalued, the expected rate of return on the market index minus the risk-free rate is lower than 5%. The *equilibrium* expected rate of return on the market index minus the risk-free rate is the compensation for risk, and is properly named the *MRP*. The difference between the actual expected rate of return on the market index, $E(R_M)$, and the risk-free rate is not truly a risk premium because the market's possible misvaluation is incorporated.

Rate of Return on a Foreign Asset

Before moving on to the global CAPM, we address the notion of a given asset's realized rate of return in different currencies. That is, the rate of return on an asset in one currency depends on the rate of return in another currency and the change in the spot FX rate between the two currencies, specifically as shown in equation (5.1a). In equation (5.1a), we are converting an asset's rate of return in euros, $R_i^{€}$, to the same asset's rate of return in U.S. dollars, $R_i^{\$}$, using the percentage change in the FX price of the euro (in U.S. dollars), $x^{\$/€}$.

Asset's Rate of Return in Different Currencies

$$1 + R_i^{\$} = (1 + R_i^{€})(1 + x^{\$/€}) \tag{5.1a}$$

For example, if an asset's rate of return in euros is 20%, and the euro appreciates by 5%, the same asset's rate of return in U.S. dollars is $(1.20)(1.05) - 1 = 0.26$, or 26%.

The rate of return in British pounds on a share of stock on the London Stock Exchange is 15%. During the same period, the British pound depreciates by 8%. What is the rate of return on the stock from the U.S. dollar perspective?

Answer: $(1.15)(1 - 0.08) - 1 = 0.058$, or 5.8%.

A NASDAQ stock's rate of return in U.S. dollars is 15%. During the same period, the British pound depreciates by 8%. What is the stock's rate of return from the British pound perspective?

Answer: $(1.15)/(1 - 0.08) - 1 = 0.25$, or 25%.

Note that equation (5.1a) is for the <u>realized</u> rate of return. Owing to the nonlinearity of the equation, you cannot use equation (5.1a) to correctly convert expected rates of return or required rates of return across currencies. We'll deal with this issue later.

If you multiply the right-hand side of equation (5.1a), you get that $R_i^{\$} = R_i^{€} + x^{\$/€} + R_i^{€}x^{\$/€}$. For purposes of simplification, the cross-product term is sometimes ignored in order to have a linear approximation. Thus, an often-used linear approximation to equation (5.1a) is given in equation (5.1b).

Asset's Rate of Return in Different Currencies
Linear Approximation

$$R_i^{\$} \approx R_i^{€} + x^{\$/€} \tag{5.1b}$$

Global CAPM

There is a tendency to think in terms of a separate CAPM for each country: a CAPM in U.S. dollars for U.S. investments, a CAPM in British pounds for UK investments, and so forth. This tendency is partly natural and partly based on the not-so-distant past when national financial markets were more segmented from each other. But this tendency is a mistake now that the world's financial markets have integrated to a large extent. Now we need to think in terms of a common risk–return trade-off for *all* assets in the internationally integrated financial markets, regardless of asset nationality or whether we choose to express the trade-off in U.S. dollars, in British pounds, or in any other currency.

We now introduce the global CAPM, in which we interpret the market index as the *global market index*, also sometimes called the world market index. Exhibit 5.1 shows some percentages of the world equity market index in 2005 of the equity capitalizations of some major countries.[6]

It is important to see that the market index in the global CAPM is the same for all investors in the market, regardless of nationality. That is, even though the global market index includes assets from different countries, the index's composition is the same regardless of which currency we choose to express the index's rate of return. Just as the rate of return on any asset in the world may be converted between currencies by equation (5.1a), the rate of return on any portfolio of assets may be expressed in terms of any currency. This idea extends to the global

Exhibit 5.1. World Equity Capitalization Major Country Percentages 2005

United States	55%
Eurozone	14%
United Kingdom	11%
Japan	11%
Canada	4%
Switzerland	3%
Australia	3%

market index. Many think the best global market index is the MSCI World Index, where MSCI stands for Morgan Stanley Capital International. The rate of return on the MSCI World Index can be expressed from the point of view of any currency, inclusive of the impact of FX changes on foreign shares.

One worry that some researchers have about the global CAPM is that real-world investors have tended to invest more in assets of their own country than would be advisable given the benefits of international diversification. This tendency is called *home bias*. Researchers are exploring why home bias occurs, and debating whether it means that local, country-specific CAPMs still have some relevance. Despite the home bias, the extent of investors' international diversification and financial markets' integration suggests that the global CAPM is a more appropriate model of risk and return in integrated financial markets than the traditional local CAPM.

In this chapter, we dwell on the global CAPM from the perspective of one currency, the U.S. dollar. Asset i's equilibrium expected rate of return, or cost of capital, in U.S. dollars, $k_i^\$$, is given in the global CAPM in equation (5.2):

Global CAPM in U.S. Dollars

$$k_i^\$ = r_f^\$ + \beta_{iG}^\$(GRP^\$) \tag{5.2}$$

The beta in the global CAPM in equation (5.2), $\beta_{iG}^\$$, is the asset's *global beta*, measured in U.S. dollars. This beta measures the sensitivity of asset i's return, adjusted into U.S. dollars if a foreign asset, relative to the return in U.S. dollars of the global market index. $GRP^\$$ represents the required risk premium for the global market index, or *global risk premium*, in U.S. dollars, which is the equilibrium expected rate of return on the global market index in U.S. dollars minus the U.S. dollar risk-free rate, $r_f^\$$. Because recent estimates for the U.S. MRP are in the 4–6% range, and as the global beta of the U.S. equity index has on average been about 1, we will use estimates in the 4–6% range for $GRP^\$$ in our various examples. While 4–6% seems like a reasonable range for $GRP^\$$ in the current environment, the best estimate may change in the future with market conditions. Note: the global risk premium expressed in other currencies is not necessarily the same number as $GRP^\$$.

The risk-free rate used in equation (5.2) is for an asset that is risk-free in U.S. dollars. It is *not* some kind of world average of risk-free rates in various currencies. The term "risk-free rate" as used here means the *nominal* interest rate on an asset that has no credit risk.

Using the global CAPM in equation (5.2) to estimate an asset's required rate of return in U.S. dollars is the same as using the traditional CAPM. Assume the U.S. dollar risk-free rate is 3% and the global risk premium is 5%. Assuming asset *i*'s global beta in U.S. dollars is 1.20, asset *i*'s estimated cost of capital is $k_i^\$ = 0.03 + 1.20(0.05) = 0.09$, or 9%.

Assume General Electric's estimated global equity beta (in U.S. dollars) is 0.69. Assume the U.S. dollar risk-free rate is 3% and the global risk premium in U.S. dollars is 4%. What is GE's estimated cost of equity in U.S. dollars with the global CAPM?

Answer: $0.03 + 0.69(0.04) = 0.058$, or 5.8%.

Figure 5.1 shows a diagram for the global CAPM in U.S. dollars. The line is the relationship between risk and expected return in U.S. dollars, *in equilibrium*, that is, for assets in the global financial market that are correctly priced in U.S. dollars. The slope of the line is the $GRP^\$$, assumed in the diagram to be 5%. The risk–return line intercepts the Y-axis at the U.S. dollar risk-free rate, assumed in the diagram to be 3%.

If an asset is correctly valued in U.S. dollars, its expected return and beta will plot exactly on the equilibrium risk–return line. If in reality, an asset is undervalued (overvalued), its actual expected return will plot above (below) what the line says the expected return should be for the risk. Misvalued assets are represented as scatter dots off the line in Figure 5.1. As we said earlier, even the market index can be misvalued and thus plot off of the equilibrium risk–return line. In U.S. dollars, a foreign asset can be misvalued for either of two reasons: (a) the asset is misvalued in its own currency or (b) the spot FX rate is misvalued. Therefore, the global market index may in principle be sometimes misvalued due to FX misvaluation(s) of the many foreign stocks in the global market index.

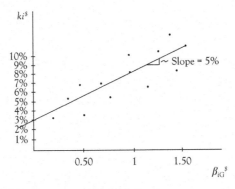

Figure 5.1. Global CAPM in U.S. dollars.

Exhibit 5.2. Global and Local Beta Estimates Selected U.S. Equities

Company	$\beta_{iG}{}^{\$}$	$\beta_{iL}{}^{\$}$
Exxon	0.85	0.73
General Electric	0.69	0.81
IBM	1.03	1.19
Merck	0.54	0.63
Microsoft	0.85	0.97

Source: Author's calculations with monthly rates of return, 2002–2007.

Global Versus Local Beta

Currently, there are no published estimates of global equity betas like there are for traditional equity betas (versus a domestic index) at sites like *Value Line*. The only way to obtain a stock's global beta estimate is to use regression analysis with historical return observations, which is fairly easy on Bloomberg. Estimated global equity betas against the MSCI World Index, in U.S. dollars, for selected U.S. firms are shown in the $\beta_{iG}{}^{\$}$ column in Exhibit 5.2. The estimated traditional equity betas, called *local betas*, are shown in the $\beta_{iL}{}^{\$}$ column for comparison. The estimation period is December 2002 through November 2007.

For example, in Exhibit 5.2, IBM's estimated global equity beta in U.S. dollars is 1.03. This estimate represents the systematic risk, in U.S. dollars, of the firm's equity shares in a globally diversified portfolio. IBM's traditional local beta estimate for the same period is 1.19. This would be IBM equity's systematic risk in a diversified portfolio of U.S. investments only.

Assume the U.S. dollar risk-free rate is 3% and the global risk premium is 5%. With IBM's global beta of 1.03, the estimated U.S. dollar cost of equity for IBM is 0.03 + 1.03(0.05) = 0.0815, or 8.15%. Using 5% also for the local U.S. market risk premium, IBM's estimated cost of equity with the traditional local U.S. CAPM would be 0.03 + 1.19(0.05) = 0.0895, or 8.95%.

Use General Electric's estimated global equity beta (in U.S. dollars) and U.S. equity beta from Exhibit 5.2. Assume the U.S. dollar risk-free rate is 3%, the global risk premium in U.S. dollars is 5%, and the U.S. market risk premium is 5%. (a) What is the estimated cost of equity in U.S. dollars for GE with the global CAPM? (b) Compare this estimate with the one for the local U.S. CAPM.

Answers: (a) GE's estimated global equity beta is 0.69. For the global CAPM, GE's estimated cost of equity in U.S. dollars is 0.03 + 0.69(0.05) = 0.0645, or 6.45%. (b) GE's estimated local U.S. equity beta is 0.81. Using the local U.S. CAPM, GE's estimated cost of equity in U.S. dollars is 0.03 + 0.81(0.05) = 0.0705, or 7.05%.

The examples above for IBM and GE show that the global CAPM and the traditional local CAPM do not give the same cost of equity estimates. Given our assumption that the U.S. equity market risk premium is equal to the global risk premium, the error one would make in using the local U.S. CAPM when the global CAPM is the correct risk–return trade-off will be driven by the difference between an asset's global beta and local beta.

Whether a stock's global beta is higher or lower than its traditional local beta depends on the drivers of the stock's returns relative to domestic and international economic conditions. In our examples for IBM and GE, the estimated local beta is higher than the estimated global beta. That is, both IBM and GE contribute less risk to a diversified global portfolio than to a diversified domestic U.S. portfolio. For Exxon, on the other hand, Exhibit 5.2 shows the estimated local beta for 2002–2007 is 0.73, lower than the estimated global beta, 0.85. So

Exxon contributes more risk to a diversified global portfolio than to a diversified domestic U.S. portfolio.

One aspect of the difference between global and local beta estimates may relate to FX exposure. For example, using monthly return observations from 1998 through 2010, the stocks on the left in Exhibit 2.6, with negative FX equity exposure estimates, had an average local beta estimate, 1.01, that was *higher* than the average global beta estimate, 0.98. The stocks on the right, with positive FX equity exposure estimates, had an average local beta estimate, 1.10, that was *lower* than the average global beta estimate, 1.17.

In other countries, there may be larger differences between the global and local beta estimates. For example, the beta estimate for Nestlé (in Swiss francs) with the local Swiss stock market index was shown to be substantially different than the beta estimate with the global market index.[7] For another example, see the box on the Australian company Fleetwood Corp, Ltd.

Fleetwood Corp, Ltd.

The Australian company Fleetwood Corp, Ltd. makes recreational vehicles and related products. With monthly return observations in Australian dollars from the end of 2006 through the end of 2011, Fleetwood's estimated local beta versus the Australian All Ordinaries index was 1.38, but the estimated global beta versus the MSCI World index was only 0.18. The All Ordinaries index of Australian stocks had a very low global beta estimate, 0.09, suggesting that Australian stocks in general tend to have very low global betas from the Australian dollar point of view.

Source: Author's computations.

Of course, the choice of time span affects any estimated beta. Part of this variation is statistical, but also a firm's true equity beta is likely to change if the firm changes its operating or financial structure, or even if the composition of the market index changes.

Some estimates of the average <u>absolute</u> difference in the cost of equity estimates, **in U.S. dollars**, of the global CAPM and the local CAPM are shown for a number of countries in Exhibit 5.3.[8]

Exhibit 5.3. Global Versus Local CAPM
Average Absolute Cost of Equity Differences

Developed			
Australia	3.67%	**Eurozone Members:**	
Canada	3.46%	Austria	0.76%
Hong Kong	2.47%	Belgium	1.37%
Israel	4.43%	Finland	3.04%
Japan	5.27%	France	1.76%
New Zealand	0.46%	Germany	0.44%
Singapore	6.40%	Greece	9.59%
Switzerland	1.80%	Ireland	6.00%
		Italy	1.23%
Non-Eurozone EU Members:		Luxembourg	1.52%
Denmark	4.15%	Netherlands	1.87%
Sweden	5.50%	Norway	2.98%
United Kingdom	1.10%	Portugal	6.40%
		Spain	4.60%
Emerging			
Asia:		**Latin America:**	
China	6.78%	Argentina	3.27%
India	0.88%	Chile	0.54%
Indonesia	3.88%	Colombia	3.95%
Korea	5.07%	Mexico	2.63%
Malaysia	7.79%	Peru	1.18%
Pakistan	0.58%	Venezuela	5.90%
Philippines	12.60%		
Sri Lanka	2.30%	**Europe:**	
Thailand	7.10%	Czech Republic	14.39%
		Hungary	1.50%
Turkey	14.20%	Poland	0.90%
Morocco	10.90%		
South Africa	1.30%	Zimbabwe	43.10%

American Depositary Receipts (ADRs)

American Depositary Receipts (ADRs) are foreign equity shares directly traded in the United States in U.S. dollars. The foreign office of a depositary, such as Bank of New York Mellon, will hold the actual foreign shares in that foreign country, while the bank's U.S. office issues U.S. dollar-denominated receipts that are more easily traded in U.S. markets. Stocks traded on both their home and foreign exchanges are said to be *cross-listed stocks*.

The first ADR was offered by JP Morgan in 1927. In 1990, there were only 352 non-U.S. stocks traded on the New York Stock Exchange (NYSE) and NASDAQ. By the end of 2002, the number was more than 850. If one includes over-the-counter and private placement issues, there are now more than 4,300 foreign companies, from 84 countries, with shares traded in the United States. This situation reflects the U.S. investors' appetite for international diversification and the desire of foreign companies to access global capital, broaden their shareholder base, and enhance company visibility. The most widely held ADRs are: Vodaphone (UK), Baidu (China), Royal Dutch Shell (UK), Daimler AG (Germany), and America Movil (Mexico).

ADRs help us see the point about foreign assets in a common risk–return trade-off in globally integrated markets. The price of an ADR should, in principle, obey the "international law of one price," or there will be a relatively easy arbitrage opportunity between the ADR shares and the actual underlying shares, called the *ordinary shares*. If the ordinary shares of Siemens are priced in Germany at €100 per share at time 0, when the spot FX rate is 1.25 $/€, then the ADRs should be priced at $125 per share in the United States. Otherwise, there would be a relatively easy arbitrage opportunity for traders who have access to both markets. The same reasoning tells us that if the ordinary Siemens shares are priced in Germany at €120 per share at time 1, when the spot FX rate is 1.50 $/€, the ADR price in the United States should be $180 per share.

Given no arbitrage opportunity between Siemens ADRs and the ordinaries, an investor in Siemens ADRs would earn the same rate of return in U.S. dollars as would an investor in the ordinaries: $180/$125 − 1 = 0.44, or 44%. This rate of return is consistent with equation (5.1a): Because the rate of return on Siemens ordinaries in euros is 20% and the euro appreciates by

20%, equation (5.1a) states that the return in U.S. dollars is $(1.20)(1.20) - 1 = 0.44$. Ignoring transaction costs, there is really no difference whether a U.S. investor holds the actual Siemens shares or the ADRs. Either way, the rate of return in U.S. dollars is the same, as the ADR returns will reflect both returns on an ordinary share and changes in the spot FX rate. So the risk and return for the Siemens ordinary shares, when viewed in U.S. dollars, needs to be consistent with the equilibrium risk–return trade-off in the same way as Siemens ADRs. In reality, some arbitrage opportunities have been observed in between ADRs and the ordinaries.[9]

ADRs often trade in a share ratio different from one for one. For example, one ADR for Telefonos de Mexico represents 20 underlying Mexican shares, while one ADR for Diageo (a British company that resulted from the merger of Guinness and Grand Metropolitan in 1997) represents four ordinary UK shares.

The ordinary shares for Diageo are denominated in British pounds and traded on the London Stock Exchange (LSE). There is one ADR share for every four ordinary shares. At time 0, the price of an ordinary share is £10 in London and the spot FX rate is 2 $/£. At time 1, the ordinary shares are priced at £12 and the spot FX rate is 1.60 $/£. (a) What is the no-arbitrage price of a Diageo ADR share at time 0? (b) What is the time-1 no-arbitrage price of an ADR share? (c) What will be the rate of return to a U.S. investor who buys the Diageo ordinary shares at time 0 and holds until time 1?

Answers: (a) An ordinary share is worth £10(2 $/£) = $20 at time 0. Because 4 ordinary shares underlie 1 ADR share, an ADR share should be priced at 4($20) = $80 at time 0. (b) An ordinary share is worth £12(1.60 $/£) = $19.20 at time 1. An ADR share should be priced at 4($19.20) = $76.80 at time 1. (c) Thus, the rate of return in U.S. dollars is $76.80/80 - 1 = -0.04$, or –4%.

The proportion of U.S. trading (in ADRs) of a foreign company's shares varies. Tomkins, a UK engineering company has relatively little U.S. trading, but GlaxoSmithKline, a UK pharmaceutical company, experiences U.S. trading of about 30%. The larger the percentage of trading in the United States, the more the price is determined in the U.S. market instead of the home market. But the no-arbitrage relationship should hold regardless of the primary market of price determination.[10]

Exhibit 5.4 shows some estimated betas in U.S. dollars for a few selected ADRs. The global beta estimate for Sony's ADR is 0.44. That Sony is headquartered in Japan has no bearing on the fact that a U.S. investor holding a globally diversified portfolio views the risk of Sony's ADRs as the global beta. For comparison, the estimated beta of Sony's ADR returns with the U.S. equity market is also shown, 0.24. The global beta estimate is higher than the local (U.S.) beta estimate for all the ADRs in Exhibit 5.4.

ADRs help us see why it is generally incorrect to use country-specific local CAPMs in a world of internationally integrated financial markets. Say we try to estimate Sony's cost of equity, both in yen using a local Japan CAPM with an estimate of Sony's traditional equity beta against a Japanese market index (in yen), and in U.S. dollars using the traditional local U.S. CAPM with an estimate of Sony's ADR beta against a U.S. market index. The mistake with this method is that there is nothing in that approach that reflects the no-arbitrage link between the Sony ordinary shares and the Sony ADRs. Sony's ordinary shares are effectively the same asset as the ADRs, but with a different currency denomination; this fact implies that the cost of equity from the different currency perspectives must be based on the asset's systematic risk relative to the same market index, but from the different currency perspectives. It would be theoretically more correct to use the global CAPM for both estimations: use the global market index from the yen perspective to estimate Sony's equity beta in yen, and use the

Exhibit 5.4. Beta Estimates (in U.S. Dollars) for Selected ADRs

Company	$\beta_{iG}^{\$}$	$\beta_{iL}^{\$}$
BHP Billiton	1.58	1.19
Diageo	0.57	0.31
Glaxosmithkline	0.45	0.32
Sony	0.44	0.24

Source: Author's calculations with monthly rates of return, 2002–2007.

global market index from the U.S. dollar perspective to estimate Sony's equity (ADR) beta in U.S. dollars.

In contrast to ADRs, violations of the "law of one price" have been regularly observed for *dual-listed shares*. In a dual-listed shares arrangement, separate but related companies in different countries pay a combined cash flow to the shareholders of the companies. One company's shares are <u>not</u> convertible into the other's, but both shares are claims on equivalent cash flow streams. Fundamentally, the shares should sell at equivalent prices, given the spot FX rate. However, researchers have found deviations from pricing parity in dual-listed shares because arbitrage is not possible. These deviations are similar to those observed between Chinese A-shares and B-shares, where A-shares may only be held by Chinese investors, whereas B-shares may only be owned by non-Chinese investors.[11]

Currency Betas

Because corporate equity returns are exposed to changes in FX rates, it makes sense that a systematic relation would exist between FX rates and an equity market index. That is, FX rates tend to have systematic risk relative to an equity market index. The relation between percentage changes in a spot FX rate and the returns on an equity market index is called a *currency beta*. In the global CAPM, given the U.S. dollar as the pricing currency, the currency beta of the euro, denoted $\beta_\epsilon^\$$, is the beta of the percentage changes in the spot FX price of the euro versus the global market index.

Some currency beta estimates, versus the global equity index, are shown in Exhibit 5.5. Generally, the currency beta estimate is positive for many currencies. Currency beta estimates for emerging market currencies tend to be higher than those of developed markets, possibly because "flight to safety" episodes tend to be correlated with high capital flight from emerging markets, creating a high FX volatility and a positive correlation between the FX price of the local currency and world equity returns. The "flight to safety" idea might also explain the relatively low currency beta estimate for the Swiss franc in Exhibit 5.5. Investors tend to increase deposits in Switzerland during times of increased worry about risk, so the Swiss franc often appreciates when other markets drop. The currency beta estimate for the Japanese yen was negative over the more recent period, perhaps due to swings in carry trade activity.

Exhibit 5.5. Currency Beta Estimates

	December 2002– November 2007	May 2007– April 2012
Australian Dollar	0.38	0.32
Brazilian Real	0.10	0.33
Euro	0.22	0.17
Indian Rupee	0.14	0.16
Japanese Yen	0.10	–0.07
Mexican Peso	0.19	0.27
New Zealand Dollar	0.30	0.31
South African Rand	0.23	0.34
South Korean Won	0.20	0.32
Swedish Krona	0.28	0.28
Swiss Franc	0.15	0.14
Taiwan Dollar	0.12	0.11
UK Pound	0.29	0.26

Source: Author's computations using month-end data from St. Louis Federal Reserve (FX Rates) and the MSCI World Index (Large + Midcap) in U.S. dollars.

The currency beta estimates in Exhibit 5.5 were made with the simple regression approach. As you can see in Exhibit 5.5, estimates of currency betas tend to change a bit over time. The changes occur for statistical reasons as well as because of changes in the economic structure of a particular country compared to the rest of the world and other changes in market conditions.

Published currency beta estimates are available for some currencies that have *currency shares*. Currency shares are exchange-traded vehicles for investors to trade foreign currency. Some currency share beta estimates are shown in Exhibit 5.6. These published estimates, from Google Finance, are versus the U.S. market index.

In academic research circles, the question of whether FX rates fluctuate systematically with an equity market index has long been controversial. However, the discussion in this chapter is supported by the following interesting research findings: (a) currencies with higher interest rates tend to have higher currency beta estimates, and currencies with lower interest rates tend to have lower currency betas (like the Swiss franc) or even negative betas (like the Japanese yen); (b) currency beta estimates tend to

Exhibit 5.6. *Currency Share Beta Estimates*

Currency	Beta
Australian Dollar	0.67
British Pound	0.29
Canadian Dollar	0.47
Euro	0.40
Japanese Yen	−0.11
Swedish Krona	0.61
Swiss Franc	0.28

Source: Google Finance 11/13/2012; Betas versus Local
U.S. Equity Market Index.

change through time, and tend to be the most extreme during crisis periods; and (c) some of the positive average returns on carry trade portfolios are compensation for global systematic risk.[12]

Risk-Adjusted UIRP Condition

The traditional uncovered interest rate parity (UIRP) condition, expressed as a linear approximation, is $E^*(x^{\$/€}) = r_f^{\$} - r_f^{€}$, where $E^*(x^{\$/€})$ is the expected percentage change in the *intrinsic* FX price of the euro, which is serving here as a representative foreign currency. The traditional UIRP condition says that if the euro is correctly valued relative to financial market conditions, the expected rate of FX change in the euro is equal to the interest rate differential, $r_f^{\$} - r_f^{€}$.

For example, if the risk-free rate in U.S. dollars is 2.5% and the risk-free rate in euros is 4.5%, the traditional UIRP condition says that the expected rate of FX change in the euro is 2.5% − 4.5% = −2%, if the time-0 actual spot FX rate is equal to the short-run intrinsic spot FX rate. The short-run intrinsic spot FX rate is the rate consistent with financial market conditions, but is not necessarily equal to the long-run intrinsic FX rate consistent with goods market prices. Like stocks, of course, FX rates are often not correctly valued even compared to the short-run intrinsic FX rate, so the *actual* expected rate of FX change in the euro may not be equal to $E^*(x^{\$/€})$.

In light of empirical research findings that do <u>not</u> support the traditional UIRP condition, some economists have argued that another factor that should affect $E^*(x^{\$/€})$ is FX risk. With this notion, a more general equation of the expected rate of intrinsic FX change is $E^*(x^{\$/€}) = r_f^\$ - r_f^€ + CRP_€^\$$, where $CRP_€^\$$ denotes the *currency risk premium* for the euro, expressed in U.S. dollars. We'll refer to this general equation as the *risk-adjusted UIRP (RA-UIRP)* condition (linear approximation).

Now we'll use the global CAPM to get a specific estimate of a currency risk premium. As part of this process, we first use the currency beta and the global CAPM to envision the cost of capital in U.S. dollars for a foreign asset that is nominally risk-free in its own currency. Because the only uncertainty in the U.S. dollar return on a euro risk-free asset is the uncertainty about the $\$/€$ spot FX rate, a euro risk-free asset has a beta in U.S. dollars that is equal to the currency beta of the euro, $\beta_€^\$$. The U.S. dollar cost of capital on a risk-free euro asset, denoted $k_{ef}^\$$, is the compensation for the systematic risk of the euro. Using the global CAPM in equation (5.2), we have that $k_{ef}^\$ = r_f^\$ + \beta_€^\$(GRP^\$)$. That is, if the global CAPM is the international risk–return trade-off, the foreign risk-free asset's required rate of return in U.S. dollars should be consistent with that trade-off, just like all assets in the integrated financial market.

Thus, $\beta_€^\$(GRP^\$)$ is the euro's currency risk premium, in U.S. dollars, if the global CAPM is the international risk–return trade-off. For example, assume $r_f^\$ = 2.5\%$, $GRP^\$ = 5\%$, and $\beta_€^\$ = 0.20$. The U.S. dollar cost of capital on a euro risk-free asset would be $0.025 + 0.20(0.05) = 0.035$, or 3.5%. The currency risk premium for the euro, in U.S. dollars, is $CRP_€^\$ = \beta_€^\$(GRP^\$) = 0.20(0.05) = 0.01$, or 1%.

Assume that the global CAPM in U.S. dollars is the risk–return trade-off for internationally traded assets and that the currency beta of the Japanese yen is –0.10. (a) What is the required rate of return in U.S. dollars on a Japanese bond that is risk-free in yen, given a U.S. dollar risk-free rate of 5.60% and a global risk premium of 6% in U.S. dollars? (b) What is the currency risk premium for the yen, expressed in U.S. dollars?

Answers: (a) $0.056 - 0.10(0.06) = 0.05$, or 5%; (b) $-0.10(0.06) = -0.006$, or –0.6%.

Next we use the global CAPM approach to the currency risk premium to state the specific RA-UIRP condition based on the global CAPM, as shown in equation (5.3).[13]

Risk-Adjusted UIRP Condition (Global CAPM)
Percentage Form—Linear Approximation

$$E^*(x^{\$/\euro}) = r_f^{\$} - r_f^{\euro} + \beta_{\euro}^{\$}(GRP^{\$}) \tag{5.3}$$

The risk-adjusted UIRP relationship in equation (5.3) adds the currency risk premium, $\beta_{\euro}^{\$}(GRP^{\$})$, to the linear approximation of the traditional UIRP condition, $E^*(x^{\$/\euro}) = r_f^{\$} - r_f^{\euro}$. The currency risk premium term adjusts the traditional UIRP condition for the systematic risk of the spot FX rate in a manner that is consistent with the intrinsic valuation of all assets by the common international risk–return relation, the global CAPM in U.S. dollars.

Now let's continue the example where $r_f^{\$} = 2.5\%$, $GRP^{\$} = 5\%$, $\beta_{\euro}^{\$} = 0.20$, and $k_{\euro f}^{\$} = 0.025 + 0.20(0.05) = 0.035$, or 3.5%. Next assume that the euro risk-free rate, $r_f^{\euro}$, is 4.5%. The global CAPM RA-UIRP condition in equation (5.3) says that the expected rate of intrinsic FX change of the euro, $E^*(x^{\$/\euro})$, is $0.025 - 0.045 + 0.20(0.05) = -0.01$, or -1%. That is, if the spot FX rate is currently correctly valued in the international financial market, the annualized expected rate of change of the euro would be -1% per year. By way of comparison, the traditional UIRP condition would say that $E^*(x^{\$/\euro}) = 0.025 - 0.045 = -0.02$, or -2%.

The expected rate of intrinsic FX change of a currency plays an important role in the conversion of an asset's cost of capital from one currency into another, as you will see in the final chapter. So if the RA-UIRP condition in equation (5.3) gives an estimate of $E^*(x^{\$/\euro})$ that improves on the estimate of the traditional UIRP condition, the important process of estimating international cost of capital is improved.

Assume the currency beta for the yen, $\beta_{\yen}^{\$}$, is -0.10. Assume the yen risk-free rate is $r_f^{\yen} = 1\%$ and the U.S. dollar risk-free rate is $r_f^{\$} = 3.5\%$. Assume the global CAPM is the international risk–return trade-off in U.S. dollars and the global risk premium is 5%. (a) Find the required rate of return in U.S. dollars on risk-free yen debt. (b) Find the expected rate of intrinsic FX change of the yen, given the global CAPM.

Answers: (a) Using the global CAPM, the required rate of return in U.S. dollars on yen risk-free debt is $0.035 + [-0.10(0.05)] = 0.03$, or 3%. (b) Using the RA-UIRP condition in equation (5.3), $E^*(x^{\$/\yen}) = r_f^\$ - r_f^\yen + \beta_\yen^\$(GRP^\$) = 0.035 - 0.01 + [-0.10(0.05)] = 0.02$, or 2%.

The RA–UIRP relationship in equation (5.3) might help explain the *forward premium puzzle*, which is the body of empirical research that finds that higher (lower) interest rate currencies tend to appreciate (depreciate), exactly the opposite of the implication of the traditional UIRP condition. Higher interest rate currencies have tended to have higher currency beta estimates, and a higher currency beta implies a higher expected rate of intrinsic FX change.

For example, assume $r_f^\$ = 2.5\%$, $r_f^\euro = 3.5\%$, $GRP^\$ = 5\%$, and $\beta_\euro^\$ = 0.40$. The global CAPM RA-UIRP condition in equation (5.3) states that the expected rate of intrinsic FX change of the euro, $E^*(x^{\$/\euro})$, is $0.025 - 0.035 + 0.40(0.05) = 0.01$, or 1%. That is, if the spot FX rate is currently correctly valued in the international financial market, the annualized expected rate of FX change of the euro would be 2%. So we'd expect the higher interest rate currency, the euro in this case, to appreciate, even though the traditional UIRP condition would forecast the euro to depreciate. The traditional UIRP condition would say that $E^*(x^{\$/\euro}) = 0.025 - 0.035 = -0.01$, or −1%.

Summary Action Points

- In international CAPM theory, the equilibrium risk–return relation is common to all assets, regardless of the assets' nationalities.
- The global CAPM is similar in form to the traditional CAPM, but the market index is a world, or global, market index. An asset's global beta tends to be different from its local beta.
- In principle, there is a no-arbitrage connection between the price of an American Depositary Receipt (ADR), the price of the underlying ordinary share in its local currency, and the spot FX rate.

- A currency risk premium may improve the estimated expected rate of intrinsic FX change of a currency, and the global CAPM is useful in estimating a currency risk premium.

Glossary

American Depositary Receipts (ADRs). U.S. dollar-denominated and U.S. market-traded receipts on foreign-issued shares.

Beta: The sensitivity of an asset's rate of return relative to the overall market, which is the asset's systematic risk.

Cost of Equity: The equilibrium expected rate of return as compensation for risk of an equity investment.

Cross-Listed Stocks: Stocks traded on both their home and foreign exchanges.

Currency Beta: The average percentage change in the FX price of a currency relative to changes in a market index.

Currency Risk Premium: The difference between the expected rate of intrinsic FX change of a currency and what would be that expected rate under the traditional UIRP condition.

Currency Shares: Exchange-traded vehicles for investors to trade foreign currency.

Dual-listed Shares: An arrangement where separate, but related companies in different countries pay a combined cash flow to the shareholders of the companies.

Expected Rate of Intrinsic FX Change (of a Currency): The expected percentage FX change in a currency, given that the currency is correctly valued relative to financial market conditions.

Forward Premium Puzzle: The body of empirical research that finds that higher interest rate currencies tend to appreciate, and vice versa, opposite to the implication of the traditional UIRP condition.

Global Beta: The beta of an asset's rate of return versus the global market index, measuring the tendency of the asset's returns to change systematically with the returns of the global market index.

Global Risk Premium: The minimum rate of return over the risk-free rate that investors (in the aggregate) require as compensation for risk in the global market index.

Home Bias: The tendency of investors to invest more in stocks of their own country than would be advisable given the benefits of international diversification.

Local Beta: The beta of an asset's rate of return versus the local (domestic) market index, measuring the tendency of the returns to change systematically with the returns of the local market index.

Market Risk Premium: The minimum rate of return over the risk-free rate that investors (in the aggregate) require as compensation for the risk in the market index.

Ordinary Shares or *Ordinaries*: The actual local market shares that underlie depositary receipts trading in another market.

Required Rate of Return: The expected rate of return required as compensation for investing capital and bearing risk.

Risk-Adjusted UIRP (RA-UIRP) Condition: The theoretical economic relationship between the spot FX rate, the expected future FX rate, the interest rate differential, and an adjustment for currency risk.

Traditional UIRP Condition: The theoretical economic relationship between the spot FX rate, the expected future FX rate, and the interest rate differential, with no adjustment for currency risk.

Discussion Questions

1. Discuss the pros and cons of using the global CAPM to estimate a firm's cost of equity.
2. The expected the rate of return on the market index is 12% and the risk-free rate is 3%. The market is undervalued. Should you use 9% as the market risk premium in the CAPM? Explain.
3. Why should a foreign stock be in the same risk–return equilibrium as U.S. stocks?

4. Why would the currency beta (in U.S. dollars) be positive for many currencies, but zero or negative for the Japanese yen?

5. Explain what is meant by the term "currency risk premium," and why a currency risk premium might be negative.

Problems

1. The rate of return in Swiss francs on a share of stock on the Swiss Stock Exchange is 15%. During the same period, the spot FX rate changes from 1 Sf/$ to 1.25 Sf/$. What is the rate of return on the stock from the U.S. dollar perspective?

2. The rate of return in Swiss francs on a share of stock on the Swiss Stock Exchange is –15%. During the same period, the spot FX rate changes from 1 Sf/$ to 1.20 Sf/$. What is the rate of return on the stock from the U.S. dollar perspective?

3. The rate of return in U.S. dollars on a share of stock on the New York Stock Exchange is 15%. During the same period, the spot FX rate changes from 1 Sf/$ to 1.25 Sf/$. What is the rate of return on the stock from the Swiss franc perspective?

4. CDG Co.'s global equity beta in U.S. dollars is 1.25. Estimate CDG's cost of equity in U.S. dollars using the global CAPM, given a U.S. dollar risk-free rate of 4% and a global risk premium of 4% in U.S. dollars.

5. Assume the U.S. equity market index has a global beta in U.S. dollars of 1. With the global CAPM, what is the U.S. equity market risk premium, given a U.S. dollar risk-free rate of 4% and a global risk premium of 5% in U.S. dollars?

6. Sony's ADR shares are traded on the New York Stock Exchange. There is one ADR share of Sony for each ordinary share. (a) If the ordinary shares are priced at ¥3,750 in Tokyo, and if the spot FX rate is 110 ¥/$, what is the no-arbitrage price of a Sony ADR share in U.S. dollars? (b) What is the time-1 price of a Sony ADR share when the ordinary shares are priced at ¥4,375 and the spot FX rate is 125 ¥/$?

7. What is the rate of return to a U.S. investor who buys Sony ADRs at time 0 and holds until time 1? Use information from the previous problem.

8. Sony's ADR shares are traded on the New York Stock Exchange. There is one ADR share of Sony for each ordinary Tokyo share. At time 0, the ordinary shares are priced at ¥4,000 in Tokyo, and the spot FX rate is 80 ¥/$. At time 1, the ordinary shares are priced at ¥5,000 in Tokyo, and the spot FX rate is 100 ¥/$. If there is no arbitrage possible between the Sony ADR shares and the ordinary shares, find the rate of return to a U.S. investor who buys Sony ADRs at time 0 and holds until time 1.

9. CSN (Companhia Siderurgica Nacional, a real company) is a Brazilian steel products company with ordinary shares traded in Brazilian real in Sao Paulo and ADRs traded on the NYSE in U.S. dollars. One ADR is equivalent to one ordinary share. The price of an ordinary share is currently Re 60 per share. The spot FX rate is 1.60 Re/$. (a) Find the no-arbitrage price in U.S. dollars of an ADR share. (b) If an ordinary share has a rate of return over the next year of –20% and the Brazilian real appreciates by 10%, find the rate of return on an ADR share in U.S. dollars.

10. Assume the Swiss franc and U.S. dollar risk-free rates are 1.50% and 3.40%, respectively, and the currency beta of the Swiss franc is 0.10. (a) Find the expected rate of intrinsic FX change of the Swiss franc using the risk-adjusted UIRP condition based on the global CAPM, assuming the global risk premium in U.S. dollars is 5%. (b) Find the currency risk premium of the Swiss franc (in U.S. dollars).

11. Assume the currency beta of the New Zealand dollar (from U.S. dollar perspective) is 0.30. The global risk premium in U.S. dollars is 5%. The risk-free rate is 3.50% in U.S. dollars and 6% in New Zealand dollars. (a) Find the expected rate of intrinsic FX change of the NZ$, given that the global CAPM holds in U.S. dollars for all international assets. (b) Compare the answer in part (a) to the one you get with the traditional UIRP condition.

For 12–15: Assume the currency beta for the British pound is 0.20. Assume the British pound risk-free rate is 5% and the U.S. dollar risk-free rate is 3%. Assume the global CAPM with a global risk premium in U.S. dollars of 5%.

12. Estimate the expected rate of intrinsic FX change of the British pound using the risk-adjusted UIRP condition based on the global CAPM.

13. Compare your answer in the previous question to the expected rate of intrinsic FX change of the British pound using the linear approximation of the traditional UIRP condition.

14. Find the required rate of return in U.S. dollars on a deposit that is risk-free in British pounds.

15. Find the currency risk premium of the British pound, from the perspective of U.S. dollars.

Answers to Problems

1. The U.S. dollar appreciates by 25% relative to the Swissie, so the Swissie depreciates by 20% relative to the U.S. dollar. The rate of return on the stock in U.S. dollars is $(1.15)(1 - 0.20) - 1 = -0.08$, or -8%.

2. Approximately: $-15\% - 16.67\% = -31.67\%$; Exactly: $(1 - 0.15)(1 - 0.1667) - 1 = -0.29$, or -29%.

3. $(1.15)(1 + 0.25) - 1 = 0.4375$, or 43.75%.

4. Using the global CAPM, $0.04 + 1.25(0.04) = 0.09$, or 9%.

5. Same as global risk premium, 5%.

6. (a) An ADR share is worth $¥3,750/(110 ¥/\$) = \$34.09$.
   (b) The new ADR share price will be $¥4,375/(125 ¥/\$) = \$35$.

7. The rate of return in U.S. dollars = $\$35/34.09 - 1 = 0.0267$, or 2.67%.

8. $\$50/50 - 1 = 0$.

9. Re $60/(1.60$ Re$/\$) = \$37.50$; $0.80(1.10) - 1 = -0.12$, or -12%.

10. (a) $E^*(x^{\$/Sf}) = 0.034 - 0.015 + 0.10(0.05) = 0.024$, or 2.40%.
    (b) $CRP_{Sf}^{\$} = E^*(x^{\$/Sf}) - (r_f^{\$} - r_f^{Sf}) = 0.024 - (0.034 - 0.015) = 0.005$, or 0.50%.

11. (a) $0.035 - 0.06 + 0.30(0.05) = -0.01$, or -1%.
    (b) $0.035 - 0.06 = -0.025$, or -2.5%.

12. $0.03 - 0.05 + 0.20(0.05) = -0.01$, or -1%.

13. $0.03 - 0.05 = -0.02$, or -2%.

14. $0.03 + 0.20(0.05) = 0.04$, or 4%.

15. $-0.01 - (0.03 - 0.05) = 0.01$, or 1%. Or, $0.20(0.05) = 0.01$, or 1%.

CHAPTER 6

Hurdle Rates For Overseas Operations

An operation's *cost of capital* is a concept that is central to valuation, investment (and divestment) decisions, measures of economic profit, and performance appraisal. Finance theory says that managers should apply a different cost of capital, or *hurdle rate*, to different operations based on risk. Applying this idea in global finance suggests that a company's managers should apply different hurdle rates to operations in different countries. As a case in point, Dan Cohrs, then vice president and treasurer at the telecommunications company GTE Corporation, said in 1996 that GTE did in fact set different hurdle rates for the company's projects in different countries.[1]

Although no single best practice has been established for this issue, the aim of this chapter is to show some basics of how a firm might estimate a cost of capital for an overseas project, division, or subsidiary. In addition to techniques for estimating a hurdle rate for a project or division in a developed country, we also look at the case of an emerging market country, where there typically are additional political risks to consider.

Risk and Divisional Hurdle Rates

The cost of capital for a division (or subsidiary or project) is sometimes called the division's hurdle rate. We have to think of the division's hurdle rate as the rate of return that would be required on investing in the division by the aggregate financial market, as compensation for risk, if the division were an independently traded, all-equity business operation with no off-balance sheet risk management positions. In principle, if the rate of return of the division's business operation is not expected to be at least the division's hurdle rate, the division is not adding shareholder value.

A division's cost of capital differs from the parent firm's overall cost of capital if the risk of the division's business operation is different from the risk of the parent firm's overall business operations. This situation is especially likely in the case of an overseas division. If a division has higher risk than the parent's overall risk, the division's hurdle rate should be higher than the parent's overall cost of capital. If the parent's overall cost of capital were used as the division's hurdle rate, the manager may make investments that do not offer enough expected reward to compensate for the risk. If a division has lower risk than the parent's overall risk, the division's hurdle rate should be lower than the parent's overall cost of capital. A manager who does not recognize this may miss out on value-adding investment opportunities by setting the hurdle rate too high.[2]

One reason an overseas division's risk is likely to differ from the parent company's overall risk is that the division and the rest of the company are likely to have different basic relationships with the global economy. For example, the sales volume or the operating costs of a Japanese division may have a different correlation with the global economy than does the rest of the company.

Explicitly or implicitly, market investors require a rate of return on their investments based on risk. The market's aggregate required rate of return on a company's shares is the company's *cost of equity*. A firm's cost of equity is one component of its *weighted average cost of capital*, or *WACC*, which you probably recall from prior finance courses. A firm's *WACC* is relatively straightforward to calculate, and *WACC*s are used for many purposes in corporate finance; thus, many companies compute a *WACC*. Finance theory tells us that a firm's *WACC* reflects the risk of the enterprise, including the impact of any debt tax shield values, and the financial risk management positions.

The *WACC* is a useful cost of capital concept for an overall firm, but impractical for individual divisions, because divisions do not have their own capital structure and market data to compute a *WACC*. Moreover, we do not know how to adjust a parent's overall *WACC* to find a hurdle rate for a division whose risk level varies from the overall risk level of the parent. Because of the problem of applying the *WACC* concept to divisions, we'll use a different approach, a standard one that is based on applying the (global) CAPM directly to divisions.[3]

For a divisional hurdle rate, the CAPM approach is easier to apply and may even be superior to the *WACC* approach on theoretical grounds. The cost of capital in the CAPM approach is technically slightly different from a *WACC*. In theory, the CAPM cost of capital discounts the expected operating cash flow stream to the intrinsic <u>business value</u>, whereas the *WACC* discounts the expected operating cash flow stream to the intrinsic <u>enterprise value</u>, assuming the *WACC* is found with <u>net debt</u> and not only "right-hand side" debt. So the difference between the *WACC* and the cost of capital we'll use is due to the debt tax shield value, which is relatively small anyway, as we argued in Chapter 2. An overseas division's hurdle rate is still difficult to estimate with precision, but we suggest some methods to consider.

As you will learn, an overseas operation's hurdle rate may be expressed in either the parent's home currency or the operation's local currency. In this chapter, we deal only with estimating foreign operation hurdle rates from perspective of the parent's home currency, which we'll assume is the U.S. dollar. In Chapter 8, we'll cover the idea of an overseas operation's hurdle rate expressed in the operation's local currency.

Operating Beta

Our approach to overseas division hurdle rates is based on the idea of *operating beta*, which is the systematic risk of a business operation, and is the beta the business operation would have in the absence of debt, cash and marketable securities, and off-balance sheet financial risk management strategies. With a division's estimated operating beta (in U.S. dollars), we can use the global CAPM in equation (5.2) to help find the division's hurdle rate (in U.S. dollars).

Estimating a division's operating beta has its own problems, because the operating beta is not directly observable and there are typically no historical divisional return data to use in statistical estimation. So we have to be somewhat creative when estimating division-specific operating betas. In this section, we discuss an approach to estimating the operating beta for an overseas division. The method is not perfect, but is relatively simple and should be helpful.

To estimate an overseas division's operating beta, we'll use the *proxy firm* approach, which means identifying a firm (or firms) in a similar business as the division and that also has traded equity data. The idea is to estimate the operating beta of the proxy firm. The proxy firm can be located in the home country or in the division's country. Sometimes, the overall parent firm is a suitable home country proxy firm if the overall firm is focused in a relatively homogeneous industry. If the proxy firm is located in the home country, we'll make an adjustment for the division's country. If the proxy firm is located in the division's country, that adjustment is not necessary.

Estimating the operating beta for a proxy firm is not as straightforward as estimating an equity beta with historical returns data, because there are typically no direct observations of the firm's business value. Instead, we use the proxy firm's estimated equity beta in an indirect approach, called *unlevering*, to estimate the proxy firm's operating beta. To properly unlever a firm's equity beta, we should consider the systematic risk of the firm's net debt and off-balance sheet financial risk management positions, which we'll do later in the chapter in equation (6.4). However, we can ignore these items in many cases and still get a reasonable estimate for the firm's operating beta with the basic beta unlevering formula in equation (6.1).

Basic Beta Unlevering Formula

$$\beta_O^{\$} = \beta_S^{\$}(1 - ND^{\$}/V_B^{\$}) \tag{6.1}$$

In equation (6.1), $\beta_O^{\$}$ is the firm's operating beta in U.S. dollars, $\beta_S^{\$}$ is the firm's equity beta in U.S. dollars, $ND^{\$}$ is the firm's net debt measured in U.S. dollars, and $V_B^{\$}$ is the firm's business value in U.S. dollars. As we said before, in many cases, you can use enterprise value for $V_B^{\$}$, ignoring the notion that there may be some tax shield value embedded in the enterprise value.[4]

As an example, assume that ANC Company is a home country proxy firm. Let ANC's estimated equity beta (in U.S. dollars) be 1.20. Assume ANC's equity market cap is $60 million and its net debt is $20 million ($30 million of debt and $10 million of cash and marketable securities). Moreover, assume that ANC has no off-balance sheet risk management positions, and its net debt is denominated entirely in U.S. dollars and has no systematic risk. Ignoring the debt tax shield value, the estimated business value is the enterprise value, $60 million + 20 million = $80 million.

The ratio of net debt to business value, $ND^\$/V_B^\$$, is \$20 million/\$80 million = 0.25. From equation (6.1), ANC's estimated operating beta (in U.S. dollars) is 1.20(1 − 0.25) = 0.90.

A firm's operating beta generally will be lower than its equity beta if net financial leverage is positive. A firm with negative net debt would have an operating beta that is higher than the equity beta.

The U.S. firm GRF Co.'s estimated equity beta in U.S. dollars is 0.80. GRF's equity market cap is \$100 million and its net debt is \$25 million (\$35 million of debt and \$10 million of cash). GRF has no off-balance sheet financial risk management positions, the value of its debt tax shields is zero, and the net debt is denominated entirely in U.S. dollars and has no systematic risk. Find GRF's estimated operating beta in U.S. dollars.

Answer: GRF's estimated business value is the enterprise value, \$125 million. The ratio of net debt to business value is \$25 million/ \$125 million = 0.20. From equation (6.1), GRF's estimated operating beta in U.S. dollars is 0.80(1 − 0.20) = 0.64.

Operating Beta for an Overseas Division

It will sometimes be possible to find a <u>foreign</u> proxy firm in the same country as the division for which you want to estimate a hurdle rate. If so, and if the proxy firm has locally-traded equity shares, you can convert a historical time series of equity returns from local currency to U.S. dollars by using historical FX rates, and then estimate the proxy firm's equity beta from the U.S. dollar perspective. Then you can unlever that equity beta estimate to get an estimate of the proxy firm's operating beta. But you have to be careful, because the proxy firm's debt is likely to be denominated in the foreign currency. Unless the currency beta happens to be zero, equation (6.1) technically does not apply. Instead, you should use equation (6.4), as covered later in the chapter. But equation (6.1) will often give a reasonable approximation, unless the currency beta is particularly high. Once you have estimated the foreign proxy firm's operating beta, you simply assume that is a good estimate of the operating beta of your division in the proxy firm's country.

If you do not know of a foreign proxy firm, you can try to use the *Lessard country beta method*. The first step is to estimate the operating beta of a home country proxy firm. In some cases, the logical proxy will be the division's parent company. For example, if a U.S. multinational telecommunications company wants to find a hurdle rate for its overseas telecommunications subsidiary, the parent's estimated operating beta is a reasonable choice for a home country proxy firm's operating beta. In more diversified situations, the best choice could be a home country proxy firm in a business similar to the division. We denote a home country proxy firm's operating beta, $\beta_{OH}^{\$}$.

The next step in the Lessard country beta method is to estimate country C's *country beta* in U.S. dollars, denoted $\beta_C^{\$}$. You'd do this by regressing the returns of the country's equity index against the returns of the global market index, expressing both index returns in U.S. dollars. The country beta is the systematic risk of an index fund of county C's stocks to globally diversified investors, from the U.S. dollar perspective. Some country beta estimates are in Exhibit 6.1. The estimates not in parentheses were calculated with daily returns covering 2 years from December 4, 2006 until December 2, 2008.[5] The estimates in parentheses are from January 1994 to December 2003.[6]

The final step in the Lessard country beta method is to multiply the home country proxy firm's operating beta times the country beta, as shown in equation (6.2), where $\beta_{OD}^{\$}$ denotes the operating beta of an overseas division. This method is *ad hoc*, but is practical. Because this method was pioneered by MIT finance professor Donald Lessard, we call equation (6.2) the *Lessard country beta method*.[7]

Lessard Country Beta Method

$$\beta_{OD}^{\$} = \beta_{OH}^{\$} \times \beta_C^{\$} \qquad (6.2)$$

For example, say a U.S. multinational operates in a relatively homogeneous industry and so is a reasonable home country proxy firm. The parent has an overall operating beta of 0.50. Using the Lessard country beta method, what would be the operating beta estimate for a division in Sweden where the estimated country beta is 1.24? Using equation (6.2), the Swedish division's operating beta estimate is 0.50(1.24) = 0.62. Because Sweden's country beta is higher than 1, it makes sense that the Swedish division's operating beta is higher than the parent's operating beta.

Exhibit 6.1. Country Beta Estimates (in U.S. dollars)

Brazil	1.80 (1.81)	Italy	1.04 (0.90)
Hungary	1.45	Belgium	1.03 (0.65)
Turkey	1.41	China	1.02 (1.26)
Norway	1.37	Australia	1.01 (0.93)
Mexico	1.31 (1.40)	Greece	0.95
Russia	1.29 (2.34)	Chile	0.95
Argentina	1.28	S. Korea	0.92 (1.55)
Austria	1.24	Portugal	0.88
Sweden	1.24 (1.25)	India	0.86 (0.63)
Canada	1.21 (1.13)	Switzerland	0.83 (0.73)
United Kingdom	1.17 (0.78)	Singapore	0.76 (1.04)
Ireland	1.16	Indonesia	0.76
South Africa	1.15 (1.09)	Hong Kong	0.70 (1.33)
Czech Republic	1.14	Thailand	0.63
France	1.14 (1.00)	New Zealand	0.60
Peru	1.12	Philippines	0.51
Germany	1.12 (1.10)	Taiwan	0.48 (1.15)
Finland	1.10	Israel	0.42
Netherlands	1.09 (1.02)	Japan	0.41 (0.83)
Spain	1.09 (0.92)	Malaysia	0.38 (0.81)
Denmark	1.08	Egypt	0.34
Poland	1.08	Morocco	0.28
United States	1.06 (1.00)		

Assume that the U.S. multinational company Specialty Chemical and Adhesives (SCA) wants to estimate the operating beta of its UK subsidiary, but there is no reasonable UK proxy firm. SCA estimates the operating beta of a typical U.S. firm in this industry is 0.90. Assume the country beta estimate in U.S. dollars of the UK equity market index is 1.17, as in Exhibit 6.1. Using the Lessard country beta method, what is the estimated operating beta of SCA's UK subsidiary?

Answer: In U.S. dollars, the operating beta estimate for the UK division is 0.90(1.17) = 1.053.

Once you have an overseas division's operating beta estimate in U.S. dollars, you can use the global CAPM in equation (5.2). If the division is in a developed country and political risk can be ignored, the global CAPM is sufficient to find the division's hurdle rate, which is the cost of capital for the division's business operation. In U.S. dollars, the division's hurdle rate is denoted $k_{OD}^{\$}$. For example, let an overseas division's operating beta estimate in U.S. dollars be 0.90. If political risk can be ignored, if the risk-free rate in U.S. dollars is 3%, and if the global risk premium in U.S. dollars is 5%, the division's $k_{OD}^{\$}$ is $r_f^{\$} + \beta_{OD}^{\$}(GRP^{\$}) = 0.03 + 0.90(0.05) = 0.075$, or 7.50%.

The U.S. multinational BBX Co. has an overseas division in a developed country and political risk can be ignored. The division's estimated operating beta in U.S. dollars is 0.80. Use the global CAPM to estimate the division's hurdle rate in U.S. dollars if the risk-free rate in U.S. dollars is 5% and the global risk premium in U.S. dollars is 4%.

Answer: Using equation (5.2), $k_{OD}^{\$}$ is $0.05 + 0.80(0.04) = 0.082$, or 8.2%.

Political Risk

For a project's or a division's hurdle rate in an emerging market country, many companies add a premium for *political risk* to the usual premium for systematic risk. Political risk is a catch-all term used to describe the additional risks posed in terms of illiquidity, civil disruptions, corruption, political intervention, expropriation, imposition of controls on funds repatriation, irresponsible economic management by the country's policymakers, and the like. We may think of the *political risk premium* for country C, denoted PRP_C, as the premium required for the political risk of investing in the country's equity index fund.

In principle, a political risk premium does not have a currency denomination, and is thus the same number from any currency perspective. Still, a country's PRP_C is difficult to measure. Many managers and analysts estimate a country's political risk premium by the country's *sovereign credit default swap (CDS) rate*. A credit default swap is an "insurance policy" against the default of a bond. As long as the said bond does not default,

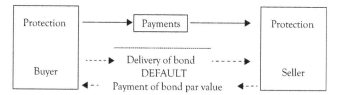

Figure 6.1. Credit default swaps.

the buyer of the insurance policy makes payments to the insurance seller based on the credit default swap rate. If the bond does default, the insurance buyer delivers the bond to the insurance seller, while the seller pays the buyer the face value of the bond. Figure 6.1 gives the basic idea.

A *sovereign credit default swap* is an "insurance policy" against the default of a sovereign bond issued by the government of a given country. Exhibit 6.2 shows some representative sovereign CDS yields for May 31, 2013. The quotes in Exhibit 6.2 are in basis points, so the CDS yield for Argentina is 3,144 basis points, or 31.44%. For Chile, the CDS yield is only 76 basis points, or 0.76%.

Technically, sovereign risk is the risk that the country's government will not service its debt obligations properly, whereas political risk applies to the country's private sector. However, the two risks are so related that analysts often use a country's CDS yield to proxy for the country's political risk premium, even though some emerging market governments could be more likely to default than to expropriate companies, in which case the sovereign CDS yield might somewhat overstate the political risk premium. We'll follow conventional practice and use an emerging market country's sovereign CDS yield for the country's PRP_C.[8]

For a given country, individual operations may pose different degrees of *political risk exposure*. The political risk exposure of operation i, denoted Φ_i, is the operation's degree of political risk relative to the overall country's political risk. Some operations may be relatively free of political risk. An example might be a tomato plant in the stable Korean food industry. At the other end of the spectrum are emerging market industries that are highly susceptible to political intervention, like the power and oil industries, or have relatively high potential for corruption.

If an operation has *average* political risk for the country, or if the manager has no opinion about the operation's political risk exposure, the

Exhibit 6.2. Sovereign Credit (Basis Points) May 31, 2013

Argentina	3,144	Korea, Rep.	75
Australia	44	Latvia	119
Austria	33	Lithuania	118
Belgium	64	Malaysia	85
Brazil	146	Mexico	102
Bulgaria	120	Netherlands	52
Chile	76	Norway	19
China	84	Panama	103
Colombia	104	Peru	109
Croatia	310	Philippines	97
Czech Republic	54	Poland	76
Denmark	26	Portugal	329
Egypt	623	Romania	182
Estonia	60	Russia	155
Finland	24	Slovakia	63
France	68	Slovenia	295
Germany	28	South Africa	191
Greece	23,389	Spain	236
Hungary	292	Sweden	20
Indonesia	162	Thailand	90
Ireland	127	Turkey	131
Israel	120	Ukraine	601
Italy	256	United Kingdom	43
Japan	78	United States	26
Kazakhstan	171	Venezuela	840

Source: Bloomberg quotes on Deutsche Bank site.

manager should assume Φ_i is equal to the average political risk exposure for the country, which by definition is 1. For operations with higher than average political risk exposure for the country, Φ_i should be higher than 1. For investments judged to have half the average political risk exposure of all the businesses in the country, $\Phi_i = 0.50$.

Often, a manager's estimate of an operation's Φ_i will be subjective, but some ideas on how to measure political risk exposure are discussed in the box titled "Brazilian Firms Embraer and Embratel." One method in that box is to estimate Φ_i by the ratio of the operation's local revenues to the average local revenues of firms domiciled in the country. For example, Embraer derives only about 3% of its revenues locally, while Embratel derives 95% of its revenues locally. Because the average Brazilian firm generates 77% of its revenues locally, the Φ_i for Embraer would be 0.03/0.77 = 0.04, and the Φ_i for Embratel would be 0.95/0.77 = 1.23.[9]

Brazilian Firms Embraer and Embratel

Professor Aswath Damodaran of New York University (NYU) suggests two methods to try to measure political risk exposure, Φ_i. He estimated Φ_i for two Brazilian firms: (a) Embraer, an aerospace company that manufactures and sells aircraft to many of the world's leading airlines; and (b) Embratel, the large Brazilian telecommunications company.

The first method is the ratio of the firm's local revenues to the local revenues of the average firm of the country. The more revenues come from outside the country, the lower the political risk exposure. Embraer derives only about 3% of its revenues locally, while Embratel derives 95% of its revenues locally. Because the average Brazilian firm generates 77% of its revenues locally, the Φ_i for Embraer would be 0.03/0.77 = 0.04, and the Φ_i for Embratel would be 0.95/0.77 = 1.23.

The second method is to estimate Φ_i as the coefficient of a time series of the firm's equity returns (converted to U.S. dollars) against the returns on a Brazilian sovereign bond (converted to U.S. dollars). For Embraer, the estimated Φ_i was 0.27. For Embratel, it was 2.00.

The hurdle rate for emerging market asset i (in U.S. dollars) is the U.S. dollar risk-free rate plus the sum of the asset's required premiums for systematic and political risk. Using the global CAPM as the basis for the premium for systematic risk, the total hurdle rate is given in equation (6.3), which we name the Damodaran model after its application by NYU finance professor Aswath Damodaran.[10]

Damodaran Model

$$k_i^{\$} = r_f^{\$} + \beta_i^{\$}(GRP^{\$}) + \Phi_i(PRP_C) \qquad (6.3)$$

For example, assume a U.S. multinational wants to estimate the hurdle rate in U.S. dollars for its subsidiary in Hungary. Assume: (a) Hungary's sovereign CDS yield is 2.92% (as in Exhibit 6.2), and so the political risk premium, PRP_C, is 2.92%. (b) The subsidiary is in an industry that has a political risk exposure, Φ_i, of 0.75. (c) The subsidiary's operating beta in U.S. dollars is 1.40. (d) The risk-free rate in U.S. dollars is 3.5%, and (e) the global risk premium in U.S. dollars is 5%. The Hungarian subsidiary's hurdle rate in U.S. dollars, applying equation (6.3), is $k_{OD}^{\$}$ = 0.035 + 1.40(0.05) + 0.75(0.0292) = 0.1269, or 12.69%.

A U.S. multinational wants to estimate the hurdle rate in U.S. dollars for its Chilean division. Management believes the industry has high political risk for Chile, and subjectively estimates the operation's Φ_i to be 1.50. The division's estimated operating beta (in U.S. dollars) is 0.70, the U.S. dollar risk-free rate is 3%, and the global risk premium in U.S. dollars is 5%. Assume that Chile's estimated sovereign CDS yield, 0.76%, is the political risk premium. Find the division's estimated hurdle rate in U.S. dollars using the Damodaran model.

Answer: $k_{OD}^{\$}$ = 0.03 + 0.70(0.05) + 1.50(0.0076) = 0.0764, or 7.64%.

One unanswered question is: How does the level of local investment affect the political risk exposure of a foreign operation? If a U.S. company produces in the United States and exports the products, does the company's foreign operation have higher or lower political risk exposure than if the foreign operation has a local plant to produce for that market? If the operation has a local plant, there is more to lose in case of political disruption, but the operation might also be seen in a more favorable light by the host government because of the jobs being provided. And what about the political risk for an overseas production operation that ships the products to markets in other countries?

Risk-Free Rates

Traditionally, the yield on a U.S. treasury bond has served as the risk-free rate in U.S. dollars. But the nonzero U.S. sovereign CDS yield in Exhibit 6.2 suggests that the risk-free rate in U.S. dollars is really the U.S. treasury yield minus the U.S. CDS rate. If the U.S. treasury yield is 1.73% and the U.S. CDS rate is 0.41%, the U.S. dollar risk-free rate is 1.73% − 0.41% = 1.32%. Similarly, if the Turkey government bond yield is 6.51% and the Turkey sovereign CDS rate is 2.59%, the Turkish lira (£) risk-free rate is 6.51% − 2.59% = 3.92%.

In addition to its use in CAPM applications, the risk-free rate in a given currency is an important input for finding the expected rate of intrinsic FX change of a currency. For example, say we want to estimate expected rate of intrinsic FX change of the Turkish lira, $E^*(x^{\$/£})$, using the traditional uncovered interest rate parity (UIRP) condition or the risk-adjusted UIRP (global CAPM) in equation (5.3). With the traditional UIRP condition (linear approximation), we'd get $E^*(x^{\$/£})$ = 0.0132 − 0.0392 = −0.026, or −2.6%. With equation (5.3), assuming the currency beta of the Turkish lira is 0.40 and the global risk premium in U.S. dollars is 5%, we'd get $E^*(x^{\$/£})$ = 0.0132 − 0.0392 + 0.40(0.05) = −0.006, or −0.6%. Note that we do NOT use the yield on lira-denominated sovereign Turkish debt as the Turkish lira risk-free rate, because that yield includes a premium for default risk. We will see later that the expected rate of intrinsic FX change is an important input for converting an asset's cost of capital from one currency to another.

The yield on rand-denominated South African sovereign bonds is 6.45%. The South African sovereign CDS rate is 1.78%. Assume the currency beta of the South African rand is 0.50. Assume the global CAPM version of the risk-adjusted UIRP condition holds, the risk-free rate in U.S. dollars is 1.32%, and the global risk premium in U.S. dollars is 5%. (a) What is the South African rand risk-free rate? (b) What is the expected rate of intrinsic FX change of the South African rand?

Answers: (a) 6.45% − 1.78% = 4.67%; (b) $E^*(x^{\$/R})$ = 0.0132 − 0.0467 + 0.50(0.05) = −0.0085, or −0.85%.

Unlevering Equity Betas and the Proxy Method

In the basic case where a proxy firm's net debt and off-balance sheet financial risk management positions have no systematic risk, we can use the simple relationship between the firm's equity beta and its operating beta in equation (6.1). If the firm's net debt and off-balance sheet financial risk management positions <u>do</u> have systematic risk, the correct formula for unlevering an estimated equity beta to find an estimated operating beta is more complicated.

A firm's net debt and off-balance sheet positions may have systematic risk if interest rates or FX rates are correlated with the market index returns. We'll ignore the systematic risk in interest rates, so that the items in net debt or the off-balance sheet positions will have no systematic FX risk if they are denominated in U.S. dollars. However, if a currency has a nonzero currency beta, any net debt or off-balance sheet positions in that currency have systematic risk that should be removed when estimating an operating beta from an equity beta. Equation (6.4) shows the advanced beta unlevering formula.

Advanced Beta Unlevering Formula

$$\beta_O^{\$} = \beta_S^{\$}(1 - ND^{\$}/V_B^{\$}) + \beta_{\epsilon}^{\$}(NL_{\epsilon}^{\$}/V_B^{\$})$$
$$+ \beta_{\pounds}^{\$}(NL_{\pounds}^{\$}/V_B^{\$}) + \beta_{\yen}^{\$}(NL_{\yen}^{\$}/V_B^{\$}) \ldots \qquad (6.4)$$

The first term after the equal sign in equation (6.4) adjusts the estimated equity beta for the overall net financial leverage, $ND^{\$}/V_B^{\$}$, the ratio of net debt to business value. (Both are shown measured in U.S. dollars.) Any or all of the net debt may be denominated in any currencies. $ND^{\$}$ does *not* include the notional principal amounts of any off-balance sheet forward FX or currency swap positions, although it should include net accumulated MTM gains/losses.

The next components of equation (6.4) adjust for any systematic FX risk in foreign currency net debt or off-balance sheet positions. $NL_{\epsilon}^{\$}$ represents the value (in U.S. dollars, at the current spot FX rate) of all euro-denominated liabilities, including both actual €-debt and the notional value of forward FX and currency swap positions on euros. Liabilities or assets in currencies other than euros, pounds, or yen are represented in equation (6.4) by the three elliptical periods (…). If the beta of a currency is positive, the use of foreign currency debt and currency swap positions in lieu of domestic currency debt reduces the equity beta. So we add back in the systematic portion of the liabilities' FX effect to the equity beta to calculate the estimated operating beta in U.S. dollars.

For example, assume a U.S. firm has only €-debt, representing 20% of the firm's business value, and has no other debt or forward FX or currency swap positions, and the currency beta of the euro, $\beta_\epsilon^\$$, is 0.25. If the firm has an equity beta of 1.25, then equation (6.4) tells us that the operating beta (in U.S. dollars) is $1.25(1 - 0.20) + 0.25(0.20) = 1.05$. You may compare this answer to the operating beta that results with equation (6.1), $1.25(1 - 0.20) = 1$, which implicitly assumes the debt is U.S. dollar debt (or the currency beta is zero).

Next, assume that the firm is levered with actual €-debt representing 20% of the firm's business value and also has a short at-market currency swap position on euros with a notional value representing 10% of the firm's business value (in U.S. dollars). Now $NL_\epsilon^\$/V_B^\$$ is 0.30, while $ND^\$/V_B^\$$ is only 0.20. Given an equity beta of 1.25 and $\beta_\epsilon^\$$ of 0.25, the firm's operating beta would be $1.25(1 - 0.20) + 0.25(0.30) = 1.075$.

The U.S. firm XYZ Co. has an equity beta (in U.S. dollars) of 1.35. XYZ's equity value is $1,400. In addition, XYZ has U.S. dollar net debt with a value of $200 and euro-denominated net debt with a value in U.S. dollars (at the current spot FX rate) of $400. XYZ also has a short currency swap position on British pounds, with a notional one-sided value (not MTM value) in U.S. dollars (at the current spot FX rate) of $200. Assume that the currency beta of the euro is 0.20 and the currency beta of the British pound is 0.25. (a) What is XYZ's operating beta (in U.S. dollars)? (b) Compare the answer in (a) to the estimate you'd find using equation (6.1).

Answers: (a) Note that XYZ's business value is $2,000, equal to the sum of the net debt value, $600, and the value of the equity, $1,400. The value of the net debt, $600, is 30% of XYZ's business value. Thus $ND^\$/V_B^\$ = 0.30$. The €-net debt with a value of $400 has a beta of 0.20. The sterling liabilities (notional swap value) are $200, which is 10% of the business value, and the currency beta of the British pound is 0.25. Thus, using equation (6.4), $\beta_O^\$ = 1.35(1 - 0.30) + 0.20(0.20) + 0.25(0.10) = 1.01$. (b) $\beta_O^\$ = 1.35(1 - 0.30) = 0.945$.

It may be helpful to think in the other direction and see the impact of capital structure on equity beta, given a firm's operating beta. We assume the U.S. firm, XYZ Co., has an operating beta, $\beta_O^\$$, of 0.90. If XYZ has no off-balance sheet risk management positions and only actual U.S. dollar net debt representing 40% of the firm's business value, XYZ's equity beta would be 0.90/(1 − 0.40) = 1.50, consistent with equation (6.1).

Now assume XYZ has only actual €-net debt, again representing 40% of the firm's business value, and has no other net debt or risk management positions, and the currency beta of the euro is 0.20. We can rearrange equation (6.4) to find that XYZ's equity beta would be (0.90 − 0.20(0.40))/(1 − 0.40) = 1.37. The equity beta is lower when the net debt is denominated in euros, 1.37, than when the debt is denominated in U.S. dollars, 1.50, because the €-net debt is hedges some of the operation's systematic risk.

Finally, assume instead that XYZ has actual €-net debt representing 20% of the firm's business value and has a short currency swap position on euros with a one-sided value representing 10% of the firm's business value (in U.S. dollars). Now $NL_\epsilon^\$/V_B^\$$ is 0.30, while $ND^\$/V_B^\$$ is only 0.20. If the currency beta of the euro is 0.20, XYZ's equity beta would be (0.90 − 0.20(0.30))/(1 − 0.20) = 1.05. In this case, there is more hedging and lower overall financial leverage than in the previous case.

Equation (6.4) is potentially useful to a manager who wants to estimate the operating beta for an overseas division by using the equity beta of a foreign proxy company. For example, say the U.S. multinational steel products company, GSP Corporation, wants to estimate the operating beta of its subsidiary operation in New Zealand using a similar firm in New Zealand, Pacific Steel (a real company). Assume the global equity beta of Pacific Steel shares (in U.S. dollars) is 0.90. Assume also that Pacific Steel has an equity market cap of NZ$ 500 million, NZ$-net debt of NZ$ 300 million, and no other net debt or off-balance sheet risk management positions. Assume the currency beta of the New Zealand dollar is 0.30. Because $NL_{NZ\$}^\$/V_B^\$$ = $300/$800 = 0.375, Pacific's operating beta in U.S. dollars, using equation (6.4), is 0.90(1 − 0.375) + 0.30(0.375) = 0.675.

The U.S. multinational steel products company, GSP Corporation, wants to estimate the operating beta its subsidiary operation in Brazil using a similar firm. CSN (Companhia Siderurgica Nacional, a real company) is a Brazilian steel products company with ordinary shares traded (in Brazilian real) in Sao Paulo and ADRs traded on the NYSE in U.S. dollars. Assume the global beta of the CSN ADR (in U.S. dollars) is 2. Assume that CSN has an equity market cap of Re 800 million, real denominated-net debt of Re 200 million, and no other net debt or financial risk management positions. The currency beta of the Brazilian real is 0.33. What is CSN's operating beta in U.S. dollars?

Answer: $2(1 - 0.20) + 0.33(0.20) = 1.67$

GSP's managers are not likely to be able to get information about the off-balance sheet risk management positions of a proxy firm the way the managers would know about their own firm's positions. So often the possibility of such positions must be ignored when applying the foreign proxy firm method of estimating an overseas division's operating beta.

Summary Action Points

- Operating beta estimates (in U.S. dollars) for an overseas division are useful, with the help of the global CAPM, in estimating the division's hurdle in U.S. dollars.
- A foreign division's operating beta is often estimated with the help of information for a proxy firm. If the proxy firm is the parent, or is located in the parent's home country, the Lessard country beta method may be used to estimate an overseas division's operating beta.
- If an overseas division is in an emerging market country, its cost of capital may need to include compensation for political risk in addition to systematic risk. A credit default swap rate is a useful estimate of a country's political risk premium.
- Credit default swap rates and local-currency sovereign debt yields may be used to estimate a currency's risk-free rate. This risk-free rate is useful in estimating the expected rate of intrinsic FX change of the currency.

Glossary

Cost of Capital for a Business Operation: The rate that discounts the operation's expected future operating cash flow steam to the intrinsic business value.

Country Beta: The beta of a country's national equity index versus the global market index.

Credit Default Swap (CDS): A market-traded "insurance policy" against the default of a bond. As long as the bond does not default, the buyer makes payments based on the price paid, the CDS yield. If the bond defaults, the buyer delivers the bond to the seller, while the seller pays the buyer the bond's face value.

Hurdle Rate: Another term for cost of capital, or required rate of return as compensation for risk.

Operating Beta: The beta an all-equity operation would have if it uses no financial risk management strategies, or the beta of the operation's business value.

Political Risk: A catch-all term used to describe the additional risks posed by emerging market investments in terms of illiquidity, civil disruptions, corruption, political intervention, expropriation, and the like.

Political Risk Exposure: An asset's political risk relative to the country's overall political risk.

Political Risk Premium: The premium that global investors require for the political risk of investing in a country's equity index fund.

Sovereign Risk: The risk that a country's government will not repay its obligations

Unlever: To find an operating variable (such as operating beta) by removing the effect of financial strategies on an equity variable (such as equity beta.)

Discussion Questions

1. Discuss the pros and cons of the various methods covered in the chapter for finding the hurdle rate for an overseas subsidiary or division.
2. Discuss the pros and cons of using a country's sovereign CDS rate as the country's political risk premium.
3. What types of industries do you think would have high political risk exposure? Low political risk exposure?
4. Explain the difference between political risk and sovereign risk.

Problems

1. CDG's equity beta in U.S. dollars is 1.25. CDG's equity market cap is $4 million and net debt is $1 million ($2 million of debt and $1 million of cash). CDG has no off-balance sheet risk management positions, and its debt and cash are denominated entirely in U.S. dollars. (a) Find CDG's operating beta. (b) The global CAPM is the international risk–return trade-off, viewed in U.S. dollars. Find CDG's cost of capital for business operations, given a U.S. dollar risk-free rate of 3% and a global risk premium of 4% in U.S. dollars.

2. The U.S. firm TZX Co. has an equity beta in U.S. dollars of 1.10. TZX's equity market cap is $6 million, and net debt is $2 million ($3 million of debt and $1 million of cash). TZX has no off-balance sheet risk management positions, and its debt and cash are denominated entirely in U.S. dollars. (a) Find TZX's operating beta in U.S. dollars. (b) The global CAPM is the international risk-return trade-off, viewed in U.S. dollars. The U.S. dollar risk-free rate = 3%. The global risk premium = 5% in U.S. dollars. Find TZX's cost of capital for business operations (in U.S. dollars).

3. The U.S. multinational PVY Co. has estimated its overall operating beta to be 0.90. The estimated (global) beta of the UK stock index is 0.85. Assume that PVY itself is a reasonable U.S. proxy firm for its UK division. Use the Lessard country beta method to find the UK division's estimated operating beta and hurdle rate in U.S. dollars. The global CAPM is the international risk–return trade-off, viewed in U.S. dollars. The U.S. dollar risk-free rate = 3%. The global risk premium = 5% in U.S. dollars.

4. The U.S. multinational GFS wants to estimate a hurdle rate for its New Zealand division. There is no proxy firm in New Zealand, but GFS's operations are in a homogeneous industry, so GFS's operating beta, 0.70, can serve as a U.S. proxy beta. The global beta of the New Zealand stock index in U.S. dollars is 0.60. Use the Lessard country beta method to find the operating beta of the New Zealand division. Ignore political risk. The U.S. dollar risk-free rate is 4% and the global risk premium is 6%. Find the New Zealand division's hurdle rate in U.S. dollars using the global CAPM.

5. A U.S. multinational wants to estimate the hurdle rate in U.S. dollars for its subsidiary in Bulgaria. Assume Bulgaria's political risk premium is equal to its sovereign CDS rate, 3.11%. The yield on Bulgarian sovereign bonds, denominated in lev (the Bulgarian currency), is 3.45%. The subsidiary is in an industry that has about <u>half</u> the average political risk for Bulgaria. The subsidiary's operating beta is 1. The currency beta of the lev is 0.40. The global CAPM is the international risk–return trade-off in U.S. dollars, the U.S. dollar risk-free rate is 2%, and the global risk premium in U.S. dollars is 5%. (a) Find the hurdle rate for the subsidiary in U.S. dollars. (b) Find the risk-free rate in Bulgarian lev. (c) Find the expected rate of intrinsic spot FX change in the lev.

For 6–9: A U.S. firm wants to estimate the hurdle rate for its subsidiary in Russia. Assume: (1) Russia has country beta 1.29. (2) The political risk exposure of the industry is 1. (3) A U.S. proxy firm has an operating beta of 0.90. Further assume: (4) The risk-free rate in U.S. dollars is 1.32%. (5) The global risk premium in U.S. dollars is 5%. (6) The global CAPM is the international risk–return trade-off in U.S. dollars. (7) The Russian political risk premium is equal to the sovereign CDS rate, 2.21%. (8) The yield on Russian sovereign bonds, in rubles, is 6.71%. (9) The currency beta of the ruble is 0.50.

6. What is the estimated operating beta of the project using the Lessard country beta method?

7. Estimate the project's hurdle rate in U.S. dollars.

8. Find the Russian ruble risk-free rate.

9. Find the expected rate of intrinsic spot FX change in the ruble.

10. The U.S. multinational PVY Co. wants to estimate the hurdle rate in U.S. dollars for its subsidiary in Tanzania. The yield on Tanzanian sovereign bonds is 9% in Tanzanian shillings. The currency beta of the shilling is 0.30. Assume Tanzania's political risk premium is equal to its sovereign CDS rate, 3.50%. The subsidiary has an operating beta in U.S. dollars of 0.75 and is in an industry that has 1.50 times the average political risk for Tanzanian companies. The global CAPM is the international risk–return trade-off, viewed in

U.S. dollars, including for the RA-UIRP condition. The U.S. dollar risk-free rate = 3%. The global risk premium = 5% in U.S. dollars. (a) What is the Tanzanian subsidiary's hurdle rate in U.S. dollars? (b) What is the risk-free rate in Tanzanian shillings? (c) Find the expected rate of intrinsic spot FX change of the Tanzanian shilling.

11. You are the manager of the Colombian division for a U.S. multinational building materials company. Your division manufactures insulation in the United States and ships it to Colombia, where it is packaged and delivered to the building industry. Assume the U.S. parent company of your division is a good U.S. proxy firm for your division. The parent has a global equity beta in U.S. dollars of 1.20. The parent's equity market cap is $700 million, debt is $400 million, and cash is $100 million. The parent's net debt has no systematic risk. The parent has no off-balance sheet financial risk management positions. The country beta of the Colombian equity market, in U.S. dollars, is 0.90. Assume the political risk premium for Colombia is 3%. Assume the industry's political risk exposure is the average for firms in Colombia. The global CAPM is the international risk–return trade-off, viewed in U.S. dollars. The U.S. dollar risk-free rate = 3%. The global risk premium = 5% in U.S. dollars. (a) Estimate the parent's operating beta. (b) Use the Lessard country beta method to estimate the division's operating beta. (c) Estimate the division's cost of capital for business operations in U.S. dollars.

For 12–16: XTZ is a U.S. multinational company with a business value of $40 billion. XTZ has actual net debt of $10 billion, all of which is denominated in U.S. dollars. XTZ has no off-balance sheet risk management positions. XTZ's estimated global equity beta in U.S. dollars is 1.20. XTZ wants to set the hurdle rate for its operation in Kazakhstan. For the operation's operating beta, XTZ will use the country beta method with XTZ's own operating beta serving as the U.S. proxy's operating beta. The operation is in an industry with a relatively low political risk exposure, so XTZ assumes the operation's political risk exposure is 0.75. The Kazakhstan currency is the tenge. Assume: (1) The global beta of the Kazakhstan stock market, in U.S. dollars, is 1.70. (2) The yield on Kazakhstan sovereign bonds, denominated in tenge, is 6%. (3) The Kazakhstan sovereign CDS rate is 2.50%. (4) The U.S. dollar global CAPM is the correct model of risk and return, including the RA-UIRP condition. (5) The U.S. dollar risk-free rate is 2.5%. (6) The global risk premium is 5% in U.S. dollars. (7) The currency beta of the tenge is 0.25.

12. Find XTZ's estimated operating beta in U.S. dollars.
13. What is the estimated operating beta (in U.S. dollars) of XTZ's Kazakhstan affiliate using the Lessard country beta method?
14. What is the Kazakhstan tenge risk-free rate?
15. What is the expected rate of intrinsic spot FX change of the tenge?
16. Assume that the sovereign CDS rate reflects the political risk premium. What is XTZ's estimated hurdle rate in U.S. dollars for the Kazakhstan operation?

17. XYZ Co.'s equity beta (in U.S. dollars) is 1. XYZ's intrinsic equity value is $6,000. In addition, XYZ has U.S. dollar net debt with a value of $1,500 and British pound-denominated net debt with a value in U.S. dollars (at the current spot FX rate) of $500. XYZ also has a long currency swap position on euros, with a notional one-sided value (not MTM value) in U.S. dollars (at the current spot FX rate) of $1,000. Assume that the beta of the euro is 0.20 and the beta of the British pound is 0.25. What is XYZ Co.'s operating beta (in U.S. dollars)?
18. The U.S. multinational steel products company, GSP Corporation, wants to estimate the operating beta of its English subsidiary using a similar firm in the United Kingdom. Assume the proxy firm has a global equity beta (in U.S. dollars) of 1.20, an equity market cap of £500 million, £-denominated net debt of £200 million, and no other net debt or off-balance sheet risk management positions. Assume the currency beta of the British pound is 0.25. Find the proxy firm's operating beta in U.S. dollars.

Answers to Problems

1. (a) CDG's business value is $5 million. The ratio of net debt to business value is $1 million/$5 million = 0.20. From equation (6.1), CDG's operating beta is 1.25(1 − 0.20) = 1. (b) Using the global CAPM, $k_O^\$ = 0.03 + 1(0.04) = 0.07$, or 7%.

2. (a) TZX's business value is \$8 million. The ratio of net debt to business value is \$2 million/\$8 million = 0.25. From equation (6.1), TZX's operating beta is 1.10(1 − 0.25) = 0.825. (b) $k_O^\$ = 0.03 + 0.825(0.05) = 0.07125$, or 7.125%.

3. The UK division's estimated operating beta 0.90(0.85) = 0.765. The division's $k_{OD}^\$$ is 0.03 + 0.765(0.05) = 0.06825, or 6.825%.

4. The estimated operating beta of the New Zealand division is 0.70 (0.60) = 0.42. GFS-New Zealand's estimated hurdle rate in U.S. dollars is 0.04 + 0.42(0.06) = 0.0652, or 6.52%.

5. (a) $k_{OD}^\$ = 0.02 + 1(0.05) + 0.50(0.0311) = 0.0856$, or 8.56%.
   (b) 3.45% − 3.11% = 0.34%.
   (c) 0.02 − 0.0034 + 0.40(0.05) = 0.0366, or 3.66%.

6. 1.29(0.90) = 1.161.

7. Equation (6.3) tells us that the project's hurdle rate in U.S. dollars is 0.0132 + 1.161(0.05) + 1(0.0221) = 0.093, or 9.3%.

8. 6.71% − 2.21% = 4.50%.

9. 1.32% − 4.50% + 0.50(5%) = −0.68%.

10. (a) $k_{OD}^\$ = 0.02 + 0.75(0.05) + 1.50(0.035) = 0.12$, or 12%.
    (b) 9% − 3.5% = 5.5%.
    (c) 3% − 5.5% + 0.30(5%) = −1%.

11. (a) The parent's operating beta = 1.20(1 − 0.30) = 0.84.
    (b) The division's operating beta = 0.90(0.84) = 0.756.
    (c) $k_{OD}^\$ = 0.03 + 0.756(0.05) + 1(0.03) = 0.0978$, or 9.78%.

12. 1.20(1 − 0.25) = 0.90.

13. 0.90(1.70) = 1.53.

14. 0.06 − 0.025 = 0.035.

15. 0.025 − 0.035 + 0.25(0.05) = 0.0025, or 0.25%.

16. 0.025 + 1.53(0.05) + 0.75(0.025) = 0.12, or 12%.

17. XYZ's business value (\$8,000) is equal to the value of all of the actual net debt (\$2,000) plus the value of the equity (\$6,000). The value of the actual net debt, \$2,000, is 25% of XYZ's business value, so $ND^\$/V_B^\$ = 0.25$. The ratio of £-net debt to business value is \$500/\$8,000 = 0.0625. The long currency swap position on euros is a net liability of −\$1,000, which is −12.5% of the business value. Thus, using equation (6.4), $\beta_O^\$ = 1(1 − 0.25) + 0.25(0.0625) + 0.20(−0.125) = 0.74$.

18. Using equation (6.4), 1.20(1 − 200/700) + 0.25(200/700) = 0.93.

CHAPTER 7

International Capital Budgeting

The theory of overseas investment decisions is generally based on the standard capital budgeting concept, which involves discounting a project's expected operating cash flows back to the present using a cost of capital that reflects the risk. The investment's *net present value* (*NPV*) is the present value of the expected cash flows minus the outlay necessary to undertake the investment. If the NPV is positive, the investment should be accepted, because the intrinsic wealth of the firm's existing shareholders would rise. If the NPV is negative, the investment should be rejected, because intrinsic wealth of the firm's existing shareholders would drop. This chapter assumes that you already understand the basics of capital budgeting. We focus on extending that coverage to international issues.

The first international issue is whether to consider the foreign investment's entire cash flow or only the portion repatriated. Our answer is immediate: Consider the investment's *entire* cash flow, not just the portion repatriated. The reason is that even the portion reinvested overseas affects the intrinsic wealth of the firm's shareholders, because the reinvestment increases the value that the overseas investment could be sold for, and thus needs to be included in the analysis. So we consider an overseas investment's entire cash flow, not just the portion repatriated.

Another important issue is the choice of currency perspective to use for the NPV analysis. For the *home currency approach*, the analyst converts the expected foreign currency cash flows into home currency equivalents using forecasted FX rates, and then discounts them using a cost of capital denominated in the home currency. In the *foreign currency approach*, the analyst uses the expected cash flows denominated in the foreign currency, and discounts them using a cost of capital denominated in the foreign currency.

We will compare these two approaches in depth in the next chapter, but in this chapter, we only use the home currency approach. We look at several international capital budgeting scenarios: (a) the acquisition of an overseas business; (b) plant modernization by an overseas subsidiary; (c) relocation of some or all of production from the home country to a foreign country, or vice versa; and (d) relocation of some or all production of a foreign subsidiary to a third country, considering the possible changes in both political risk and currency risk.

Foreign Direct Investment

A multinational will make a *foreign direct investment* (*FDI*) into an overseas plant in order to avoid tariffs or other foreign country import barriers, to engage in operational hedging, and so forth. The construction of a new facility is referred to as a *greenfield investment*. However, a cross-border acquisition or merger is often the preferred FDI mode of entry or expansion into foreign markets, where an existing local firm may be acquired by a multinational that wishes to avoid the construction time and other frictions of a greenfield investment. Other reasons for foreign acquisitions include: consolidating worldwide excess capacity, combining firms in fragmented industries ("roll-ups"), exploiting developed marketing channels, eliminating a competitor, achieving critical mass required for new approaches to R&D and production, obtaining an innovation (patent, knowledge, technology), or entering a market to exploit an innovation. In 2007, total worldwide FDI was almost $2 trillion, with roughly half being greenfield investments and the other half being cross-border mergers and acquisitions (M&A).

Cross-Border Mergers and Acquisitions

The total volume of cross-border M&A has been growing worldwide, from 23% of the total merger volume in 1998 to 45% in 2007. Recent cross-border M&A activity has mostly been non-conglomerate, instead involving firms in the same industry (*horizontal M&A*) or along the supply/distribution chain (*vertical M&A*). In 1999, about 70% of all global M&As were horizontal. The major industries in which these horizontal combinations occurred were the automobile, pharmaceutical, chemical, food, beverage, tobacco, and more recently telecommunications and utilities. Some of the more well-known ones include Daimler-Benz (Germany)-Chrysler (U.S.); Vodaphone (UK)-AirTouch Communications (U.S.); British Petroleum (UK)-Amoco and ARCO (U.S.); Alcatel (France)-DSC Communications (U.S.); Deutsche Telecom (Germany)-Voice Stream Wireless (U.S.); and Sony (Japan)-Columbia Pictures (U.S.).

About 90% of cross-border M&A activity in 1999 occurred in developed countries. The great majority of global combinations were between firms in the major Western industrial countries. At that time, the foreign targets of U.S. firms (outward U.S. FDI) were primarily located in the United Kingdom, Canada, and Europe. Japan was a relatively minor target of outward U.S. FDI. British firms were the source of the most acquisitions of U.S. firms and in a wide variety of industries. Other acquirers of U.S. firms came from Japan, the Netherlands, Canada, Germany, France, and other European countries.

The prior trends have been changing. According to *The World Investment Report 2011*, 25% of global M&A activity in 2010 was undertaken in emerging and developing countries. At the same time, investors from these economies are becoming increasingly important players in cross-border M&A markets, which previously were dominated by developed country players.

In a sample of almost 57,000 international M&A deals for the years 1990–2007, 80% targeted a non-U.S. firm, while 75% of the acquirers were from outside the United States. The vast majority of cross-border mergers involved private firms as either bidder or target: 96% of the deals involved a private target, 26% involved a private acquirer, and 97% had either private acquirers or targets.

Converting Expected Cash Flows

As we said, in the home currency approach to international capital budgeting, a project's expected foreign currency cash flows are converted to equivalent expected home currency cash flows. The standard practice is to simply multiply the expected foreign currency operating cash flow by the expected spot FX rate. That is, letting $E(O_N^{\text{€}})$ denote the expected time-N operating cash flow in euros (the representative foreign currency) and $E(X_N^{\$/€})$ denote the expected time-N spot FX rate, the standard practice is to find $E(O_N^{\$})$ by $E(O_N^{\text{€}}) \times E(X_N^{\$/€})$.

The standard practice is technically correct, however, only in the special case where the foreign currency cash flow and the spot FX rate are *independent*, which means that the foreign currency cash flow has zero FX operating exposure to the U.S. dollar. The standard practice calculation does <u>not</u> give the correct expected cash flow in U.S. dollars in the more general situation where the foreign currency cash flow and the FX rate are <u>not</u> independent, that is, when the foreign currency cash flow has a non-zero FX operating exposure to the U.S. dollar. Instead, equation (7.1) gives a close approximation to the correct expected time-N cash flow in U.S. dollars, the assumed home currency.[1]

Expected Operating Cash Flow in U.S. Dollars

$$E(O_N^{\$}) \approx E(O_N^{\text{€}}) \times E(X_N^{\$/€})[1 - \xi_{O\$}^{\text{€}}\sigma_{\text{€}}^2]^N \qquad (7.1)$$

Equation (7.1) adjusts the "standard-practice" formula, $E(O_N^{\text{€}}) \times E(X_N^{\$/€})$, by multiplying by the term $[1 - \xi_{O\$}^{\text{€}}\sigma_{\text{€}}^2]^N$, where $\xi_{O\$}^{\text{€}}$ denotes the foreign project's FX operating exposure to the home currency (the U.S. dollar) and $\sigma_{\text{€}}^2$ denotes the variance (squared volatility) of the percentage changes in the spot FX rate. Note that the FX exposure is to the U.S. dollar. If you happen to instead know the cash flow's FX exposure to the euro, you can use the relationship that $\xi_{O\text{€}}^{\$} + \xi_{O\$}^{\text{€}} = 1$ to find $\xi_{O\$}^{\text{€}}$.

For example, assume that the U.S. firm XRT Co. is considering the acquisition of a private business in Austria, in the Eurozone. XRT expects that under its ownership, the acquisition will generate €10,000 in operating cash flow each year into perpetuity. An analysis shows that the acquisition target's FX operating exposure to the U.S. dollar, $\xi_{O\$}^{\text{€}}$, is 0.40. Assume the expected time-1 spot FX rate is 1.3055 \$/€ and the volatility of the euro, $\sigma_{\text{€}}$, is 0.21. Equation (7.1) says that $E(O_1^{\$})$ is (approximately) €10,000(1.3055 \$/€)[1 − 0.40(0.21)^2] = \$12,825. Using the standard practice of implicitly assuming no FX exposure to the U.S. dollar, you would get €10,000(1.3055 \$/€) = \$13,055, which would *overestimate* the time-1 expected operating cash flow in U.S. dollars.

If the foreign asset's FX exposure to the home currency is negative, the standard practice calculation will *underestimate* the correct expected cash flow in the home currency. The next example demonstrates this point.

TXR Co. is a U.S. firm considering an acquisition in Brazil with FX operating exposure to the U.S. dollar of –0.80. The target's expected time-1 operating cash flow is Re 100,000. The expected time-1 spot FX rate is 0.50 $/Re. The volatility of the real is 0.14. (a) Use equation (7.1) to find the approximate expected time-1 operating cash flow in U.S. dollars. (b) Compare the answer in (a) with that of the standard practice approach.

Answers: (a) Re $100,000(0.50 \text{ \$/Re})[1 - (-0.80)(0.14)^2] = \$50,784$. (b) Re $100,000(0.50 \text{ \$/Re}) = \$50,000$. Here, the standard practice answer underestimates the equation (7.1) answer because the foreign asset's FX exposure to the home currency is negative.

Illuminating Example

Assume three equally likely outcomes for the time-1 spot FX rate: 1.667 $/€, 1.25 $/€, and 1 $/€. The expected time-1 spot FX rate is thus (1.667 $/€ + 1.25 $/€ + 1 $/€)/3 = **1.3055 $/€**. You can verify that the standard deviation of the percentage differences between the spot FX rate and the mean is about 0.21. That is, $\sigma_\epsilon = \mathbf{0.21}$. Note that the three spot FX rate outcomes, when reciprocated into direct terms from the euro perspective, are 0.60 €/$, 0.80 €/$, and 1 €/$, respectively, with an expected spot FX rate of 0.80 €/$.

Using a "what if" analysis, if the spot FX rate is 0.60 €/$, the U.S. dollar is 25% lower than expected. So given $\xi_{OS}^\epsilon = \mathbf{0.40}$, the operating cash flow in euros is lower than expected by 0.40(25%) = 10%, and thus would be 10% lower than €10,000, or €9,000. Similarly, if the time-1 spot FX rate is 1 €/$, the U.S. dollar is 25% higher than expected. So the operating cash flow in euros would be higher than expected by 0.40(25%) = 10%, and thus would be €11,000.

So in U.S. dollars, the actual time-1 operating cash flow will be one of three equally likely outcomes: (1) €9,000(1.667 $/€) = $15,000; (2) €10,000(1.25 $/€) = $12,500; or (3) €11,000(1 $/€) = $11,000. The expected time-1 operating cash flow in U.S. dollars is thus ($15,000 + 12,500 + 11,000)/3 = **$12,833**. So the approximation using equation (7.1), $12,825, is pretty close to the actual answer, and much closer than the standard-practice answer, $13,055.

Probability	$X_1^{\$/€}$	$X_1^{€/\$}$	$O_1^{€}$	$O_1^{\$}$
1/3	1.667 $/€	0.60 €/$	€9,000	$15,000
1/3	1.25 $/€	0.80 €/$	€10,000	$12,500
1/3	1.00 $/€	1.00 €/$	€11,000	$11,000
Expected	1.3055 $/€	0.80 €/$	€10,000	$12,833

Currency volatility estimates are available in many places. Some example estimates are shown in Exhibit 7.1.

Exhibit 7.1. **Currency Volatility Estimates**

	2002–2007	2007–2012
Australian Dollar	0.09	0.13
Brazilian Real	0.10	0.14
Euro	0.07	0.10
Indian Rupee	0.04	0.08
Japanese Yen	0.07	0.09
Mexican Peso	0.06	0.11
New Zealand Dollar	0.09	0.13
South African Rand	0.12	0.14
South Korean Won	0.05	0.11
Swedish Krona	0.09	0.11
Swiss Franc	0.08	0.11
Taiwan Dollar	0.04	0.05
UK Pound	0.07	0.09

Source: Author's computations using month-end data from St. Louis Federal Reserve.

Acquisition Analysis

For the rest of the chapter, we'll do applications of international capital budgeting using the home currency approach. We begin by completing the XRT example of the previous section, where XRT is considering the acquisition target in Austria. Let's make the following additional assumptions:

(1) The cost of capital for the acquisition, in U.S. dollars, is 8%. Note that the cost of capital for the target depends on the target's risk, per the previous chapter, and is not XRT's overall cost of capital.

(2) The sellers of the Austrian business are asking €100,000 for the operation.

(3) The euro is expected to appreciate indefinitely at the rate of **1%** per year.

In our example, we have already assumed that the time-1 expected spot FX rate is 1.3055 $/€, so the time-0 spot FX rate must be (1.3055 $/€)/ 1.01 = **1.293 $/€**, given the assumed 1% appreciation forecast. Here, we use the formula: $E(X_1^{\$/€}) = X_0^{\$/€}(1 + E(x^{\$/€}))$. Typically, you'd observe the actual time-0 spot FX rate, and then develop spot FX rate forecasts. Perhaps you would use the expected rate of intrinsic FX change, discussed in Chapter 5, if you have no reason to think the time-0 spot FX rate is misvalued relative to financial market conditions.

Given the assumptions, should XRT make the acquisition? Using equation (7.1), we have already found that the future operating cash flow stream in U.S. dollars is expected to start with (approximately) $12,825 at time 1. After that, because the operating cash flow stream is expected to be level in euros, and because the euro is expected to appreciate at the rate of 1% per year, the operating cash flows in U.S. dollars are expected to grow at a rate equal to $g^{\$} = (1 + g^{€})[1 + E(x^{\$/€})][1 - \xi_{0S}^{€}\sigma_{€}^{2}] - 1$, where $g^{€}$ is the cash flow growth rate in euros. Here, $g^{\$}$ equals $(1.00)[1.01][1 - 0.40(0.21)^2] - 1$ = −0.0078, or −0.78%, per year. To see this point, note that *if the spot FX rate forecast for each successive year is 1% higher than the previous year's, and you apply equation (7.1) year by year, you'd get that each successive expected home currency cash flow is lower than the previous one by 0.78%.*

Because the cost of capital is 8%, we can use the constant growth formula, equation (2.1), to find the target's intrinsic business value in U.S. dollars: $12,825/(0.08 − (−0.0078)) = $146,071. In U.S. dollars, the outlay for the acquisition (at time 0) is $(1.293 \ \$/€)(€100,000) = \$129,300$. Using the traditional NPV criterion, XRT should make the acquisition, because there is a positive NPV of $\$146,071 - 129,300 = \$16,771$.

In this example, we assumed for simplicity a zero expected growth rate in the euro cash flow stream. If the expected growth rate in the euro cash flows is 2%, and the euro is expected to appreciate at the rate of 1%, then the expected cash flow growth rate in U.S. dollars is $(1.02)(1 - 0.0078) - 1 = 0.012$, or approximately 1.2%. The next example applies this idea.

Extend the earlier TXR Co. example where the Brazilian target's FX operating exposure to the U.S. dollar is –0.80. Make the following additional assumptions: (1) The Brazilian real is expected to <u>depreciate</u> indefinitely at the rate of 0.50% per year. (2) The cash flows in Brazilian real are expected to grow at the annual rate of 2.5%. (3) The cost of capital for the acquisition, in U.S. dollars, is 8%. (4) The sellers of the Brazilian business are asking Re 1.68 million for the company. (a) Given the assumption that the expected time-1 spot FX rate is 0.50 $/Re, find today's spot FX rate. (b) What is the expected growth rate in the target's cash flows from the U.S. dollar point of view? (c) Should TXR make the acquisition? (d) What would be TXR's acquisition decision if it uses the standard practice for finding expected cash flow in U.S. dollars of multiplying the expected foreign currency cash flow by the expected spot FX rate?

Answers: (a) $(0.50 \ \$/Re)/(1 - 0.005) = 0.5025 \ \$/Re$. (b) $(1 + 0.025)(1 - 0.005)(1 - 0.80(0.14)^2) - 1 = 0.0359$, or 3.59%. (c) We know from the previous TXR example that the future operating cash flow stream in U.S. dollars is expected to start at time 1 with (approximately) $50,784$. After that, the operating cash flows in U.S. dollars are expected to grow at the rate of 3.59% per year. Because the cost of capital is 8%, we can use the constant growth formula to find the target's intrinsic value in U.S. dollars is $\$50,784/[0.08 - 0.0359] = \$1,151,565$. In U.S. dollars, the outlay for the project is $(0.5025 \ \$/Re) \times (Re \ 1.68 \ million) = \$844,200$. Using the traditional NPV criterion, TXR should acquire the target, because the NPV is positive: $\$1,151,565 - 844,200 = \$307,365$. (d) With the standard-practice calculation, TXR would assume that the time-1 expected U.S. dollar operating cash flow is $50,000$, and so would estimate the target's intrinsic business value is $50,000/[0.08 − 0.02] = $833,333. The NPV estimate is negative, $833,333 − 844,200 = −$10,867, so TXR would mistakenly reject the acquisition that actually has a positive NPV.

Incremental Cash Flow Application

Often, a capital budgeting analysis involves thinking in terms of *incremental* cash flows. Examples include projects to (a) expand production capacity because of growth in product demand in a given market; and (b) replace old equipment with modern, more efficient equipment. For our scenario, we'll assume that XRT has acquired the Austrian target, but quickly discovers that if the plant equipment is modernized, the production process will be significantly improved. Assume that the plant modernization would require a time-0 outlay of €15,000. At the same time, the operating costs would be reduced by €1,000 per year. Thus, the expected operating cash flows in euros would be €11,000 per year instead of €10,000. Should XRT approve the plant modernization proposal?

This capital budgeting project involves an incremental perpetuity in euros of €1,000 per year. Using the same assumptions about the FX rate and FX exposure as above, and using equation (7.1), the initial incremental expected operating cash flow in U.S. dollars is (approximately) €1,000(1.3055 $/€)[1 − 0.40(0.21)^2] = $1,282. The present value of the incremental expected operating cash flows, from the U.S. dollar point of view, is $1,282/(0.08 − (−0.0078)) = $14,601. In U.S. dollars, the time-0 outlay would be €15,000(1.293 $/€) = $19,395. The modernization proposal should be rejected, because the NPV is negative, $14,601 − 19,395 = −$4,794.

Use the following scenario and re-do XRT's Austrian plant modernization analysis in the text example. Assume that the plant modernization would require an outlay of €8,000. At the same time, the operating costs would be reduced by €800 per year. Thus the expected operating cash flows in euros would be €10,800 per year instead of €10,000. Should XRT approve the modernization proposal?

Answer: This project involves an incremental perpetuity in euros of €800 per year. Using the same FX rate and FX exposure assumptions as in the text example, and using equation (7.1), the initial incremental expected operating cash flow in U.S. dollars would be (approximately) €800(1.3055)[1 − 0.40(0.21)^2] = $1,026. The present value of the incremental expected operating cash flows, from the U.S. dollar point of view, is $1,026/(0.08 − (−0.0078)) = $11,686. In U.S. dollars, the outlay would be €8,000(1.293 $/€) = $10,344. The modernization proposal should be accepted because the NPV is positive, $11,686 − 10,344 = $1,342.

Change in Risk

When you use expected incremental cash flows in an NPV analysis, you are making the implicit assumption that the adoption of the project would not change the risk of the operation and thus would not affect the cost of capital. In many domestic capital budgeting situations, this implicit assumption is acceptable. However, in international capital budgeting applications, it is easy to think of situations where the project will affect the operation's risk and cost of capital. For example, assume that XRT Co. has rejected the Austrian plant modernization proposal discussed above. Instead, XRT is now looking at a proposal to produce some components for the Austrian operation in a "cheap labor" country, namely, Poland.

A proposal to shift a portion (or all) of production to a different country involves two potential changes to the operation's risk. One potential risk change is related to currency. In our present scenario, we'll ignore any change in currency risk. Poland has (for now) its own currency, the zloty, not the euro. But in anticipation of eventually joining the Eurozone, the Polish zloty is controlled to "track" the euro fairly closely. So in this situation, changing the currency denomination of some of the operating costs is not likely to significantly affect the Austrian operation's risk. Later in the chapter, we'll cover a similar scenario where the currency risk changes.

The other type of potential risk change is in the political risk. If you compare the sovereign credit default swap (CDS) rates for Austria and Poland in Exhibit 6.2, you'll see that Poland's CDS yield is 76, which is 43 basis points higher than Austria's, 33. We interpret this information as saying that the financial market perceives Poland to have higher political risk than Austria. In addition to the change in political risk due to shifting of some production processes to Poland, the operation's political risk exposure may also change. Some Austrian government officials may look less favorably on the business after some Austrians have lost their jobs to Poles. It is hard to say how this situation might play out, but government approvals might become more difficult, or something similar.

The operation's new political risk involves two countries. One simple way to handle this situation is to assume that the overall political risk for the operation is driven by the higher political risk country, which is Poland in this case. There is plenty of room for judgment here. Some capital budgeting analyses might justify a weighted average approach to the new political risk. Also, for simplicity, we assume the operation's political risk exposure is 1, whether the relocation occurs or not. Because Poland's sovereign CDS rate is 43 basis points higher than Austria's, the operation's new cost of capital would be higher by 43 basis points. So the operation's new cost of capital (in U.S. dollars) would be 8% + 0.43% = 8.43%.

When the capital budgeting proposal involves a change in the cost of capital like this, you cannot do an NPV analysis with incremental cash flows. Instead, you need to compare two business alternatives. In the XRT case, you need to compare the intrinsic business value after the move with the intrinsic business value before the move and the investment outlay needed to make the move. **To find the NPV of the proposal, you need to find the change in the intrinsic business value, and then subtract the investment outlay.**

We already know the intrinsic business value before the move, $146,071. Let's assume that the initial outlay at time 0 to shift the component production to Poland is €30,000, and that the operating costs would drop by €1,500 per year. So the expected time-1 operating cash flow in euros is €11,500. Given that the Polish zloty closely tracks the euro, we expect the operating cash flow stream in euros to continue to be a level perpetuity. In U.S. dollars, the new expected initial operating cash flow is (approximately) €11,500(1.3055 $/€)[1 − 0.40(0.21)^2] = $14,748. And in U.S. dollars, we'll still expect −0.78% annual growth, due to the expected annual appreciation of the euro by 1%. So the operation's new intrinsic business value, in U.S. dollars, would be $14,748/(0.0843 − (−0.0078)) = $160,130.

The new intrinsic business value of $160,130 is higher than the intrinsic business value before the shift, $146,071. But the time-0 outlay for the shift, in U.S. dollars, is €30,000(1.293 $/€) = $38,790. So the proposal's NPV is negative, $160,130 − 146,071 − 38,790 = −24,731.

Use the following scenario and redo XRT's proposal to move component production for the Austrian acquisition to Poland. Assume that the proposal would require an outlay of €20,000. At the same time, the future operating costs would be reduced by €2,500 per year. Thus, the expected operating cash flows would be €12,500 per year instead of €10,000. The cost of capital in U.S. dollars is presently 8%. Assume the operation's political risk exposure is 1 whether the move is made or not, and that the sovereign CDS rate for Poland is 76 and for Austria is 33. (a) What would be the new cost of capital for the operation? (b) Should XRT approve the proposal?

Answer: (a) If the component production is moved to Poland, the new political risk premium is 43 basis points higher. Assuming the operation's political risk exposure is 1, the new cost of capital in U.S. dollars would be 8% + 0.43% = 8.43%. (b) In U.S. dollars, the new expected initial operating cash flow is (approximately) €12,500(1.3055 $/€)[1 − 0.40(0.21)^2] = $16,031. And in U.S. dollars, we expect −0.78% annual growth in the operating cash flow, due to the expected annual euro appreciation of 1%. So the operation's new intrinsic business value, in U.S. dollars, would be $16,031/(0.0843 − (−0.0078)) = $174,061. The new intrinsic business value would be higher by $27,990 than the existing one, $146,071, and the proposal should be accepted because it has a positive NPV of $27,990 − €20,000(1.293 $/€) = $2,130.

Operational Hedging and Cost of Capital

You may recall that if a firm changes its operational hedging strategy, the firm's FX operating exposure to a currency changes. Changes in operational hedging can occur when a company changes the country source of materials and other production inputs, and thus changes the currency of some portion of the operating costs. Another primary way for a company to change the level of operational hedging is to change the country location of all or part of the production process. Perhaps a U.S. exporter will close a plant in the United States and build or buy a plant in the export market. This production *offshoring* should increase operational hedging and thus reduce the FX operating exposure. Or, a firm could do the reverse, shut down a plant in the overseas market and increase production in the home country. This production *reshoring* would reduce operational hedging and thus increase FX operating exposure.

One simple benefit of lower FX operating exposure is the reduced volatility of operating cash flows and thus a reduction in the expected costs of financial distress. Similarly, a reduction in operational hedging would raise the expected costs of financial distress. So the capital budgeting analysis of a production relocation decision should, in principle, incorporate the change in the expected costs of financial distress, in addition to the change in expected cash flows and the net investment outlay to close production in one country and make the production operational in the other country. However, estimating the expected costs of financial distress is not easy in practice.

In this section we focus on an additional consideration: If the foreign currency has systematic risk, meaning a nonzero currency beta, the operational hedging decision will affect the operating beta and thus the cost of capital. We'll ignore changes in political risk here. Our analysis will make use of equation (7.2), which applies if the only reason that assets i and j have different betas is that they have different FX exposures to the euro.[2]

Beta, FX Exposure, and Currency Beta

$$\beta_j^{\$} = \beta_i^{\$} + \beta_\epsilon^{\$}(\xi_{j\epsilon}^{\$} - \xi_{i\epsilon}^{\$}) \qquad (7.2)$$

Equation (7.2) says that the difference between the betas for asset j and asset i is equal to the product of the currency beta of the euro and the difference between the FX exposures to the euro of assets j and i. To illustrate, we assume that if the U.S. exporter, AEM Co., offshores a manufacturing process to the export market, the Eurozone, the company's FX operating exposure to the euro would drop from 1.50 to 0.50, because of the operational hedging of producing in the overseas market country.

Now we want to know the impact of the offshoring on AEM's operating beta and cost of capital. Because AEM still sells the same products in the same market, the Eurozone, the company's operating beta would change with the offshoring because the FX operating exposure to the euro would drop from 1.50 to 0.50. We can characterize AEM producing in the United States as asset i, and AEM producing in the Eurozone as asset j, and use equation (7.2) to examine the impact of the production relocation on AEM's operating beta.

To apply equation (7.2), assume AEM's operating beta is presently 0.80. Assume also that the currency beta of the euro is 0.20. Because AEM's FX operating exposure to the euro before the relocation is 1.50, and after the relocation is 0.50, equation (7.2) says that AEM's new operating beta would be $0.80 + 0.20$ $(0.50 - 1.50) = 0.60$, after the offshoring of production to the Eurozone. That is, by moving production to the Eurozone, AEM would lower its operating beta to 0.60 (from 0.80), because the euro has systematic risk, $\beta_\epsilon^\$ = 0.20$, and because AEM would reduce its FX operating exposure to the euro. Assume the global CAPM in U.S. dollars is the international risk–return relationship, and that in U.S. dollars, the risk-free rate is 4% and the global risk premium is 5%. So AEM's cost of capital is currently $k_O^\$ = r_f^\$ + \beta_O^\$(GRP^\$) = 0.04 + 0.80(0.05) =$ 0.08, or 8%. AEM's *pro forma* cost of capital, given the decision to offshore the manufacturing process to Europe, would be $k_O^\$ = r_f^\$ + \beta_O^\$(GRP^\$) = 0.04 +$ $0.60(0.05) = 0.07$, or 7%, lower than the current cost of capital, 8%.

The U.S. firm BBX Co. makes and exports machine components to the United Kingdom. BBX's FX operating exposure to the British pound is 2. Assume BBX's operating beta is 0.80, given that the production is in the United States. If BBX decides to offshore production to the United Kingdom, the FX operating exposure to the British pound will fall to 1, due to operational hedging. Assume that political risk does not change. (a) If the British pound's currency beta is 0.25, find BBX's new operating beta if it offshores production to the United Kingdom. (b) Assume the global CAPM is the risk–return trade-off, the risk-free rate in U.S. dollars is 3%, and the global risk premium in U.S. dollars is 5%. Compare the new cost of capital to the current cost of capital.

Answers: (a) Using equation (7.2), BBX's new operating beta is $0.80 + 0.25(1 - 2) = 0.55$. (b) The new cost of capital would be $0.03 + 0.55(0.05) = 0.0575$, or 5.75%. The current cost of capital is $0.03 + 0.80(0.05) = 0.07$, or 7%.

Because most currency beta estimates are positive, an increase in operational hedging by an exporter typically implies a lower operating beta and thus a lower cost of capital, and vice versa, as we saw in the examples above. However, there are rare cases of a negative currency beta estimate, most notably for the Japanese yen. In such a case for an exporter, an increase in operational hedging and a drop in FX operating exposure typically imply a *higher* operating beta and cost of capital, and vice versa. However, we do not spend time on an example of this case, due to its rarity.

Of course, an *importer* can also decide to change its FX operating exposure by changing the currency denomination of certain operating costs. Say a U.S. firm initially imports raw materials or components from the Eurozone, and the price of the imports is fixed in euros. Assume the firm's FX operating exposure to the euro is –2, and the operating beta is 1.25. If the firm decides to change suppliers, and sources more from the United States, the FX operating exposure to the euro will drop (in absolute value), say to –1. What will happen to the importer's operating beta if the currency beta of the euro is 0.20? Using equation (7.2), the importer's new operating beta will be 1.25 + 0.20(–1 – (–2)) = 1.45. So the importer's operating beta is *higher* if the FX operating exposure is lower (in absolute value).

If a U.S. importer is sourcing from Japan, given a negative currency beta estimate of the Japanese yen, however, the effect of a change in FX operating exposure will go the other way. The importer's operating beta would be lower if the FX operating exposure is lower (in absolute value), and vice versa. The next example covers this scenario.

The U.S. firm TDY Co. imports machine components from Japan. TDY's initial FX operating exposure to the Japanese yen is –1.75 and the operating beta is 0.80. If TDY changes the source of some components to the United States, the FX operating exposure would drop (in absolute value) to –1.25. (a) If the Japanese yen's currency beta is –0.10, find TDY's new operating beta if it makes the sourcing change. (b) Assume the global CAPM is the risk–return trade-off, the risk-free rate in U.S. dollars is 3%, and the global risk premium in U.S. dollars is 5%. Compare the new cost of capital to the current cost of capital.

Answers: (a) Using equation (7.2), TDY's new operating beta is 0.80 + (−0.10)(−1.25 − (−1.75)) = 0.75. (b) The new cost of capital is 0.03 + 0.75(0.05) = 0.0675, or 6.75%. The current cost of capital is 0.03 + 0.80(0.05) = 0.07, or 7%. So in the rare case where the estimated currency beta is negative, if an importer reduces the (absolute value of) FX operating exposure, the cost of capital is lower.

Effect on Cost of Capital (k) of Higher Operational Hedging and Lower FX Operating Exposure (Absolute Value)

	Exporter	Importer
Currency Beta		
Positive	$k \downarrow$	$k \uparrow$
Negative	$k \uparrow$	$k \downarrow$

NPV of a Project that Changes FX Operating Exposure

As we saw earlier, incorporating a cost of capital change in a capital budgeting analysis requires that we use a slightly different procedure than the traditional one with expected incremental cash flows. The reason is that you only use expected incremental cash flows in the analysis when the cost of capital does *not* change as a result of the investment being made. Here, however, the cost of capital does change as a direct result of the investment decision, so we have to use the more general approach of finding the intrinsic business value before and after the investment.

For example, we extend the AEM example from before. Assume that from the U.S. dollar perspective, AEM initially expects operating cash flows of $1,600 per year into perpetuity. So with AEM's initial cost of capital of 8%, AEM's intrinsic business value is initially $1,600/0.08 = $20,000. Assume further that if the production relocation is undertaken, the new expected annual operating cash flow would be $1,500. So with AEM's new cost of capital of 7%, the new intrinsic business value would be $1,500/0.07 = $21,429, an increase of intrinsic business value of

$21,429 − 20,000 = $1,429. Assume further that the necessary outlay to do the relocation is $1,000. The NPV would be $1,429 − 1,000 = $429, and so the relocation should be made.

Note that if you ignore the change in the cost of capital, and use the traditional procedure of discounting the incremental expected cash flows using the initial cost of capital, you would mistakenly calculate the NPV to be −$100/ 0.08 − 1,000 = −$2,250. And you might mistakenly reject the project because you did not consider the impact of the investment on the cost of capital.

Extend the previous example on BBX Co. Assume that BBX initially expects annual operating cash flows of $2.8 million into perpetuity. If BBX offshores production to the United Kingdom, the expected annual operating cash flows would be $2.875 million per year. Assume the net investment outlay to complete the offshoring would be $5 million. (a) What is the NPV of the production offshoring proposal? Should BBX offshore production to the United Kingdom? (b) What would be the incorrect NPV of the offshoring proposal if BBX ignores the cost of capital change?

Answers: (a) NPV = $2.875 million/0.0575 − $2.8 million/0.07 − 5 million = $50 million − 40 million − 5 million = $5 million, so approve the relocation proposal. (b) The incremental expected perpetual annual operating cash flow is $2.875 million − 2.8 million = $0.075 million. The proposal's incorrect NPV would be $0.075 million/0.07 − 5 million = $1.07 million − 5 million = −$3.93 million.

It is also instructive to look at the same scenario in reverse, where the proposal is to reshore production from a foreign country back to the home country, here the United States. Here, there is a possibility that if you ignore the cost of capital change, you will accept a proposal that you should reject. This is the opposite of the scenario above where ignoring the cost of capital change leads to rejecting a proposal that should be accepted.

For example, assume that AEM initially produces overseas, expects annual operating cash flows of $1,500 into perpetuity, and has a cost of capital of 7%. AEM is thinking of reshoring the production back to the United States, which would lower the production costs and hence increase expected annual operating cash flows, to $1,600. Assume the net outlay to make the relocation is $1,000. The traditional capital budgeting analysis would discount the expected incremental operating cash flows at 7%, to get $100/0.07 = $1,429, and the NPV would seem to be positive, $1,429 – 1,000 = $429. But this solution would not account for the increase in the cost of capital to 8%, because of the reduced level of operational hedging. The correct answer is that the intrinsic business value would drop from $1,500/0.07 = $21,429, to $1,600/0.08 = $20,000, so the NPV of the relocation would be –$1,429 – 1000 = –$2,429. The relocation proposal has a negative NPV and should thus be rejected.

Assume that the U.S.-owned BBX currently produces in the United Kingdom and expects annual operating cash flows of $2.875 million into perpetuity. BBX's FX operating exposure to the British pound is 1 and the cost of capital is 5.75%. If BBX reshores production to the United States, the expected annual operating cash flows would be $3.275 million per year, the FX operating exposure to the British pound would increase to 2, and the cost of capital would rise to 7%. Assume the investment outlay to complete the reshoring is $5 million. (a) Should BBX reshore production to the United States? (b) What would be the incorrect NPV if BBX ignores the cost of capital change? **Answers:** (a) NPV = $3.275 million/0.07 – 2.875 million/0.0575 – 5 million = $46.79 million – 50 million – 5 million = –$8.21 million, so reject the reshoring proposal. (b) The incremental expected perpetual annual operating cash flow is $3.275 million – 2.875 million = $0.40 million. The proposal's incorrect NPV would be $0.40 million/0.0575 – 5 million = $6.96 million – 5 million = $1.96 million.

Extend the TDY Co. example above. Initially, TDY's FX operating exposure to the Japanese yen is –1.75, operating beta is 0.80, and perpetual expected annual operating cash flow is $700,000. If TDY changes the source of some components to the United States, the FX operating exposure would drop (in absolute value) to –1.25, and the expected annual cash flow stream would drop to $679,000. There is no investment outlay to make this change in FX operating exposure. The Japanese yen's currency beta is estimated to be –0.10. (a) Should TDY accept the proposal to relocate a portion of sourcing to the United States? (b) What would be the incorrect NPV of the proposal if TDY ignores the cost of capital change?

Answers: (a) The NPV is $679,000/0.0675 – 700,000/0.07 – 0 = $10.059 million – 10 million = $59,000, so accept the sourcing relocation proposal. (b) The incremental expected annual operating cash flow would be –$21,000, so the proposal's incorrect NPV would be –$21,000/0.07 – 0 = –$300,000.

MIGA and OPIC

The *Multilateral Investment Guarantee Agency (MIGA)* was created in 1988 as a member of the World Bank Group to promote foreign direct investment into emerging economies to improve people's lives and reduce poverty. MIGA fulfills this mandate and contributes to development by offering political risk insurance (guarantees) to investors and lenders, and by helping developing countries attract and retain private investment. More information may be obtained from: http://www.miga.org/.

The *Overseas Private Investment Corporation (OPIC)* is a development agency of the U.S. government. OPIC helps U.S. businesses invest overseas, fosters economic development in new and emerging markets, complements the private sector in managing the risks associated with foreign direct investment, and supports U.S. foreign policy. By expanding economic development in host countries, OPIC-supported projects can encourage political stability, free market reforms, and U.S. best practices. Because OPIC charges market-based fees for its products, it operates on a self-sustaining basis at no net cost to taxpayers. More information may be obtained from: http://www.opic.gov/.

FX Operating Exposure and Third Country Production

Previously, we covered the case where a U.S. firm has a subsidiary in Austria, which proposed to relocate some or all of the production process to Poland. The choice of Poland, whose currency tracks the euro because Poland has planned to join the European Monetary Union (EMU), was partially for convenience so that we could avoid the currency risk issue while covering the political risk issue. Now we are ready to address the currency risk issue in a capital budgeting application where production is in one foreign country and the product market is in a different foreign country.

Our new scenario involves the Swiss electronics manufacturer, CHS Plc, a subsidiary of the U.S. parent BXM Inc. CHS's main market is the Eurozone, and product prices are fixed in euros. From its U.S. dollar perspective, CHS poses two FX exposures for BXM. The revenues in euros are a positive (long) FX operating exposure to the euro, and the manufacturing costs in Swiss francs are a negative (short) FX operating exposure to the Swiss franc.

BXM has estimated that the operating beta for CHS, in U.S. dollars, is 1.25. Choosing to ignore political risk in this case, and given the U.S. dollar risk-free rate of 3%, the global risk premium estimate of 5%, and the global CAPM, BXS estimates the cost of capital in U.S. dollars for CHS is $0.03 + 1.25(0.05) = 0.0925$, or 9.25%.

CHS proposes to relocate some of its basic manufacturing processes to Germany. One motivation is the CHS management view that the euro will likely depreciate relative to the Swiss franc. The operational hedging aspect of the relocation would reduce BXM's FX operating exposure to the euro. Also, the FX operating exposure to the Swiss franc would be smaller (in absolute value). Let's assume that the manufacturing relocation would reduce BXM's FX operating exposure to the euro, from 2.50 to 1.50, and would change the FX operating exposure to the Swiss franc, from -1.80 to -1.20. Given currency betas of 0.25 for the euro and 0.10 for the Swiss franc, and a double application of equation (7.2), the new operating beta for CHS, in U.S. dollars, would be $1.25 + 0.25(1.50 - 2.50) + 0.10(-1.20 - (-1.80)) = 1.06$. So the new cost of capital for CHS in U.S. dollars would be $0.03 + 1.06(0.05) = 0.083$, or 8.3%.

The U.S. firm DRV has a subsidiary in Australia. The subsidiary produces and distributes entirely in Australia. DRV has determined that from the U.S. dollar point of view, the subsidiary's operating beta is 1.40 and the FX operating exposure to the Australian dollar is 1.30. The subsidiary is proposing to offshore some of its basic manufacturing processes to Malaysia. If the proposal is accepted, from the U.S. dollar point of view, the subsidiary would have a new FX operating exposure to the Australian dollar of 2.30 and an FX operating exposure to the Malaysian ringgit of –1.25. The currency betas are 0.50 for the Australian dollar and 0.20 for the ringgit. What would be the subsidiary's new operating beta, from the U.S. dollar perspective?

Answer: 1.40 + 0.50(2.30 – 1.30) + 0.20(–1.25 – 0) = 1.65. Because the operating beta would be higher, the cost of capital would be higher.

Summary Action Points

- In the home currency approach to international capital budgeting, the analyst converts the expected foreign currency cash flows into home currency equivalents using forecasted FX rates, and then discounts them using a cost of capital denominated in the home currency.
- The correct conversion of an expected foreign currency cash flow to the home currency often depends on the cash flow's FX exposure and the currency's volatility, and is usually slightly more involved than the simple standard practice of multiplying the expected foreign currency cash flow by the forecasted spot FX price of the foreign currency.
- A capital budgeting proposal to relocate production to a different country should take into consideration the impact of the move on political risk, currency risk, and the cost of capital.
- If the currency beta of the foreign currency is not zero, a firm's operating beta will change when the FX operating exposure changes. The resulting change in the firm's cost of capital needs to be considered as part of the financial evaluation of the capital budgeting proposals that change FX operating exposure.

Glossary

Foreign Currency Approach (to International Capital Budgeting): The analyst uses the expected cash flows denominated in the foreign currency, and discounts them using a cost of capital denominated in the foreign currency.

Greenfield Investment: The construction of a new plant or facility.

Home Currency Approach (to International Capital Budgeting): The analyst converts the expected foreign currency cash flows into home currency equivalents using forecasted FX rates, and then discounts them using a cost of capital denominated in the home currency.

Horizontal M&A: Merger or acquisition involving firms in the same industry.

Multilateral Investment Guarantee Agency (MIGA): Organization connected to the World Bank that promotes foreign direct investment into emerging economies by insuring political risk.

Offshoring: A change of production location by an exporter from the home country to the export market.

Overseas Private Investment Corporation (OPIC): A development agency of the U.S. government that helps U.S. businesses invest overseas and foster economic development in new and emerging markets.

Reshoring: A change of production location by an exporter from the export market to the home country.

Vertical M&A: Merger or acquisition involving firms of a supply or distribution chain.

Discussion Questions

1. In overseas investment decisions, should one consider the investment's overall cash flow or just the portion to be repatriated? Explain.
2. The expected cash flow in home currency is equal to the product of the expected cash flow in the foreign currency and the expected spot FX price of the foreign currency. Evaluate this statement.
3. If the currency beta is positive, what is the impact on the cost of capital of offshoring production to the export market country? Explain.
4. What is the impact on the cost of capital of an importer that reduces sourcing from an exporting country, if that country's currency beta is positive? Explain.

5. What is the impact on the cost of capital of an importer that reduces sourcing from an exporting country, if that country's currency beta is negative? Explain.

Problems

1. Assume that the U.S. firm XRZ Co. is considering the acquisition of a private business in Australia. XRZ expects that under its management, the acquisition will generate A$100,000 in operating cash flow each year into perpetuity. An analysis shows that the acquisition target's FX operating exposure to the U.S. dollar is 0.60. The cost of capital for the target in U.S. dollars is 10%. The sellers are asking A$1,000,000 for the Australian business. Assume: (1) the time-0 spot FX rate is 1.20 $/A$; (2) the expected rate of FX change in the Australian dollar is 1.25% per year; and (3) the volatility of the Australian dollar is 0.13. (a) Find the expected time-1 spot FX rate. (b) Find the (approximate) expected time-1 operating cash flow in U.S. dollars using equation (7.1), and compare this answer to the answer you'd get with the standard practice of assuming zero FX exposure to the U.S. dollar. (c) Find the target's intrinsic business value in U.S. dollars. (d) Should XRZ make the acquisition?

2. Assume that the U.S. firm RTZ Co. has a subsidiary in the United Kingdom. The subsidiary is expected to generate £100,000 in operating cash flow each year into perpetuity. An analysis shows that the subsidiary's FX operating exposure to the U.S. dollar is 0.70. The cost of capital in U.S. dollars for subsidiary is 8.50%. RTZ is evaluating a plant modernization proposal by the UK subsidiary that would require an outlay of £150,000. At the same time, the expected operating costs would be reduced by £10,000 per year. Thus the expected operating cash flows in British pounds would be £110,000 per year instead of £100,000. Assume: (1) the time-0 spot FX rate is 1.50 $/£; (2) the expected rate of change in the FX price of the British pound is –0.80% per year; and (3) the volatility of the British pound is 0.10. (a) Find the expected time-1 spot FX rate. (b) Find the (approximate) expected time-1 operating cash

flow in U.S. dollars using equation (7.1). (c) Find the NPV of the modernization proposal in U.S. dollars. Should RTZ approve the modernization proposal?

3. Assume that the U.S. firm AGM Co. has a subsidiary in Germany. The subsidiary is expected to generate €100,000 in operating cash flow each year into perpetuity. An analysis shows that the subsidiary's FX operating exposure to the U.S. dollar is 0.70. The cost of capital in U.S. dollars for the subsidiary is 9%. AGM is evaluating a proposal to relocate some basic portions of the production process to Poland, which would require a time-0 outlay of €400,000. At the same time, the expected operating costs would be reduced by €30,000 per year. Thus the expected operating cash flows in euros would be €130,000 per year instead of €100,000. Assume that Poland's CDS yield is 250 and Germany's is 100. The political risk exposure of the operation is 1, whether the proposal is accepted or not. Ignore any impact of the change in currency from euros to zloty for the operating costs. Assume: (1) the time-0 spot FX rate is 1.25 $/€; (2) the expected rate of change in the FX price of the euro is 1.40% per year; and (3) the volatility of the euro is 0.15. (a) Find the expected time-1 spot FX rate. (b) For the subsidiary, before and after the relocation, find the (approximate) expected time-1 operating cash flow in U.S. dollars using equation (7.1). (c) Find the subsidiary's intrinsic business value in U.S. dollars before the relocation. (d) What is the new cost of capital for the German subsidiary? (e) Should AGM approve the proposal to relocate some of the production to Poland?

4. The U.S. exporter UVC may move its assembly process to the Eurozone. If so, UVC's FX operating exposure to the euro will fall from 3.80 to 1.80. UVC's operating beta (in U.S. dollars) is currently 1.35. (a) If the euro's currency beta is 0.20, find what UVC's new operating beta would be. (b) Assume the global CAPM. Find UVC's cost of capital (in U.S. dollars) before and after, if the risk-free rate in U.S. dollars is 4%, and if $GRP^\$ = 5\%$.

For 5–7: The U.S. firm ZXR Co. exports machine components to the United Kingdom. Given that the production of the components is in the

United States, ZXR has FX operating exposure to the British pound of 2.50, an operating beta of 0.90, and expected annual operating cash flows of $3 million into perpetuity. Assume that if ZXR moves the final stages of the production process to the United Kingdom, the FX operating exposure to the British pound will drop from 2.50 to 1.50, because of operational hedging, and the expected annual operating cash flow will drop to $2.75 million into perpetuity. The net investment outlay to relocate the production would be $5 million. Assume the global CAPM in U.S. dollars is the risk–return trade-off for all international assets, the risk-free rate in U.S. dollars is 2.5%, the global risk premium in U.S. dollars is 5%, and the British pound's currency beta is 0.30.

5. Find ZXR's new operating beta if the firm offshores the final stages of production to the United Kingdom.
6. Find ZXR's new cost of capital if the firm offshores the final stages of production to the United Kingdom.
7. Find the NPV of the production relocation proposal.

For 8–10: The U.S. firm GBC Co. currently sources and produces entirely in the United States and has an FX operating exposure to the Japanese yen of 0. GBC's operating beta is 1.20, and the perpetual expected annual operating cash flow is $900,000. GBC is considering a proposal to change the source of some raw material to Japan, which would change the FX operating exposure to the yen to –0.80, and the expected annual cash flow stream would rise to $927,000. There is no investment outlay to make the sourcing change. The Japanese yen's currency beta is –0.10. In U.S. dollars, the risk-free rate is 3% and the global risk premium is 5%.

8. Find the initial and new cost of capital for GBC.
9. Find the NPV of the proposal to increase sourcing from Japan.
10. What would be the incorrect NPV of the proposal if GBC ignores the cost of capital change?

11. The U.S. firm DRV has a subsidiary in Australia. The subsidiary produces and distributes entirely in Australia. DRV has determined that from the U.S. dollar point of view, the subsidiary has an operating beta of 1.35 and an FX operating exposure to the Australian

dollar of 1. The subsidiary is proposing to offshore some of its basic manufacturing processes to Thailand. If the proposal is accepted, from the U.S. dollar point of view, the subsidiary would have a new FX operating exposure to the Australian dollar of 1.80 and an FX operating exposure to the Thai baht of −0.80. The currency betas are 0.50 for the Australian dollar and 0.30 for the baht. What would be the subsidiary's new operating beta, from the U.S. dollar perspective?

Answers to Problems

1. (a) (1.20 $/A$)(1.0125) = 1.215 $/A$. (b) A$100,000(1.215 $/A$)[1 − 0.60(0.13)^2] = $120,268. Using the standard practice of implicitly assuming no FX exposure to the U.S. dollar, one would overestimate the time-1 expected operating cash flow in U.S. dollars, €100,000(1.215 $/€) = $121,500. (c) $120,268/(0.10 − 0.0022) = $1,229,734. (d) The NPV is $1,229,734 − (1.20 $/A$)(A$1,000,000) = $29,734. Because the NPV > 0, make the acquisition.

2. This capital budgeting project involves an incremental perpetuity in British pounds of £10,000 per year. (a) (1.50 $/£)(1 − 0.008) = 1.488 $/£. (b) £10,000(1.488 $/£)[1 − 0.70(0.10)^2] = $14,776. (c) The present value of the incremental expected operating cash flows, from the U.S. dollar point of view, is $14,776/(0.085 − (−0.0149)) = $147,908. In U.S. dollars, the time-0 outlay would be £150,000(1.50 $/£) = $225,000. The modernization proposal should be rejected, because the NPV is negative, $147,908 − 225,000 = −$77,092.

3. (a) (1.25 $/€)(1 + 0.014) = 1.2675 $/€. (b) Before: €100,000(1.2675 $/£) × [1 − 0.70(0.15)^2] = $124,754; After: €130,000(1.2675 $/£)[1 − 0.70(0.15)^2] = $162,180. (c) $124,754/(0.09 − (−0.002)) = $1,356,022. (d) 0.09 + (0.025 − 0.01) = 0.105. (e) The new intrinsic business value, in U.S. dollars, would be $162,180/(0.105 − (−0.002)) = $1,515,710. In U.S. dollars, the time-0 outlay would be €400,000(1.25 $/€) = $500,000. The proposal should be rejected, because the NPV is negative, $1,515,710 − 1,356,022 − 500,000 = −$340,312.

4. (a) The new operating beta is $1.35 + 0.20(1.80 - 3.80) = 0.95$. (b) The old cost of capital in U.S. dollars is $0.04 + 1.35(0.05) = 0.1075$, or 10.75%. The new cost of capital in U.S. dollars is $0.04 + 0.95(0.05) = 0.0875$, or 8.75%.

5. $0.90 + 0.30(1.50 - 2.50) = 0.60$.

6. $0.025 + 0.60(0.05) = 0.055$.

7. $\$2.75/0.055 - 3/0.07 - 5 = \$2.14$ million.

8. The initial cost of capital is $0.03 + 1.20(0.05) = 0.09$. Using equation (7.2), the new operating beta would be $1.20 + (-0.10)(-0.80 - 0) = 1.28$. The new cost of capital would be $0.03 + 1.28(0.05) = 0.094$.

9. $\$927,000/0.094 - 900,000/0.09 - 0 = \$9.86$ million $- 10$ million $= -\$0.14$ million, so reject the sourcing relocation proposal.

10. The incremental expected perpetual annual operating cash flow is $27,000, so the proposal's incorrect NPV would be $27,000/0.09 - 0 = \$300,000$.

11. Using a double application of equation (7.2), we get that the new operating beta would be $1.35 + 0.50(1.80 - 1) + 0.30(-0.80 - 0) = 1.51$.

Cross-Border Valuation

In the previous chapter, we used the home currency approach to international capital budgeting, where the analyst converts the expected foreign currency cash flows into home currency equivalents using forecasted FX rates, and then discounts them using a cost of capital denominated in the home currency. As we have said, in the foreign currency approach, the analyst uses the expected cash flows denominated in the foreign currency, and discounts them using a cost of capital denominated in the foreign currency.

The typical textbook advice is that the currency perspective is irrelevant in cross-border valuation analyses, given consistent conversions of expected cash flows and cost of capital across currencies. We'll show that a critical condition behind this typical advice is that the spot and forecasted FX rates are the intrinsic FX rates. You will also see that when the time-0 spot FX rate is misvalued, or when managers' FX forecasts differ from expected intrinsic spot FX rates, the NPV analyses in the different currency perspectives may lead to different decision outcomes. This important result means that an FX misvaluation or a forecast of a future FX misvaluation may affect an international investment decision.

Cost of Capital in Different Currencies

Any asset's cost of capital may be viewed from the perspective of different currencies. So you must be careful to specify which currency you are using to express a cost of capital. For example, a firm's cost of equity might be 10% expressed in U.S. dollars and 8% expressed in Swiss francs, regardless of whether the firm is domiciled in the United States, Switzerland, or anywhere else. The different numbers in different currencies are different ways to express the same cost of equity. This idea is the same as saying that a firm's equity has only one value, but it is a different number when expressed in different currencies. That is, you can express a firm's equity value either as $100 or Sf 160 assuming a spot FX rate of 1.60 Sf/$. This is a similar idea as a firm's cost of equity being 10% in U.S. dollars or 8% in Swiss francs.

In theory, the intrinsic value of a Swiss company's equity, expressed in Swiss francs, is found by discounting the expected future Swiss franc cash flows to the equityholders, using the firm's Swiss franc cost of equity. The company's ADR, which receives the same cash flows after conversion into U.S. dollars, has an intrinsic value in U.S. dollars that is the present value of the converted expected cash flows, using the firm's cost of equity in U.S. dollars. As we know from Chapter 5, the ADR's intrinsic value should be equal to the intrinsic value of the ordinary shares, given the spot FX rate. So the valuation process in Swiss francs must be linked to the valuation process in U.S. dollars. A cost of equity for the ordinaries in Swiss francs that is *consistent* with the cost of equity in U.S. dollars for the ADRs is based on this linkage.

Financial managers often want to express a foreign asset's cost of capital in the overseas local currency, given that the asset's cost of capital is known in the parent company's home currency. For example, a U.S. multinational company may have estimated the cost of capital for a foreign subsidiary in U.S. dollars, but the parent will want to supply the subsidiary's managers with a *consistent* cost of capital in their own local currency, so that they can have a hurdle rate for making local, decentralized investment decisions.

For example, consider the hypothetical Eurozone subsidiary, AEM Co., with an estimated operating beta in U.S. dollars of 1.20. Assume $r_f^\$ = 4\%$ and $GRP^\$ = 5\%$. The global CAPM tells us that AEM's cost of capital in U.S. dollars, $k_O^\$$, is $0.04 + 1.20(0.05) = 0.10$, or 10%. AEM's $k_O^\$$ of 10% is the proper capitalization rate for AEM's expected operating cash flows, as measured in U.S. dollars, if we want to find the subsidiary's intrinsic business value in U.S. dollars. However, because AEM's future operating cash flow stream is in euros, we also may think of AEM's business value in euros. The question is what discount rate should be used to find AEM's intrinsic business value in euros, which is the present value in euros of the expected euro operating cash flow stream. In other words, what is AEM's cost of capital *in euros*, k_O^ϵ, consistent with its 10% $k_O^\$$?

For some technical reasons beyond our scope, it is difficult to use a risk–return model in a foreign currency consistent with the global CAPM in equation (5.2), so we find a given asset's cost of capital in a foreign currency, based on a given cost of capital in U.S. dollars, using the conversion approach in equation (8.1).

Cost of Capital Conversion

$$1 + k_i^\$ = (1 + k_i^€)(1 + E^*(x^{\$/€})) + (\xi_{i€}^\$ - 1)\sigma_€^2 \qquad (8.1)$$

Although we typically want to solve for asset i's cost of capital in euros, $k_i^€$, given the cost of capital in U.S. dollars, it is easier to show the formula in the form of equation (8.1). To apply equation (8.1), you need the expected rate of intrinsic FX change in the euro, $E^*(x^{\$/€})$. For example, assume that $r_f^€ = 6\%$ and the currency beta of the euro is 0.10. Then given our assumptions that $r_f^\$ = 4\%$ and $GRP^\$ = 5\%$, and using the linear approximation RA-UIRP condition in equation (5.3), $E^*(x^{\$/€}) = 4\% - 6\% + 0.10(5\%) = -1.5\%$. If we were to ignore the $(\xi_{i€}^\$ - 1)\sigma_€^2$ term at the end of equation (8.1), the cost of capital conversion would be relatively easy: Given that AEM's U.S. dollar cost of capital is 10%, we'd plug into equation (8.1) to get $1.10 = (1 + k_O^€)(1 - 0.015)$, and then solve for $k_O^€$. AEM's cost of capital in euros would be $1.10/0.985 - 1 = 0.11675$, or 11.675%.

However, we do need to consider the $(\xi_{i€}^\$ - 1)\sigma_€^2$ term at the end of equation (8.1). This term is for the statistical interaction between the asset's returns and spot FX rate changes, and is mathematically necessary when the asset's returns in euros and spot FX rate changes are not independent. But the term unfortunately does not lend itself to an easy intuitive economic interpretation. The term says to subtract one from the asset's FX exposure to the euro, $\xi_{i€}^\$ - 1$, and then multiply this difference by the squared (annualized) volatility of the euro, $\sigma_€^2$. So to make this adjustment for AEM's cost of capital, we need AEM's FX operating exposure to the euro, $\xi_{O€}^\$$, and the volatility of the euro, $\sigma_€$, which we assume are 0.75 and 0.10, respectively. Then, the $(\xi_{O€}^\$ - 1)\sigma_€^2$ term for AEM is $(0.75 - 1)0.10^2 = -0.0025$.[1]

Equation (8.1) says that $1.10 = (1 + k_O^€)(1 - 0.015) - 0.0025$, so AEM's $k_O^€$ is $1.1025/0.985 - 1 = 0.1193$, or **11.93%**. The main reason why AEM's cost of capital is different when represented in euros (11.93%) rather than U.S. dollars (10%) is the impact of the expected rate of intrinsic FX change in the euro, $E^*(x^{\$/€}) = -1.5\%$. The secondary reason why AEM's euro cost of capital is different from 10% is based on the statistical interaction between AEM's returns and FX rates, reflected in AEM's FX operating exposure to the euro. Perhaps not much harm would be done in many cases if you ignore the statistical interaction term when dealing with developed country currencies. But this term can be significant when the currency volatility is high, as with emerging market currencies.[2]

The result that AEM's estimated cost of capital expressed in euros is 11.93% is based on its estimated cost of capital in U.S. dollars of 10% and the other given assumptions, including AEM's FX operating exposure to the euro of 0.75. AEM really has only one basic cost of capital that compensates for the systematic risk of the business, and 10% and 11.93% are equivalent expressions of that cost of capital in the two different currencies. While AEM's cost of capital in euros is a different number than its cost of capital in U.S. dollars, the two are equivalent in economic content. Figure 8.1 summarizes the ideas in cost of capital conversion from U.S. dollars to euros.

In the special case of a foreign asset with returns in local currency that are independent of spot FX rate changes, meaning that from the euro perspective, the asset's FX exposure to the U.S. dollar is zero, the asset's returns in U.S. dollars have only a pure FX conversion exposure to the euro, $\xi_{i€}^{\$} = 1$. Only in this special case no adjustment is needed for the interaction between returns and FX changes, and equation (8.1) simplifies to $1 + k_i^{\$} = (1 + k_i^{€})(1 + E^*(x^{\$/€}))$.

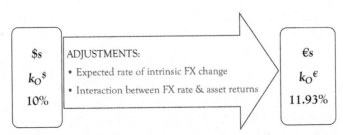

Figure 8.1. Cost of capital conversion across currencies.

A simpler conversion is possible if we ignore both the currency risk premium and the statistical adjustment term involving the asset's FX exposure. With the traditional UIRP condition, the cost of capital conversion would simply use the expression: $(1 + k_i^{\$})/(1 + k_i^{€}) = (1 + r_f^{\$})/(1 + r_f^{€})$, in which the cost of capital differential ratio is equal to the risk-free rate differential ratio. This approach to cost of capital conversion is often an acceptable approximation to the more "precise" one in equation (8.1), at least for developed country currencies, and is easier to apply. In our example, we'd approximate AEM's $k_O^{€}$ to be $1.10(1.06)/1.04 - 1 = 0.121$, or 12.1%. Even easier is the linear approximation of the same idea: $k_i^{\$} - k_i^{€} = r_f^{\$} - r_f^{€}$, in which case AEM's approximate $k_O^{€}$ is $0.10 + 0.06 - 0.04 = 0.12$, or 12%.

A U.S. multinational's Japanese division has an FX operating exposure to the yen of 1.60 and a hurdle rate in U.S. dollars of 9%. The risk-free rates are 5% in U.S. dollars and 2% in yen, and the volatility of the yen is 0.08. Assume the linear approximation RA-UIRP condition (global CAPM) in U.S. dollars. The currency beta of the yen is −0.10 and $GRP^{\$} = 5\%$. (a) Find the division's hurdle rate in yen. (b) How close to the correct hurdle rate is the simple interest rate differential linear approximation?

Answers: (a) Using equation (5.3): $E^{*}(x^{\$/¥}) = r_f^{\$} - r_f^{¥} + \beta_{¥}^{\$}(GRP^{\$}) = 0.05 - 0.02 - 0.10(0.05) = 0.025$, or 2.50%. Using equation (8.1), $1.09 = (1 + k_O^{¥})(1 + 0.025) + (1.60 - 1)0.08^{2}$; so the division's $k_O^{¥}$ is $1.08616/1.025 - 1 = 0.0597$, or 5.97%. (b) $k_O^{¥} = k_O^{\$} - (r_f^{\$} - r_f^{¥}) = 0.09 - (0.05 - 0.02) = 0.06$, or 6%.

Note that we convert an asset's cost of capital <u>not</u> using a managers' actual forecasted rate of FX change, but rather using the expected rate of <u>*intrinsic*</u> FX change, even if it is different from the managers' FX forecast. The reason is that the cost of capital is a compensation for risk, regardless of the currency perspective. We take the view that there is a single relationship between risk and *required* return for globally traded assets, even though specific assets might be mispriced at any time in one or more currencies. Only the expected rate of change in the short-run <u>*intrinsic*</u> FX price of the foreign currency is based on risk, and thus preserves a consistent risk and required return relationship across different currencies for globally traded assets.

A reminder: *the short-run intrinsic spot FX rate is the correctly valued FX rate per the financial market. The short-run intrinsic FX rate is not necessarily equal to the long-run intrinsic FX rate, which is based on FX valuation relative to the goods market. In this chapter, the intrinsic spot FX rate refers to the short-run intrinsic spot FX rate.*

Framework for Cross-Border Valuation

Now we begin to address issues in cross-border valuation. Reviewing our notation, $E(X_N^{\$/€})$ refers to the *actual* forecasted time-N spot FX rate, and $E^*(X_N^{\$/€})$ will represent the expected *intrinsic* time-N spot FX rate. Similarly, $X_0^{\$/€}$ denotes the actual time-0 spot FX rate, and $X_0^{*\$/€}$ denotes the intrinsic time-0 spot FX rate. Also, $E(x^{\$/€})$ refers to the actual forecasted rate of FX change in the euro, with $E^*(x^{\$/€})$ representing the expected rate of intrinsic FX change in the euro. So to get the expected intrinsic spot FX rate for time N, we use equation (8.2).

Expected Time-N Intrinsic Spot FX Rate

$$E^*(X_N^{\$/€}) = X_0^{*\$/€}(1 + E^*(x^{\$/€}))^N \qquad (8.2)$$

To help the presentation, we use a hypothetical scenario of the U.S. multinational ABC Co., which is considering acquiring VPC Plc, an operation that produces and sells aircraft components in the Eurozone. To emphasize the main issues, we'll make two simplifying assumptions for the time being. First, VPC will only be in business for 1 year, and will generate only next year's operating cash flow, in euros. VPC's actual time-1 cash flow in euros, $O_1^{€}$, is uncertain with an expectation, $E(O_1^{€})$, of €2,000. Second, while VPC's $O_1^{€}$ is uncertain, we'll assume that changes in the spot FX rate do not affect $O_1^{€}$. That is, from the euro perspective, VPC has zero FX operating exposure to the U.S. dollar. This assumption implies that from the U.S. dollar perspective, VPC's FX operating exposure to the euro, $\xi_{O€}^{\$}$, is 1. We'll relax the two simplifying assumptions later, after we have established some basic ideas.

ABC's managers have estimated VPC's cost of capital is 11% in U.S. dollars. That is, $k_O^{\$} = 0.11$. Here is a common scenario where the corporate managers have estimated an overseas project's cost of capital in the home currency but have measured the expected operating cash flow stream in the foreign currency.

Let's first apply the foreign currency approach and find VPC's time-0 intrinsic business value in euros. To do this, we first need to convert VPC's $k_O^{\$}$ from U.S. dollars to euros, using equation (8.1). For this purpose, we need to determine the expected rate of intrinsic FX change of the euro, $E^*(x^{\$/\euro})$. Let's use the global CAPM RA-UIRP condition in equation (5.3). We assume that the risk-free rates are 3.5% in U.S. dollars and 6% in euros, the currency beta of the euro is 0.20, and the $GRP^{\$}$ is 5%. So $E^*(x^{\$/\euro}) = 0.035 - 0.06 + 0.20(0.05) = -0.015$. That is, $E^*(x^{\$/\euro}) = -1.50\%$. Given that VPC's $k_O^{\$}$ is 11% and $\xi_{O\euro}^{\$}$ is 1, we rearrange equation (8.1) to find VPC's cost of capital in euros: $k_O^{\euro} = (1 + k_O^{\$})/(1 + E^*(x^{\$/\euro})) - 1 = 1.11/0.985 - 1 = 0.1269$. That is, $k_O^{\euro} = 12.69\%$. Now we find VPC's time-0 intrinsic business value in euros as the present value of the expected future cash flow in euros: $V_B^{\euro} = E(O_1^{\euro})/(1 + k_O^{\euro}) = \euro2,000/1.1269 = \euro1,775$. In general, $V_i^{\euro}$ denotes asset i's intrinsic value in euros. In this case, we know that asset i is the VPC business operation, so we suppress the i subscript, but use the B subscript to denote our focus on business value.

Next, perform a similar present value analysis, but in the home currency, U.S. dollars. We already have VPC's cost of capital in U.S. dollars, 11%, so we need the expected time-1 operating cash flow, measured in U.S. dollars. To get this number, we need to convert the expected time-1 operating cash flow from euros using the forecasted time-1 spot FX rate. In the next sections, we'll continue this scenario, exploring cases when today's spot FX rate is correctly valued and other cases when it is not. We'll also cover cases where managers' forecast of the future FX rate is equal to the expected intrinsic spot FX rate and cases where it is not.

Cross-Border Valuation With Correctly-Valued FX Rates

We first assume that ABC's managers forecast that the future spot FX rate will be equal to the expected intrinsic spot FX rate. Given this assumption, we'll show that if the parameters of the valuation analysis in each currency are consistent, the present value of the project's expected cash flow in U.S.

dollars is equivalent to the present value in euros, given the time-0 intrinsic spot FX rate.

For simplicity, assume that the time-0 intrinsic spot FX rate, $X_0^{*\$/€} =$ 1 $/€. Thus using equation (8.2), the expected time-1 intrinsic spot FX rate is 1 $/€$(1 - 0.015) = 0.985$ $/€. That is, $E^*(X_1^{\$/€}) = $ **0.985 $/€.** Because we assume (for now) that ABC forecasts the time-1 spot FX rate to be the intrinsic spot FX rate, the actual forecasted spot FX rate, $E(X_1^{\$/€})$, is also 0.985 $/€. So VPC's expected time-1 operating cash flow, viewed in U.S. dollars, is $E(O_1^{\$}) = 0.985$ $/€(€2,000) = $1,970, using equation (7.1) and recalling that the euro cash flow is independent of the spot FX rate ($\xi_{O\$}^{€} = 0$). Because VPC's cost of capital in U.S. dollars is 11%, VPC's intrinsic business value in U.S. dollars is: $V_B^{\$} = $1,970/1.11 = $ **$1,775.** So VPC's intrinsic business value in euros, which we found earlier is €1,775, is equivalent to VPC's intrinsic business in U.S. dollars, $1,775, given the time-0 intrinsic spot FX rate, $X_0^{*\$/€}$, of 1 $/€.

The Eurozone firm DYA will generate one operating cash flow, expected to be €1 million at time 1. From the perspective of U.S. dollars, DYA's FX operating exposure to the euro is 1 and cost of capital is 8.50%. XYZ Company, a U.S. multinational, is evaluating the acquisition of DYA. Assume $r_f^{\$} = 3\%$ and $r_f^{€} = 6\%$, the currency beta of the euro is 0.20, and the actual time-0 spot FX rate of 1.50 $/€ is the time-0 intrinsic spot FX rate. Assume the global CAPM RA-UIRP condition with $GRP^{\$} = 5\%$. XYZ forecasts that the time-1 spot FX rate will be the intrinsic spot FX rate. (a) Find DYA's intrinsic business value in euros. (b) Find the expected time-1 intrinsic spot FX rate. (c) Find DYA's intrinsic business value in U.S. dollars. (d) Show that the intrinsic business values in euros and U.S. dollars are equivalent given the time-0 intrinsic spot FX rate.

Answers: (a) $E^*(x^{\$/€}) = 3\% - 6\% + 0.20(5\%) = -2\%$. Using equation (8.1), given $\xi_{O€}^{\$} = 1$, DYA's $k_O^{€}$ is found by solving $(1 + k_O^{\$}) = (1 + k_O^{€}) \times (1 + E^*(x^{\$/€}))$; so $k_O^{€} = 0.1071$, or 10.71%. $V_B^{€} = $ €1 million/1.1071 = €0.9032 million. (b) The expected time-1 intrinsic spot FX rate, $E^*(X_1^{\$/€})$, is 1.50 $/€$(1 - 0.02) = 1.47$ $/€. (c) DYA's expected time-1 operating cash flow in U.S. dollars is 1.47 $/€(€1 million) = $1.47 million. So $V_B^{\$}$ is

$1.47 million/1.085 = $1.355 million. (d) At the time-0 intrinsic spot FX rate of 1.50 $/€, V_B^{ϵ} is equivalent to $V_B^{\$}$, because 1.50 $/€(€0.9032 million)= $1.355 million.

Now let's bring the project's investment outlay into the analysis. Assume that VPC's owners are asking **€1,900** for the business. Thus, €1,900 would be ABC's investment outlay, viewed in euros, I^{ϵ}. Looking at the proposal from the euro point of view, the NPV would be $V_B^{\epsilon} - I^{\epsilon} =$ €1,775 − 1,900 = −€125. That is, NPV^{ϵ} = −**€125**. From the euro perspective, the acquisition has a negative NPV, implying rejection.

Next we find the NPV in U.S. dollars, assuming that the actual time-0 spot FX rate is 1 $/€ and is thus correctly valued in the financial market. ABC's investment outlay from the U.S. dollar perspective, $I^{\$}$, would thus be 1 $/€(€1,900) = $1,900. Thus the NPV in U.S. dollars is $1,775 − 1,900 = −$125. That is, $NPV^{\$}$ = −**$125**.

In this case of correctly valued FX rates, the two currency perspectives lead to equivalent NPV amounts, given that the inputs to the analysis are consistent across the currencies. Thus, the two currency perspectives result in the same decision outcome. In principle, it does not matter which currency is chosen for the NPV analysis, because the same accept/reject decision is reached by conducting the NPV analysis in euros, with a euro cost of capital and an expected euro cash flow, or in U.S. dollars, with a U.S. dollar cost of capital and an expected cash flow converted from euros into U.S. dollars.

You will sometimes see these conclusions stated as general propositions that always hold. As you will see next, that generalization is incorrect. **The home and foreign currency approaches to international capital budgeting give equivalent NPVs _only if_ the FX rates are the intrinsic FX rates.**

Misvalued Time-0 Spot FX Rate

Next assume that the euro is *undervalued* at time 0. For example, assume the time-0 actual spot FX rate is $X_0^{\$/\epsilon}$ = **0.85 $/€**, whereas the time-0 intrinsic spot FX rate is 1 $/€. Now ABC's investment outlay from the U.S. dollar perspective would be 0.85 $/€(€1,900) = $1,615. That is, $I^{\$}$ = **$1,615**. VPC's $V_B^{\$}$ is not affected by the time-0 spot FX misvaluation of the euro, given that the FX forecast is still the expected time-1 intrinsic spot FX rate, 0.985 $/€. That is, $V_B^\$$ is still $1,970/1.11 = $1,775, regardless of the time-0 spot FX rate. So $NPV^\$ = $1,775 - 1,615 = 160. That is, $NPV^\$ = \$160$.

Note that even though the NPV in U.S. dollars is affected by whether the time-0 actual spot FX rate is correctly valued, the NPV in euros is NOT affected. Regardless of the actual time-0 spot FX rate, $NPV^€ = €1,775 - 1,900 = -€125$. So we see that the two NPVs are NOT necessarily equivalent to each other when the time-0 spot FX rate is not correctly valued. Indeed in this case, it matters which currency is chosen for the NPV analysis, because in the ABC example, the NPV in euros is negative and the NPV in U.S. dollars is positive. A <u>reject decision</u> is implied by the $NPV^€$, but an <u>accept decision</u> is implied by the $NPV^\$$. Of course, what is going on is that the FX market conditions allow ABC to convert U.S. dollars into euros for the investment outlay at time 0 at a "bargain" spot FX rate, yet expect to convert the acquisition's future cash flow at a correctly valued future spot FX rate. The time-0 spot FX misvaluation is temporary and forecasted to be corrected by time 1.

It should be relatively easy to grasp an example of the opposite situation, where the euro is *overvalued* at time 0, and the acquisition's $NPV^€$ is positive, but the $NPV^€$ is negative. For example, assume that VPC's owners are only asking €1,700 for the business and that the time-0 actual spot FX rate is 1.20 $/€. The acquisition has a positive $NPV^€$: €1,775 - 1,700 = €75. But in U.S. dollars, the outlay for the acquisition is 1.20 $/€(€1,700) = $2,040. So $NPV^\$$ is negative, $1,775 - 2,040 = -$265.

Extend the previous XYZ/DYA example. DYA's owners are asking €800,000 for the business. Assume the time-0 actual spot FX rate is 1.80 $/€ and the time-0 intrinsic spot FX rate is 1.50 $/€. XYZ believes that the temporary overvaluation of the euro will be corrected before the time-1 cash flow arrives. Find the NPV of XYZ's proposed acquisition in euros and in U.S. dollars.

Answer: $NPV^€ = €903,200 - 800,000 = €103,200$. $I^\$ = (1.80 \ \$/€) \times (€800,000) = \$1.44$ million. $NPV^\$ = \$1.355$ million $- \$1.44$ million $= -\$85,000$.

Toronto-Dominion Bank, October 2007

"Helped by the strength of the Canadian dollar, TORONTO-DOMINION BANK agreed to buy COMMERCE BANCORP, an American retail bank, for $8.5 billion in October 2007. The deal cemented the Canadian bank's presence in America's north-east."

This news quote suggests that the FX rate played a role in this acquisition decision. Perhaps the "strength of the Canadian dollar" was a view that the Canadian dollar was overvalued and the U.S. dollar undervalued, at that time. Such an FX misvaluation may have implied that the acquisition of COMMERCE BANCORP would have a positive NPV to TORONTO-DOMINION BANK. If the Canadian dollar had been correctly valued, the acquisition may not have had a positive NPV.

Forecasts of Misvalued Spot FX Rates

In this section, managers forecast a future spot FX rate that differs from the expected intrinsic spot FX rate. As you might guess, the two present values of the cash flow will not be the same across the currencies, even converting with the time-0 intrinsic spot FX rate.[3]

Let's pick up the ABC/VPC example and assume again that the expected time-1 intrinsic spot FX rate is 0.985 $/€, but that ABC's managers' forecast for the time-1 spot FX rate is 0.90 $/€. That is, $E(X_1^{\$/€})$ = **0.90 $/€**. To correctly value VPC in U.S. dollars, we first need to break the expected cash flow in U.S. dollars, 0.90 $/€(€2,000) = **$1,800**, into two components. The first component is the cash flow that we'd expect with the expected time-1 *intrinsic* spot FX rate of 0.985 $/€, which we already know is **$1,970**. Denote this expected cash flow $E^*(O_1^\$)$. For the second component, we subtract $E^*(O_1^\$)$ from the actual expected time-1 cash flow, $1,800. That difference, $E(O_1^\$) - E^*(O_1^\$)$, is $1,800 - 1,970 = **-$170**.

The reason for breaking the $1,800 expected cash flow into two components is that we need to discount the components at different rates, because of the different risks. We need to discount the component based on the expected time-1 intrinsic spot FX rate, $1,970, at VPC's cost of capital in U.S. dollars, 11%. We already know that the present value of this component is $1,970/1.11 = **$1,775**. Because the other component, the difference of –$170, is due solely to FX market conditions and not VPC's business operation, we need to discount the difference component at a required rate of return that reflects the systematic FX risk of the euro. So the correct discount rate for the difference component is the required rate of return in U.S. dollars on a one-year risk-free euro asset. We assumed earlier that the currency beta is 0.20 and the $GRP^\$$ is 0.05. Using the global CAPM with $r_f^\$$ = 3.50%, the discount rate for the difference component should be 3.50% + 1% = 4.50%. So the present value of the difference component is –$170/1.045 = **–$163**. Adding the component present values, the present value of the $1,800 expected time-1 cash flow is $1,775 – 163 = **$1,612**.

So when the managers forecast a future spot FX rate that is NOT the expected intrinsic spot FX rate, the present value of the cash flow is NOT the same for the two valuation avenues, even using the time-0 intrinsic spot FX rate. If you convert the U.S. dollar cost of capital to euros, find the present value in euros, and then convert to U.S. dollars using the time-0 intrinsic spot FX rate, you get $1,775. If you find the present value in U.S. dollars by converting the expected euro cash flow to U.S. dollars at the forecasted time-1 spot FX rate, and find the present value of the two components using the component discount rates, you get $1,612.

Let's combine this scenario with a time-0 actual spot FX rate of 0.85 $/€, reflecting an undervalued euro at time 0. We have a situation where managers forecast that the time-0 euro undervaluation will be partially, but not completely, corrected by time 1. Managers forecast that the time-1 spot FX rate will be 0.90 $/€, relative to the expected time-1 intrinsic spot FX rate of 0.985 $/€. Recall that at the time-0 actual spot FX rate of 0.85 $/€, the outlay in U.S. dollars to acquire VPC is $1,615. In the case here where the forecasted time-1 actual spot FX rate is 0.90 $/€, the acquisition's U.S. dollar NPV is negative, $NPV^\$$ = $1,612 – 1,615 = –$3. With the forecasted time-1 spot FX rate equal to the expected intrinsic spot FX rate of 0.985 $/€, we found earlier that the NPV in U.S. dollars is positive, $160.

Extend the previous example of XYZ and DYA. DYA's owners are asking €800,000 for the business. The time-0 actual spot FX rate is 1.80 $/€, whereas the time-0 intrinsic spot FX rate is 1.50 $/€. XYZ's managers believe that the current misvaluation of the euro will not be fully corrected when the time-1 cash flow arrives. Instead, managers forecast a time-1 spot FX rate of 1.65 $/€. (a) Find the NPV in euros of the proposed acquisition. (b) Find the NPV in U.S. dollars of the proposed acquisition.

Answers: (a) The acquisition's $NPV^€$ is the same as before, €903,200 – 800,000 = €103,200. (b) The expected time-1 operating cash flow in U.S. dollars is 1.65 $/€ (€1 million) = $1.65 million. Of this expected cash flow, there is a $1.47 million component based on the expected time-1 intrinsic spot FX rate, and a $0.18 million component that is a forecasted windfall FX gain. Because the currency beta of the euro is 0.20, the discount rate for the FX windfall component is 3% + 0.20(5%) = 4%, using the global CAPM. $V_B^$$ is thus $1.47 million/1.085 + 0.18 million/1.04 = $1.355 million + 0.173 million = $1.528 million. Because $I^$$ is (1.80 $/€)(€800,000) = $1.44 million, $NPV^$$ = $1.528 million – 1.44 million = $0.088 million.

Debate: Foreign Versus Home Currency Approaches

We have seen that the home and foreign currency approaches give equivalent NPVs with intrinsic FX rates, but with any FX misvaluation, at time 0 or forecasted, the home currency approach incorporates the FX misvaluation whereas the foreign currency approach does not. Which approach should you use?

Some think that an investment decision should not include windfall FX gains and losses and thus that the foreign currency NPV gives the correct investment decision. Proponents of this approach make two arguments. The first is that managers do not know enough about FX rates to make useful FX valuations, and so the managers should stick to managing their business instead of trying to estimate FX values.

Second, even if managers could reliably judge FX values, they could better exploit their judgment using a financial market transaction instead of a business investment. To see this point, consider the earlier ABC/VPC scenario where the euro is undervalued at time 0, but forecasted to be correctly valued by time 1. ABC would be better off to invest the $1,615 in a risk-free euro deposit instead of acquiring VPC. ABC would pay $1,615 for an asset that is intrinsically worth $1,900, for an NPV of $285. According to this viewpoint, acquiring VPC, with a U.S. dollar NPV of $160, should be rejected in favor of the euro deposit with an NPV of $285. In other words, why package the business investment together with a currency speculation, when the currency speculation by itself is better?

A different school of thought favors the home currency approach *because* the foreign currency NPV ignores the windfall FX gains/losses. Proponents of this approach argue that if managers have an informed view on FX rates, why should they ignore this information when making investment decisions? Maybe the managers' FX information came from a top-notch FX research organization.

Second, a financial market transaction like a euro deposit is usually not a realistic alternative to a business investment. For one thing, acquiring VPC is consistent with ABC's business, but speculating in a euro deposit is not. That is, currency speculation may be frowned-upon on its own, but may be "OK" if embedded in a business decision. For another thing, managers are likely to want to avoid the volatility that the MTM changes in the euro deposit would create in reported earnings. From ABC's home currency perspective, acquiring VPC adds less value than investing in a euro deposit, but acquiring VPC may still be a more practical way for ABC's managers to add value, given their view that the euro is currently undervalued and their forecast that the current FX misvaluation will soon be corrected.

On one point, there is agreement: If a company wants to manage an overseas investment's FX operating exposure with financial hedging, say with foreign currency debt, this tactic has its own windfall FX change that will tend to offset the windfall FX effects of the investment. It seems plausible that an optimal level of financial hedging would trade-off the hedging benefit of lower financial distress costs with the nonhedging benefit of capturing windfall FX gains. A model of this type is beyond our scope. Another consideration is if the company already has some natural short exposure to the foreign currency that will serve as an operational hedge. If so, then financial hedging of the FX operating exposure of a proposed investment is less needed, and a new project with a predicted windfall FX gain might be acceptable.

The debate is difficult to resolve, because both sides make reasonable points. Assessing whether a spot FX rate is misvalued is difficult even for economists, let alone managers. Yet we often see opinions about currency misvaluation. And both sides make good points about the "bundling" of a corporate investment with FX speculation. Academic researchers have empirically studied whether FDI relates to spot FX rates, but the evidence is inconclusive, particularly on how FDI relates to FX misvaluations.[4]

So the choice is yours: **use the home currency approach if you want to incorporate your view on FX misvaluation in the NPV analysis, or use the foreign currency approach if you want to avoid doing so.** The rest of the chapter addresses the same issues for more general, but also more complicated scenarios.

Forecasting Misvalued FX Rates: Multiperiod Scenario

Until now, we have used a single-period framework to focus on basic issues. Let's now look at the more realistic situation of multiperiod cash flows. Assume again that $X_O^{*\$/€} = 1$ \$/€ and $X_O^{\$/€} = 0.85$ \$/€. Also, for any horizon up to 5 years: the risk-free rate in U.S. dollars is 3.5%, the risk-free rate in euros is 6%, and the currency beta of the euro is 0.20. So for any horizon up to 5 years, the annual expected rate of intrinsic FX change, $E^*(x^{\$/€})$, is −1.50%, and the required return in U.S. dollars on a risk-free euro bond is 4.50%. The expected intrinsic spot FX rates, found using equation (8.2), are shown in Exhibit 8.1.

Now say we forecast that the actual future spot FX rate will converge to the intrinsic spot FX rate in 5 years' time, according to the pattern shown in Exhibit 8.1. Let's find the present value in U.S. dollars of a project that is expected to generate an operating cash flow of €2,000 for each of the next 5 years. Again assume the project's $k_O^\$ = 11\%$ and $\xi_{O€}^\$ = 1$, and so the project's cost of capital in euros is 12.69%, as before. While some might prefer to use a spreadsheet here, the present value in euros of the project's expected cash flows is €2,000/1.1269 + 2,000/1.1269² + 2,000/1.1269³ + 2,000/1.1269⁴ + 2,000/1.1269⁵ = **€7,088**.

Next we use the expected intrinsic spot FX rates and convert the expected euro operating cash flows to U.S. dollars, denoted $E^*(O_N^\$)$ in

Exhibit 8.1. *Five-Year Project Scenario*

N	$E^*(X_N^{\$/€})$	$E(X_N^{\$/€})$	$E^*(O_N^{\$})$	$E(O_N^{\$})$	$E(O_N^{\$}) - E^*(O_N^{\$})$
1	0.985 \$/€	0.90 \$/€	\$1,970	\$1,800	–\$170
2	0.970 \$/€	0.91 \$/€	\$1,940	\$1,820	–\$120
3	0.956 \$/€	0.92 \$/€	\$1,912	\$1,840	–\$72
4	0.941 \$/€	0.93 \$/€	\$1,882	\$1,860	–\$22
5	0.927 \$/€	0.927 \$/€	\$1,854	\$1,854	

Exhibit 8.1. The present value in U.S. dollars of these U.S. dollar operating cash flows is $\$1,970/1.11 + 1,940/1.11^2 + 1,912/1.11^3 + 1,882/1.11^4 + 1,854/1.11^5 = \$7,088$. The present value of the differences, between the actual forecasted cash flows, $E(O_N^{\$})$ in Exhibit 8.1, and $E^*(O_N^{\$})$, is $-\$170/1.045 - 120/1.045^2 - 72/1.045^3 - 22/1.045^4 = -\$359$. So the present value in U.S. dollars of the project's expected operating cash flows is $\$7,088 - 359 = \$6,729$. Note that if the investment outlay for the project is €7,500, the project would have a positive $NPV^{\$}$, $\$6,729 - 0.85 \ \$/€ \ (€7,500) = \$354$, but a negative $NPV^{€}$, $€7,088 - 7,500 = -€412$.

The Eurozone firm DYA expects €1 million per year in operating cash flow for 5 years. XYZ Company, a U.S. firm, is considering acquiring DYA. XYZ estimates that in U.S. dollars, DYA's FX operating exposure to the euro is 1 and the cost of capital is 8.50%. Assume $r_f^{\$} = 3\%$ and $r_f^{€} = 6\%$, the currency beta of the euro is 0.20, the time-0 actual and intrinsic spot FX rates are 1.80 \$/€ and 1.50 \$/€, the global CAPM RA-UIRP condition applies, and $GRP^{\$}$ is 5%. XYZ forecasts that the spot FX rate will gradually converge to the intrinsic spot FX rate by year 5, as follows: $E(X_1^{\$/€}) = 1.70 \ \$/€$; $E(X_2^{\$/€}) = 1.60 \ \$/€$; $E(X_3^{\$/€}) = 1.50 \ \$/€$; $E(X_4^{\$/€}) = 1.40 \ \$/€$. (a) Find DYA's intrinsic business value in euros. (b) Make a table in the format of Exhibit 8.1. (c) Find DYA's intrinsic business value in U.S. dollars.

Answers: (a) $E^*(x^{\$/€}) = 3\% - 6\% + 0.20(5\%) = -2\%$. Using equation (8.1), given $\xi_{O€}^{\$} = 1$, $k_O^{€} = 1.085/(1 - 0.02) - 1 = 0.1071$, or 10.71%. $V_B^{€}$ is €1 million/1.1071 + 1 million/1.1071^2 + 1 million/1.1071^3 + 1 million/1.1071^4 + 1 million/1.1071^5 = €3.723 million.

(b)

N	$E^*(X_N^{\$/\epsilon})$	$E(X_N^{\$/\epsilon})$	$E^*(O_N^{\$})$	$E(O_N^{\$})$	$E(O_N^{\$}) - E^*(O_N^{\$})$
1	1.470 $/€	1.70 $/€	$1.470 m	$1.70 m	$0.230 m
2	1.441 $/€	1.60 $/€	$1.441 m	$1.60 m	$0.159 m
3	1.412 $/€	1.50 $/€	$1.412 m	$1.50 m	$0.088 m
4	1.384 $/€	1.40 $/€	$1.384 m	$1.40 m	$0.016 m
5	1.356 $/€	1.356 $/€	$1.356 m	$1.356 m	

(c) With the expected intrinsic spot FX rates, the present value in U.S. dollars is \$1.47 million/1.085 + 1.441 million/1.085^2 + 1.412 million/1.085^3 + 1.384 million/1.085^4 + 1.356 million/1.085^5 = \$5.585 million. Because 4% is the required return in U.S. dollars on a euro risk-free asset, the present value in U.S. dollars of the windfall cash flow differences is \$0.23 million/1.04 + 0.159 million/1.04^2 + 0.088 million/1.04^3 + 0.016 million/1.04^4 = \$0.46 million. $V_B^{\$}$ = \$5.585 million + 0.46 million = \$6.045 million.

Foreign Currency Cash Flows not Independent of FX Rates

Until now, we have conveniently assumed that the local currency cash flows of an overseas project are independent of FX rate changes, or equivalently that the project has an FX operating exposure of 1 to the foreign currency, from home currency perspective. This assumption makes the analysis relatively easy, because it implies that an expected cash flow measured in the home currency is simply the product of the expected cash flow in the foreign currency and the forecasted spot FX rate. However, if the local currency cash flows of an overseas project are _not_ independent of FX rate changes, we must make an adjustment to the product of the expected cash flow in the foreign currency and the forecasted spot FX rate to find the expected cash flow in the home currency. This adjustment involves a term for the asset's FX exposure and the volatility of the FX rate, as we saw in Chapter 7.

All the results we saw earlier still hold: If the FX rates are correctly valued, the home currency and foreign currency NPVs are equivalent. And if the FX rates are NOT correctly valued, the home currency and foreign currency NPVs are NOT equivalent.

We briefly demonstrate the first point with some example numbers from earlier. AEM is a Eurozone subsidiary with a cost of capital in U.S. dollars of 10% and an FX operating exposure to the euro of **0.75**. Given $E^*(x^{\$/€}) = -1.5\%$ and $\sigma_€ = 0.10$, we found earlier that AEM's cost of capital in euros is 11.93%. Assume AEM expects only one cash flow of €2,000 at time 1. AEM's intrinsic business value in euros is thus €2,000/1.1193 = €1,787. Now assume that the time-0 intrinsic spot FX rate is 1 \$/€, so using equation (8.2), the expected time-1 intrinsic spot FX rate is 1 \$/€(1 − 0.015) = 0.985 \$/€. Using equation (7.1), noting that $\xi_{O€}^{\$} + \xi_{O\$}^{€} = 1$, AEM's expected time-1 cash flow from the U.S. dollar perspective is €2,000 (0.985 \$/€)(1 − 0.25(0.10²)) = \$1,965. AEM's intrinsic business value in U.S. dollars is thus \$1,965/1.10 = \$1,786. So the two intrinsic business values are equivalent at the time-0 intrinsic spot FX rate, except for a small discrepancy the crept in due to the fact that equation (7.1) is an approximation.

In the rest of the section, we continue to deal with an overseas operation with an FX operating exposure to the foreign currency that is not equal to 1, but tackle the more complicated scenario where the foreign currency is forecasted to be misvalued for multiple periods. For this scenario, we use a "short-cut" that involves converting the present value of the expected operating cash flows in euros to U.S. dollars using the time-0 intrinsic spot FX rate.

To establish this "short-cut," note first that if the forecasted future spot FX rates are equal to the expected intrinsic spot FX rates, the present value of a project's future expected cash flows in U.S. dollars may be found directly by first finding the present value of the project's future expected cash flows in the foreign currency, and then converting to U.S. dollars at the time-0 intrinsic spot FX rate, as in equation (8.3). We let $V_B^{*\$}$ denote the present value of an investment's future operating cash flows, measured in U.S. dollars, when the forecasted future FX rates are equal to the expected intrinsic spot FX rates. We'll call $V_B^{*\$}$ the investment's *intrinsic FX business value in the home currency.*

Intrinsic FX Business Value in Home Currency

$$V_B^{*\$} = X_0^{*\$/€}(V_B^€) \tag{8.3}$$

This approach turns out to be general and useful, and is valid even if a project's cash flows in the foreign currency are related to the spot FX rate. For this case, we will find the present value of an overseas project's operating cash flows, measured in the home currency, using the following steps:

Step 1: Convert the (assumed to be known) cost of capital from the home currency to the foreign currency using equation (8.1), and find the intrinsic business value in the foreign currency.

Step 2: Find the intrinsic FX business value in the home currency, using equation (8.3).

Step 3: Find the present value in the home currency of the differences between the cash flows converted at the actual forecasted spot FX rates and the cash flows converted at the expected intrinsic spot FX rates, which we'll show may be done without having to find the expected cash flows in the home currency.

Step 4: Add the results of Step 2 and Step 3 to find the investment's intrinsic business value in the home currency.

For an example, we take a project that will generate 5 years of euro cash flows, with the expected cash flow being €2,000 each year. We assume that the project's cost of capital in U.S. dollars is 11%, and this time that the project's FX operating exposure to the euro is 0.50. That is, $\xi_{O\epsilon}^{\$} = \mathbf{0.50}$. Assume the same FX rate assumptions as in the 5-year example of the previous section, and the volatility of the euro is 0.10. For Step 1, we use equation (8.1) to find the project's cost of capital in euros: $(1.11) = (1 + k_O^{\epsilon})(1 - 0.015) + (0.50 - 1)0.10^2$. So $k_O^{\epsilon} = 0.132$, or 13.2%. Then, we get the intrinsic business value in euros: €$2,000/1.132 + 2,000/1.132^2 + 2,000/1.132^3 + 2,000/1.132^4 + 2,000/1.132^5 = \mathbf{€7,000}$. You can see the impact of the FX operating exposure (and the currency volatility) on the intrinsic business value, all else equal, by comparing this answer to the one in the previous section, €7,088.

For Step 2, we apply equation (8.3) to find the intrinsic FX business value in U.S. dollars, 1 $/€(€7,000) = $7,000. We see Step 3 in Exhibit 8.2. Rather than finding the operating cash flows expected in U.S. dollars for the two sets of FX rate forecasts, we simply multiply each year's spot FX rate difference, between the actual FX rate forecast and the expected intrinsic spot FX rate, times the expected operating cash flow in euros (€2,000 each year) to get the

Exhibit 8.2. Five-Year Project Scenario (Short-Cut)

N	$E^*(X_N^{\$/€})$	$E(X_N^{\$/€})$	$E(X_N^{\$/€}) - E^*(X_N^{\$/€})$	$E(O_N^{\$}) - E^*(O_N^{\$})$
1	0.985 \$/€	0.90 \$/€	–0.085 \$/€	–\$170
2	0.970 \$/€	0.91 \$/€	–0.060 \$/€	–\$120
3	0.956 \$/€	0.92 \$/€	–0.036 \$/€	–\$72
4	0.941 \$/€	0.93 \$/€	–0.011 \$/€	–\$22
5	0.927 \$/€	0.927 \$/€	0	0

differences in U.S. dollars between actual forecasted cash flows and the cash flows for the expected intrinsic spot FX rates.

To finish Step 3, we find the present value of those differences, $-\$170/1.045 - 120/1.045^2 - 72/1.045^3 - 22/1.045^4 = -\$359$, just as we found before. Finally, for Step 4, we find the investment's intrinsic business value in U.S. dollars, $\$7,000 - 359 = \textbf{\$6,641}$.

The Eurozone firm DYA will generate uncertain future operating cash flows in euros for 5 years, expected to be €1 million per year. XYZ Company, a U.S. firm, is considering the acquisition of DYA. XYZ estimates that from the U.S. dollar perspective, DYA's FX operating exposure to the euro is <u>1.50</u> and the cost of capital is 8.50%. Assume $r_f^{\$} = 3\%$ and $r_f^{€} = 6\%$, the currency beta of the euro is 0.20, <u>the volatility of the euro is 0.10</u>, and the time-0 intrinsic and actual spot FX rates are 1.50 \$/€ and 1.80 \$/€, respectively. Assume the global CAPM RA-UIRP condition applies, and $GRP^{\$}$ is 5%. XYZ forecasts that the spot FX rate will gradually converge to the expected intrinsic spot FX rate by year 5, as follows: $E(X_1^{\$/€}) = 1.70$ \$/€; $E(X_2^{\$/€}) = 1.60$ \$/€; $E(X_3^{\$/€}) = 1.50$ \$/€; $E(X_4^{\$/€}) = 1.40$ \$/€. (a) Find DYA's intrinsic business value in euros. (b) Make a table in the format of Exhibit 8.2. (c) Find DYA's intrinsic business value in U.S. dollars.

Answers: (a) $E^*(x^{\$/€}) = 3\% - 6\% + 0.20(5\%) = -2\%$. With equation (8.1) and $\xi_{O€}^{\$} = 1.50$, $k_O^{€} = 1.08/(1 - 0.02) - 1 = 0.102$, or 10.2%. $V_B^{€} = $ €1 million/1.102 + 1 million/1.102^2 + 1 million/1.102^3 + 1 million/1.102^4 + 1 million/1.102^5 = €3.77 million.

(b)

N	$E^*(X_N^{\$/€})$	$E(X_N^{\$/€})$	$E(X_N^{\$/€}) - E^*(X_N^{\$/€})$	$E(O_N^{\$}) - E^*(O_N^{\$})$
1	1.470 \$/€	1.70 \$/€	0.230 \$/€	\$0.230 m
2	1.441 \$/€	1.60 \$/€	0.159 \$/€	\$0.159 m
3	1.412 \$/€	1.50 \$/€	0.088 \$/€	\$0.088 m
4	1.384 \$/€	1.40 \$/€	0.016 \$/€	\$0.016 m
5	1.356 \$/€	1.356 \$/€		

(c) Using equation (8.3), $V_B^{*\$}$ = 1.50 \$/€ (€3.77) = \$5.66 million. Because 4% is the required rate of return in U.S. dollars on a risk-free euro-denominated bond, the present value in U.S. dollars of the differences between the actual forecasted cash flows and those converted with expected intrinsic spot FX rates is \$0.23 million/1.04 + 0.159/1.04^2 + 0.088/1.04^3 + 0.016/1.04^4 = \$0.46 million. So $V_B^{\$}$ = \$5.66 million + 0.46 million = \$6.12 million.

Summary Action Points

- An asset's cost of capital from the perspective of a foreign currency needs to be consistent with the same asset's cost of capital in the home currency.
- The conventional view is that an asset's intrinsic value will be the same in one currency as in another, given the spot FX rate. Similarly, it is often asserted that it is irrelevant whether we analyze an overseas investment's NPV in the home currency or the foreign currency, as long as consistent cross-border cash flow forecasts and costs of capital are used. These assertions are implicitly based on correctly valued FX rates.
- Given an FX misvaluation, the choice of currency perspective of the NPV analysis is relevant, due to expected windfall FX gains or losses.
- The home currency approach to international capital budgeting incorporates the windfall FX gains and losses, whereas the foreign currency approach does not. In this environment, managers' FX valuation and forecasts might affect their overseas investment decisions.

Discussion Questions

1. Discuss situations where managers should consider the level of FX rates in overseas investment analysis.

2. Discuss situations where managers should not consider the level of FX rates in overseas investment analysis.

3. Do you think managers incorporate their FX forecasts into international investment decisions?

4. Do you think managers *should* incorporate their FX forecasts into international investment decisions?

Problems

1. The U.S. firm PVY has estimated the cost of capital for an acquisition target in Spain to be 8% in U.S. dollars. From the euro point of view, the target's operating cash flows have no FX exposure to the U.S. dollar. The global CAPM holds in U.S. dollars, including for the linear approximation RA-UIRP condition. Assume $r_f^\$ = 3.5\%$, $r_f^\euro = 5\%$, $GRP^\$ = 4\%$, the volatility of the euro = 10%, and the currency beta of the euro = 0.20. Find the cost of capital for the Spanish target in euros.

For 2–6: The global CAPM holds in U.S. dollars, including the linear approximation RA-UIRP condition. The U.S. dollar risk-free rate = 3.50%, the Swedish krona risk-free rate = 5.50%, $GRP^\$ = 5\%$, the volatility of the Swedish krona = 0.10, the currency beta of the Swedish krona = 0.28, and the time-0 intrinsic spot FX rate = 6.25 Sk/$.

The U.S. multinational VYP Co. is evaluating a Swedish acquisition target that will generate only a single operating cash flow 1 year from now, expected to be Sk10 million. From the U.S. dollar perspective, the target's FX operating exposure to the Swedish krona is 1. The target's owners are asking Sk 9 million. VYP has estimated the target's cost of capital is 10% in U.S. dollars. VYP forecasts that the future spot FX rate will be the intrinsic spot FX rate.

2. Find the cost of capital for the Swedish target in Swedish kronor.

3. Find the intrinsic business value of the Swedish target in Swedish kronor.

4. Find the intrinsic business value of the Swedish target in U.S. dollars.

5. Find the NPV of the Swedish target in U.S. dollars assuming that the actual spot FX rate is the intrinsic spot FX rate, 6.25 Sk/$.

6. Find the NPV of the Swedish acquisition in U.S. dollars assuming that the krona is overvalued in the time-0 spot FX market and that the actual spot FX rate is 5 Sk/$.

For 7–8: The British firm BGD Ltd. will generate one uncertain British pound operating cash flow, expected to be £1 million at time 1. In U.S. dollars, BGD's FX operating exposure to the British pound is 1 and cost of capital is 10%. XYZ Company, a U.S. multinational, wants to evaluate the acquisition of BGD. Assume the risk-free rates are 3.5% in U.S. dollars and 4% in British pounds, and the currency beta of the British pound is 0.30. Assume the global CAPM RA-UIRP condition with $GRP^\$ = 5\%$. XYZ's managers believe that the time-0 intrinsic spot FX rate is 1.60 $/£. The actual time-0 spot FX rate is 1.50 $/£.

7. XYZ's managers forecast that the time-1 spot FX rate will be the expected intrinsic spot FX rate. (a) What is BGD's intrinsic business value in British pounds? (b) What is the expected time-1 spot FX rate? (c) What is BGD's intrinsic business value in U.S. dollars? (d) Show that the intrinsic business values in British pounds and U.S. dollars are equivalent at the time-0 intrinsic spot FX rate.

8. BGD's owners will sell the company to XYZ for £925,000. (a) For XYZ, what is the acquisition's NPV in British pounds? (b) What is the acquisition's NPV in U.S. dollars?

9. The British firm LVI expects operating cash flows for 5 years of £1 million per year. XYZ Co., a U.S. firm, is considering the acquisition of LVI. XYZ estimates that from the U.S. dollar perspective, LVI's FX operating exposure to the British pound is 1 and the cost of capital is 9.50%. Assume $r_f^\$ = 3\%$, $r_f^£ = 5\%$, the currency beta of the British pound is 0.30, the intrinsic time-0 spot FX rate is 1.60 $/£, and the actual time-0 spot FX rate is 1.40 $/£. Assume the global CAPM RA-UIRP condition with $GRP^\$ = 5\%$. XYZ's managers forecast the spot FX price of the British pound will gradually converge to the intrinsic spot FX rate by year 5, as follows: $E(X_1^{\$/£}) = 1.45$ $/£; $E(X_2^{\$/£}) = 1.50$ $/£; $E(X_3^{\$/£}) = 1.52$ $/£; $E(X_4^{\$/£}) = 1.54$ $/£; $E(X_5^{\$/£}) = E^*(X_5^{\$/£})$. (a) Find LVI's intrinsic business value in British pounds. (b) Make a table in the format of Exhibit 8.1. (c) Find LVI's intrinsic business value in U.S. dollars.

For 10–11: Assume $r_f^\$ = 3\%$, $r_f^\pounds = 5\%$, the currency beta of the British pound is 0.30, the volatility of the British pound is 0.08, the time-0 intrinsic spot FX rate is 1.60 $/£, and the time-0 actual spot FX rate is 1.70 $/£. Assume the global CAPM RA-UIRP condition with $GRP^\$ = 5\%$.

The British firm TXZ Ltd. will generate only one future operating cash flow, an uncertain time-1 British pound operating cash flow expected to be £1 million. LMP Company, a U.S. multinational, wants to evaluate the acquisition of TXZ. LMP estimates that from the U.S. dollar perspective, TXZ's <u>FX operating exposure to the British pound is 1.50</u> and the cost of capital is 10%.

10. LMP's managers forecast that the time-1 spot FX rate will be the intrinsic spot FX rate. (a) What is TXZ's intrinsic business value in British pounds? (b) What is TXZ's intrinsic business value in U.S. dollars?

11. TXZ's owners will sell the company to LMP for £900,000. (a) For LMP, what is the acquisition's NPV in British pounds? (b) What is the acquisition's NPV in U.S. dollars?

12. The British firm LVI will generate uncertain future operating cash flows in British pounds for 5 years, expected to be £1 million per year. XYZ Co. is a U.S. firm considering the acquisition of LVI. XYZ estimates that from the U.S. dollar perspective, LVI's <u>FX operating exposure to the British pound is 1.50,</u> and the cost of capital is 9.50%. XYZ forecasts that the spot FX rate will gradually converge to the intrinsic spot FX rate by year 5, as follows: $E(X_1^{\$/\pounds}) = 1.45$ $/£; $E(X_2^{\$/\pounds}) = 1.50$ $/£; $E(X_3^{\$/\pounds}) = 1.52$ $/£; $E(X_4^{\$/\pounds}) = 1.54$ $/£; $E(X_5^{\$/\pounds}) = E^*(X_5^{\$/\pounds})$. Assume $r_f^\$ = 3\%$, $r_f^\pounds = 5\%$, the currency beta of the British pound is 0.30, the volatility of the British pound is 0.08, and the intrinsic time-0 spot FX rate is 1.60 $/£. Assume the global CAPM RA-UIRP condition with $GRP^\$ = 5\%$. (a) Find LVI's intrinsic business value in British pounds. (b) Find LVI's intrinsic business value in U.S. dollars.

Answers to Problems

1. $E^*(x^{\$/\euro}) = 3.5\% - 5\% + 0.20(4\%) = -0.7\%$. From the U.S. dollar point of view, the FX operating exposure to the euro is 1. So $k_O^\euro = 1.08/(1 - 0.007) - 1 = 0.0876$, or 8.76%.

2. $E^*(x^{\$/Sk}) = 3.50\% - 5.50\% + 0.28(5\%) = -0.60\%$. Using equation (8.1), $k_O^{Sk} = 1.10/(1 - 0.006)) - 1 = 0.1066$, or 10.66%.

3. Sk10 million/1.1066 = Sk9.036 million.

4. Using equation (8.2), the expected time-1 intrinsic spot FX price of the krona is 0.16 \$/Sk(1 − 0.006) = 0.159 \$/Sk. The expected time-1 cash flow, in U.S. dollars, is \$1.59 million. The present value is \$1.59 million/1.10 = \$1.445 million. We get the same intrinsic value of the future cash flows by using equation (8.3): (0.16 \$/Sk) × (Sk9.036 million) = \$1.445 million.

5. $I^\$$ = (Sk 9 million)/(6.25 Sk/\$) = \$1.44 million. $NPV^\$$ = \$1.445 million − 1.44 million = \$0.005 million, or \$5,000.

6. $I^\$$ = (Sk 9 million)/(5 Sk/\$) = \$1.80 million. $NPV^\$$ = \$1.445 million − 1.80 million = −\$0.355 million.

7. (a) $E^*(x^{\$/£})$ = 3.5% − 4% + 0.30(5%) = 1%. Using equation (8.1), given $\xi_{O£}^\$$ = 1, BGD's $k_O^£$ = 1.10/1.01 − 1 = 0.0891, or 8.91%. BGD's $V_B^£$ is £1 million/1.0891 = £0.918 million.

   (b) $E(X_1^{\$/£})$ = $E^*(X_1^{\$/£})$ = 1.60 \$/£(1.01) = 1.616 \$/£.

   (c) Because XYZ forecasts the time-1 spot FX rate to be the expected intrinsic spot FX rate, BGD's $E(O_1^\$)$ = (1.616 \$/£)(£1 million) = \$1.616 million. BGD's $V_B^\$$ is \$1.616 million/1.10 = \$1.469 million.

   (d) At the time-0 intrinsic spot FX rate of 1.60 \$/£, BGD's $V_B^£$ of £0.918 million, is equivalent to its $V_B^\$$ of \$1.469 million, because £0.918 million(1.60 \$/£) = \$1.469 million.

8. (a) £918,000 − 925,000 = −£7000.

   (b) \$1,469,000 − £925,000(1.50 \$/£) = \$81,500.

9. (a) $E^*(x^{\$/£})$ = 3% − 5% + 0.30(5%) = −0.5%. Using equation (8.1), given $\xi_{O£}^\$$ = 1, LVI's $k_O^£$ is 1.095/(1 − 0.005) − 1 = 0.10, or 10%. LVI's $V_B^£$ is £1 million/1.10 + 1 million/1.10² + 1 million/1.10³ + 1 million/1.10⁴ + 1 million/1.10⁵ = £3.79 million.

   (b)

N	$E^*(X_N^{\$/£})$	$E(X_N^{\$/£})$	$E^*(O_N^\$)$	$E(O_N^\$)$	$E(O_N^\$)$ − $E^*(O_N^\$)$
1	1.592 \$/£	1.45 \$/£	\$1.592 m	\$1.45 m	\$0.142 m
2	1.584 \$/£	1.50 \$/£	\$1.584 m	\$1.50 m	\$0.084 m
3	1.576 \$/£	1.52 \$/£	\$1.576 m	\$1.52 m	\$0.056 m
4	1.568 \$/£	1.54 \$/£	\$1.568 m	\$1.54 m	\$0.028 m
5	1.560 \$/£	1.56 \$/£	\$1.560 m	\$1.56 m	

(c) Converting the expected British pound cash flows to U.S. dollars at the expected intrinsic spot FX rates, we get a present value of $1.592 million/1.095 + 1.584 million/1.095^2 + 1.576 million/1.095^3 + 1.568 million/1.095^4 + 1.56 million/1.095^5 = $6.06 million. Or, using equation (8.3), 1.60 $/£(£3.79 million) = $6.06 million. Because 3% + 0.30(5%) = 4.50% is the required rate of return in U.S. dollars on a risk-free pound-denominated bond, the present value in U.S. dollars of the differences between the actual forecasted cash flows and those converted at the expected intrinsic spot FX rates is equal to: $0.142 million/1.045 + 0.084 million/1.045^2 + 0.056 million/1.045^3 + 0.028 million/1.045^4 = $0.29 million. So LVI's $V_B^\$$ is $6.06 million + 0.29 million = $6.35 million.

10. (a) $E^*(x^{\$/£})$ = 3.5% − 4% + 0.30(5%) = 1%. Using equation (8.1), given $\xi_{O£}^\$$ = 1.50, TXZ's $k_O^£$ is (1.10 − 0.50(0.08^2))/1.01 − 1 = 0.0859, or 8.59%. TXZ's $V_B^£$ = £1 million/1.0859 = £0.921 million.

(b) £0.921 million(1.60 $/£) = $1.473 million.

11. (a) £921,000 − 900,000 = £21,000.

(b) $1,473,000 − £900,000(1.70 $/£) = −$57,000.

12. (a) $E^*(x^{\$/£})$ = 3% − 5% + 0.30(5%) = −0.5%. Using equation (8.1), given $\xi_{O£}^\$$ = 1.50, LVI's cost of capital in British pounds is found by solving 1.095 − 0.50($0.08)^2$ = (1 + $k_O^£$)(1 − 0.005); so $k_O^£$ = 1.0918/0.995 − 1 = 0.0973, or 9.73%. LVI's $V_B^£$ = £1 million/1.0973 + 1 million/1.0973^2 + 1 million/1.0973^3 + 1 million/1.0973^4 + 1 million/1.0973^5 = £3.82 million.

(b) If the expected British pound cash flows are converted to U.S. dollars at the expected intrinsic spot FX rates, we use equation (8.3) to get a present value of (1.60 $/£)(£3.82 million) = $6.11 million. Because 3% + 0.30(5%) = 4.50% is the required rate of return in U.S. dollars on a risk-free pound-denominated bond, the present value in U.S. dollars of the differences between the actual forecasted cash flows and those converted at the expected intrinsic spot FX rates is equal to: $0.142 million/1.045 + 0.084 million/1.045^2 + 0.056 million/1.045^3 + 0.028 million/1.045^4 = $0.23 million. So LVI's $V_B^\$$ = $6.11 million + 0.23 million = $6.40 million.

CASE

New Plant for Houston Marine Electronics

Sitting behind his desk, Ben Nunnally told Reid Click, "We need to do an analysis of HME's request for more plant capacity." Their meeting was taking place in May 2013 in Nunnally's office at Adventure and Recreation Technologies, Inc. (ART), in Boise, Idaho. Nunnally had been the company's chief financial officer and treasurer since before the company went public in the 1980s, and Click had been with the company for 5 years as an assistant treasurer.

ART is the parent company of three businesses: (1) Divemaster scuba equipment; (2) Houston Marine Electronics (HME) sonar equipment; and (3) Watercraft canoes and kayaks. ART's strategy across its three business segments is to use sophisticated research and cutting-edge technology to create the world's best-known brands of outdoor recreational products.

The previous week, the HME division's CEO, William "King" Kennedy, and CFO, Stafford Johnson, had traveled to the ART headquarters in Boise and made a presentation to Nunnally and Click. The presentation outlined the increasing orders from Australia for HME's sonar equipment and the lack of production capacity to keep up with the growing demand. HME had several plants in the United States, and all were producing at full capacity. HME had recently signed a 2-year contract with the Australian boat builder Gold Coast Ships, and HME's operations managers were already straining to stay on schedule. In the meantime, HME's head of sales, Steve Magee, reported that a number of other Australian and New Zealand boat builders had expressed a keen interest in putting HME's sonar equipment in their boats. Simply put, Kennedy and Johnson were letting the ART corporate officers know that HME needed more production capacity. The HME executives also knew that

ART had accumulated about $60 million in cash, some of which could be used for the capital expenditure.

Nunnally continued talking to Click, "Magee is optimistic that HME's sonar units will penetrate the Australian market quickly. He told me that he expects Australian **revenues of A$4 million next year, A$8 million the year after, and then A$10 million each year after that.**"

Nunnally continued, "There is no doubt that HME needs an additional plant dedicated entirely to the Australian business. I am pretty sure that the numbers will support the overseas expansion as a sound business move. Still, I am asking you to prepare a formal capital budgeting analysis. For the capacity that HME needs, we'd need **to invest $12 million for a plant in the United States.** And we know from our present operations that the **annual operating costs in a U.S. plant are about 75% of revenue, for an operating cash flow margin of 25%.**"

Nunnally added, "One thing on the table is the plant location. The "old man" (ART's CEO, John Griffin) wants us to consider three location options: 1) The United States; 2) Australia; and 3) Malaysia. As you know, our Divemaster business has a facility in Malaysia that has helped trim that division's operating costs. You can call the Divemaster CFO, Alain Krapl, and get some useful information for the analysis."

Click returned to his office and immediately began to think about the project. He decided to perform the capital budgeting analysis in U.S. dollars. He understood the three inputs he needed for the NPV were: (a) the expected operating cash flow stream; (b) the discount rate; and (c) the investment outlay.

Expected Operating Cash Flows for the Australian Business

Click looked first at the option of building a new facility in Australia. At the time, the spot FX rate was 1 $/A$. Based on the *Economist* magazine's Big Mac approach to purchasing power parity, Click estimated that the Australian dollar was 5% overvalued relative to the long-run intrinsic spot FX rate. So he assumed that if a plant cost $12 million in the United States, a 5% higher **outlay for a plant in Australia would be $12.60 million**. He also assumed that an Australian plant would operate on the same operating cash flow margin as a U.S. plant, so operating costs would be 75% of revenues. Thus, using Magee's revenue forecast, Click expected the business's **operating cash flows would be A$1 million next year, A$2 million the year after, and then A$2.5 million each year after that.**

Next, Click wanted to convert the operating cash flow forecast from Australian dollars to U.S. dollars. Click observed that the 10-year government bond yields were 1.90% for the United States and 3.20% for Australia, and the sovereign credit default swap (CDS) rates were 0.29% for the United States and 0.38% for Australia. Click wanted to estimate the currency risk premium, so he used monthly data for 2007–2011 to estimate a currency beta of the Australian dollar of 0.41. Using an assumed market risk premium of 5%, Click estimated an expected rate of intrinsic FX change of the Australian dollar of **0.84% per year.** For lack of any better idea, he assumed that Australian dollar was correctly valued relative to short-run financial market conditions. He thus forecasted that the spot FX rate would be 1 $/A$(1.0084) = 1.0084 $/A$ next year, (1.0084 $/A$) (1.0084) = 1.0169 $/A$ the following year, and so forth. (Q1)

Click had no reason to expect any economic effects of FX changes on the revenues that would be generated in Australia, so from the U.S. dollar perspective, the operating cash flows would have an FX operating exposure to the Australian dollar of 1. Based on the FX forecast, Click found the expected operating cash flows in U.S. dollars: A$1 million(1.0084 $/A$) = **$1.0084 million for year 1**; A$2 million(1.0169 $/A$) = **$2.0338 million for year 2**; A$2.50(1.0254 $/A$) = **$2.5635 million for year 3**, and 0.84% per year growth after that. (Q2)

Cost of Capital and NPV for the Australian Business

Click had recently helped estimate ART's overall cost of capital. He had successfully argued that ART's equity beta should be estimated relative to the world index (measured in U.S. dollars) and not a U.S. stock index. Using historical monthly equity rates of return for 2007–2011, Click had estimated ART's global equity beta to be 1.28 (versus a local equity beta of 1.43 relative to the S&P 500 index.) This relatively high beta estimate is consistent with the notion that recreational products are "luxuries" that have a relatively high income elasticity of demand. At the other end of the spectrum, companies that sell "necessities" with low income elasticity of demand, such as food and basic apparel, tend to have low betas. During 2007–2011, ART had gradually paid off all of its $60 million in debt and accumulated $60 million in cash. Click reasoned that because ART's net debt had averaged about zero during 2007–2011, he was comfortable with using **1.28 for ART's operating beta.** (Q3)

Click knew that he could not just assume ART's overall operating beta estimate of 1.28 is valid for an operation in Australia. He decided to use two approaches to estimating the Australian business's operating beta. The first approach is the Lessard country beta method. He estimated **an Australian country beta of 0.63** (in U.S. dollars versus the world index). Click was confident that ART was a reasonable choice for a U.S. proxy firm for the Australian sonar business. Using the Lessard country beta method, Click estimated the operating beta of a new HME operation in Australia would be 0.806. (Q4)

Click's wanted to use an Australian proxy company for the second approach. Searching on "Australia recreational product companies," he decided to use Fleetwood Corp, Ltd., a maker of recreational vehicles and related products. After downloading Fleetwood's monthly adjusted stock prices in Australian dollars for 2007–2011 from Yahoo Finance, Click estimated Fleetwood's equity beta (in U.S. dollars) versus the world index was 0.80. Fleetwood's net debt was a negligible number, so Click's estimate of Fleetwood's operating beta in U.S. dollars was 0.80. (Q5)

The closeness of the two operating beta estimates gave Click the confidence to move forward with a single estimate of **operating beta for the Australian business, 0.80**. He assumed: (a) a global risk premium of 5%; and (b) a U.S. dollar risk-free rate of 2.60%, calculated as the difference between the 30-year Treasury yield of 2.89% and the U.S. sovereign CDS rate, 0.29%. (Click preferred to use the 30-year Treasury yield, 2.89%, for the risk-free rate when estimating a cost of capital, but use the 10-year Treasury yield, 1.90%, when estimating the expected rate of intrinsic FX change.) Click added the 0.38% Australian sovereign CDS spread, assuming the business's political risk exposure is 1. He estimated a **cost of capital for the Australian business, in U.S. dollars, of 6.98%**. (Q6)

Finally, Click needed to estimate the expected longevity of the sonar business in Australia. He thought, "Tough question. Some unforeseen technology or competitor could knock us out anytime." He decided to be conservative and base the NPV analysis on **10 years** of expected operating cash flows. He calculated that if the new plant were located in Australia, the **NPV in U.S. dollars would be $3.86 million**. (Q7)

NPV if Plant is in the United States

A plant in the United States would have two advantages relative to one in Australia. First, the cost to build would be only $12 million. Second, the operating cost per unit, viewed in U.S. dollars, would be stable for a U.S. plant but would be expected to increase at 0.84% per year for an Australian plant. For the projected output, the U.S. plant's projected operating costs would be $3 million for year 1, $6 million for year 2, and $7.5 million for year 3 and beyond.

Of course, shipping would cost more, but Click ignored this relatively minor cost. More significantly, producing in the United States instead of Australia would mean that HME would <u>not</u> be practicing operational hedging, and so would imply more risk. How much more <u>systematic</u> risk depends on the FX operating exposure to the Australian dollar and the currency beta of the Australian dollar.

For U.S. production, Click estimated an **FX operating exposure to the Australian dollar of 4**. He based this estimate on HME's operating margin of 25% and simple "what if" thinking: If the Australian dollar depreciates by 10% and so revenue measured in U.S. dollars drops by 10%, say from $100 to $90, the operating cash flow would drop by 40%, from $25 to $15. Considering the higher FX operating exposure, Click estimated an **operating beta of 2.03** with U.S. production, which implied a cost of capital of **12.75%**. Click saw that with the Australian dollar's high currency beta, 0.41, the big difference in FX operating exposure made a big difference in the operating beta. He calculated an NPV of **$2.04 million**. (Q8)

NPV if Plant is in Malaysia

Click turned his attention to the Malaysian plant option. At the time, the spot FX rate was 3 RM/$. Based on the *Economist* magazine's Big Mac approach to purchasing power parity, Click estimated that the Malaysian ringgit was about 40% underlined relative to the long-run intrinsic spot FX rate. So he assumed that if the plant cost $12 million in the United States, it would cost 40% less for same capacity in Malaysia, and the **investment for a Malaysian plant would be $7.20 million**. Click also expected the operating costs would be 40% lower, from the U.S. dollar point of view. On the basis of the U.S. plant's projected operating costs of $3 million for year 1, $6 million for year 2, and $7.5 million for year 3 and beyond, Click forecasted the operating costs in Malaysian ringgits: **RM 5.4 million in FY 2014, RM 10.8 million in FY 2015, and RM 13.5 million in the subsequent years**.

Next, Click wanted to convert the Malaysian ringgit operating cost forecast to U.S. dollars. Click observed that the 10-year government bond yields were 1.90% for the United States and 3.05% for Malaysia. The sovereign CDS rates were 0.29% for the United States and 0.79% for Malaysia. Click wanted to estimate the currency risk premium, so he used monthly data for 2007–2011 to estimate a currency beta of the ringgit of 0.10. Using an assumed market risk premium of 5%, Click estimated an expected rate of intrinsic FX change of the ringgit of –0.15% per year. But Click was not comfortable with forecasting a depreciation of a currency that was already 40% undervalued based on purchasing power. So he omitted an FX trend and assumed the spot FX rate would oscillate around 3 RM/$ for the next 10 years. (Q9)

With Malaysian production, ART's FX operating exposure to the Australian dollar would still be 4, and the FX operating exposure to the ringgit would be –3. Click based this estimate on HME's operating margin of 25% and simple "what if" thinking: Given revenue of $100, if the ringgit appreciates by 10% and so operating costs measured in U.S. dollars rise by 10%, from $75 to $82.5, the operating cash flow in U.S. dollars would drop by 30%, from $25 to $17.5. Based on the estimated FX operating exposure to the ringgit, Click computed an **operating beta of 1.73**.

Click added a political risk premium of 0.79%, based on the Malaysian sovereign CDS rate, and assumed the operation's political risk exposure to be the country's average, which is 1. He calculated the cost of capital would be **12.04%**, lower than with U.S. production despite the political risk premium. Click calculated an NPV in U.S. dollars of **$22.15 million**. (Q10)

Click thought, "Wow, producing in Malaysia makes a big difference in the NPV." He called the Divemaster CFO, Alain Krapl, to get some feedback. Krapl said that the operating costs of the Malaysian plant are lower than for a comparable U.S. plant, but not by 40%. He suggested that Click assume the outlay and the operating costs would be lower than in the United States by 25%, which was a number in line with Divemaster's experience. Click calculated an alternative NPV of **$14.79 million**.

Krapl added, "Malaysia has one of the fastest growing economies in Asia, and the government's goal is developed nation status by 2020. So the operating costs and the ringgit could both rise in the future. And "old man" Griffin and your boss Nunnally know all this because I told them in a recent meeting. You might also see how a 1% per year increase in operating costs and a 1% per year appreciation of the ringgit would affect your NPV." Click calculated an alternative NPV of **$11.82 million**. (Q11)

Click was ready to write his report. But then he read on the Internet that legendary currency speculator George Soros was predicting a 15% drop in the Australian dollar in the very near future. Click thought, "If Soros is correct, the Australian dollar is overvalued, and the short-run intrinsic spot FX rate, consistent with the financial markets, is only 0.85 $/A$." He decided to prepare an additional analysis based on this possibility. He assumed that the drop would come after the investment outlay was made for the plant, but before the first operating cash flow would arrive. Click calculated a new NPV for the Australian plant option of **$1.39 million**. If the plant is in the United States, the new NPV is **–$5.46 million**. For the Malaysian plant option, the NPV for the "what if" case of a 25% cost reduction and a 2% growth rate in operating costs (in U.S. dollars) is **$4.07 million**. (Q12)

Questions (Read Chapters 5–8 First!)

1. How did Click estimate 0.84% per year for the expected rate of intrinsic FX change for the Australian dollar? Use data in Appendix II to replicate the estimate of 0.41 for the Australian dollar's currency beta.

2. How would the analysis change if the Australian dollar revenues were subject to FX economic exposure?

3. Use data in Appendix I to estimate ART's equity betas relative to the world index and the S&P index. Explain why ART's operating beta estimate is the same as its equity beta estimate.

4. Show how Click calculated the operating beta estimate of 0.806. Use data in Appendix I to replicate the Australia country beta estimate of 0.63.

5. Use data in Appendix I to replicate Fleetwood's equity beta estimate of 0.80.

6. Show how Click found the cost of capital estimate of 6.98%. What would be the cost of capital expressed in Australian dollars?

7. Show how Click found the NPV of $3.86 million. If Click had done an analysis using the foreign currency approach to international capital budgeting, the NPV in Australian dollars should be equivalent, because the spot FX rate, 1 $/A$, is assumed to be equal to the short-run intrinsic spot FX rate. Show that the NPV in Australian dollars is indeed equivalent, A$3.86 million.

8. Show how Click got the operating beta of 2.03 and the cost of capital of 12.75%. Show how Click found the NPV of $2.04 million.

9. How did Click estimate –0.15% per year for the expected rate of intrinsic FX change for the ringgit? Use data in Appendix II to replicate the estimate of 0.10 for the ringgit's currency beta.

10. Show how Click estimated the operating beta of 1.73 and the cost of capital of 12.04%. Why is the cost of capital lower than for U.S. production? Show how Click found the NPV of $22.15 million.

11. Show how Click found the alternative NPVs: $14.79 million and $11.82 million.

12. Show how Click calculated the new NPVs for the Soros' prediction scenario. For the Australian plant option, show that the NPV is not equal to the NPV in U.S. dollars using the foreign currency approach to international capital budgeting.

Appendix I

Date	ART Rtn	S&P Rtn	World Rtn$	All Ordinaries A$	All Ordinaries $	All Ordinaries Rtn$	Fleetwood A$	Fleetwood $	Fleetwood Rtn$
11/30/2006				5644	4356		4.89	3.77	
12/29/2006	0.004	0.013	0.020	5758	4525	0.039	4.96	3.90	0.033
1/31/2007	−0.003	0.014	0.012	5817	4558	0.007	5.67	4.44	0.140
2/28/2007	−0.015	−0.022	−0.005	5979	4676	0.026	5.68	4.44	0.000
3/30/2007	0.011	0.010	0.018	6158	4878	0.043	5.82	4.61	0.038
4/30/2007	0.030	0.043	0.043	6342	5239	0.074	6.17	5.10	0.106
5/31/2007	0.001	0.033	0.028	6311	5205	−0.007	5.51	4.54	−0.108
6/29/2007	0.062	−0.018	−0.008	6188	5207	0.000	5.94	5.00	0.100
7/31/2007	0.149	−0.032	−0.022	6248	5412	0.039	6.17	5.34	0.069
8/31/2007	−0.185	0.013	−0.001	6581	5472	0.011	6.33	5.26	−0.015
9/28/2007	0.145	0.036	0.046	6779	5724	0.046	7.01	5.92	0.125
10/31/2007	0.011	0.015	0.030	6594	5926	0.035	7.02	6.31	0.066
11/30/2007	0.064	−0.044	−0.042	6421	5779	−0.025	6.96	6.26	−0.007
12/31/2007	−0.035	−0.009	−0.013	5697	4974	−0.139	6.18	5.40	−0.139
1/31/2008	−0.176	−0.061	−0.079	5675	4998	0.005	5.81	5.12	−0.052
2/29/2008	−0.002	−0.035	−0.006	5410	4923	−0.015	5.6	5.10	−0.004
3/31/2008	−0.077	−0.006	−0.010	5657	5229	0.062	6.11	5.65	0.108
4/30/2008	−0.064	0.048	0.051	5774	5369	0.027	6.62	6.16	0.090
5/30/2008	−0.002	0.011	0.015	5333	5060	−0.058	6.28	5.96	−0.032
6/30/2008	−0.023	−0.086	−0.083	5053	4811	−0.049	6.05	5.76	−0.033
7/31/2008	0.008	−0.010	−0.025	5216	5026	0.045	6.24	6.01	0.044
8/29/2008	0.016	0.012	−0.014	4631	4101	−0.184	6.25	5.53	−0.080
9/30/2008	−0.212	−0.091	−0.127	3983	3281	−0.200	4.39	3.62	−0.346
10/31/2008	−0.337	−0.169	−0.210	3673	2543	−0.225	2.93	2.03	−0.439
11/28/2008	−0.172	−0.075	−0.067	3659	2404	−0.055	2.58	1.70	−0.165
12/31/2008	−0.195	0.008	0.032	3478	2327	−0.032	2.56	1.71	0.010
1/30/2009	0.362	−0.086	−0.092	3297	2244	−0.036	3.09	2.10	0.228
2/27/2009	−0.364	−0.110	−0.108	3532	2298	0.024	4.23	2.75	0.308

(Continued)

(Continued)

Date	ART Rtn	S&P Rtn	World Rtn$	All Ordinaries A$	$	Rtn$	Fleetwood A$	$	Rtn$
3/31/2009	0.046	0.085	0.073	3745	2488	0.083	4.73	3.14	0.142
4/30/2009	0.255	0.094	0.106	3813	2725	0.095	4.89	3.49	0.112
5/29/2009	−0.022	0.053	0.087	3948	3010	0.105	4.48	3.42	−0.023
6/30/2009	−0.111	0.000	−0.005	4250	3412	0.134	4.92	3.95	0.157
7/31/2009	0.187	0.074	0.081	4484	3599	0.055	5.93	4.76	0.205
8/31/2009	0.491	0.034	0.040	4739	3959	0.100	6.95	5.81	0.220
9/30/2009	−0.077	0.036	0.039	4647	3998	0.010	6.01	5.17	−0.109
10/30/2009	−0.028	−0.020	−0.018	4716	4267	0.067	5.9	5.34	0.032
11/30/2009	0.086	0.057	0.040	4883	4485	0.051	6.35	5.83	0.093
12/31/2009	0.028	0.018	0.018	4597	4147	−0.075	6.4	5.77	−0.010
1/29/2010	0.086	−0.037	−0.042	4651	4239	0.022	6.48	5.91	0.023
2/26/2010	0.015	0.029	0.014	4893	4338	0.023	7.41	6.57	0.112
3/31/2010	0.054	0.059	0.060	4834	4405	0.015	7.83	7.14	0.086
4/30/2010	0.120	0.015	0.000	4454	4124	−0.064	7.21	6.68	−0.064
5/28/2010	0.131	−0.082	−0.101	4325	3785	−0.082	7.57	6.63	−0.008
6/30/2010	−0.218	−0.054	−0.035	4507	3847	0.016	7.97	6.80	0.027
7/30/2010	0.132	0.069	0.078	4439	3880	0.008	8.25	7.21	0.060
8/31/2010	−0.218	−0.047	−0.038	4637	4179	0.077	9.4	8.47	0.175
9/30/2010	0.288	0.088	0.089	4733	4423	0.058	10.46	9.77	0.154
10/29/2010	0.114	0.037	0.037	4676	4590	0.038	10.53	10.34	0.058
11/30/2010	−0.093	−0.002	−0.022	4847	4799	0.045	11.12	11.01	0.065
12/31/2010	−0.033	0.065	0.071	4850	4809	0.002	11.89	11.79	0.071
1/31/2011	0.216	0.023	0.022	4924	4913	0.022	11.52	11.49	−0.025
2/28/2011	0.014	0.032	0.034	4929	4971	0.012	10.63	10.72	−0.067
3/31/2011	−0.016	−0.001	−0.010	4899	4952	−0.004	9.75	9.85	−0.081
4/29/2011	0.092	0.028	0.042	4789	5062	0.022	9.58	10.13	0.028
5/31/2011	−0.039	−0.014	−0.021	4660	4985	−0.015	9.94	10.63	0.050
6/30/2011	0.073	−0.018	−0.016	4501	4772	−0.043	10.04	10.65	0.001
7/29/2011	0.041	−0.021	−0.018	4370	4708	−0.013	9.91	10.68	0.003
8/31/2011	−0.113	−0.057	−0.073	4070	4276	−0.092	10.32	10.84	0.015

(Continued)

(Continued)

Date	ART Rtn	S&P Rtn	World Rtn$	All Ordinaries A$	All Ordinaries $	All Ordinaries Rtn$	Fleetwood A$	Fleetwood $	Fleetwood Rtn$
9/30/2011	−0.028	−0.072	−0.090	4361	4488	0.050	11.16	11.49	0.060
10/31/2011	0.209	0.108	0.098	4185	4235	−0.056	10.89	11.02	−0.041
11/30/2011	−0.113	−0.005	−0.025	4111	4160	−0.018	10.92	11.05	0.003
12/30/2011	−0.069	0.009	−0.001	4155	4209	0.012	11.14	11.29	0.021

Appendix II

Date	World Return	$/A$	A$ FX Return	RM/$	RM FX Return
11/30/2006		0.772		3.655	
12/29/2006	0.020	0.786	0.018	3.565	0.025
1/31/2007	0.012	0.784	−0.003	3.519	0.013
2/28/2007	−0.005	0.782	−0.002	3.508	0.003
3/30/2007	0.018	0.792	0.013	3.507	0.000
4/30/2007	0.043	0.826	0.043	3.456	0.015
5/31/2007	0.028	0.825	−0.002	3.422	0.010
6/29/2007	−0.008	0.842	0.020	3.447	−0.007
7/31/2007	−0.022	0.866	0.029	3.449	0.000
8/31/2007	−0.001	0.831	−0.040	3.487	−0.011
9/28/2007	0.046	0.844	0.015	3.482	0.001
10/31/2007	0.030	0.899	0.064	3.386	0.028
11/30/2007	−0.042	0.900	0.001	3.360	0.008
12/31/2007	−0.013	0.873	−0.030	3.347	0.004
1/31/2008	−0.079	0.881	0.009	3.278	0.021
2/29/2008	−0.006	0.910	0.033	3.231	0.014
3/31/2008	−0.010	0.924	0.016	3.186	0.014
4/30/2008	0.051	0.930	0.006	3.165	0.006
5/30/2008	0.015	0.949	0.020	3.217	−0.016
6/30/2008	−0.083	0.952	0.004	3.262	−0.014

(Continued)

(*Continued*)

Date	World Return	$/A$	A$ FX Return	RM/$	RM FX Return
7/31/2008	−0.025	0.964	0.012	3.257	0.002
8/29/2008	−0.014	0.886	−0.081	3.329	−0.022
9/30/2008	−0.127	0.824	−0.070	3.451	−0.035
10/31/2008	−0.210	0.693	−0.159	3.527	−0.022
11/28/2008	−0.067	0.657	−0.051	3.603	−0.021
12/31/2008	0.032	0.669	0.018	3.560	0.012
1/30/2009	−0.092	0.681	0.017	3.574	−0.004
2/27/2009	−0.108	0.650	−0.044	3.633	−0.016
3/31/2009	0.073	0.664	0.021	3.688	−0.015
4/30/2009	0.106	0.715	0.076	3.616	0.020
5/29/2009	0.087	0.762	0.067	3.539	0.022
6/30/2009	−0.005	0.803	0.053	3.524	0.004
7/31/2009	0.081	0.803	−0.001	3.557	−0.009
8/31/2009	0.040	0.835	0.041	3.528	0.008
9/30/2009	0.039	0.860	0.030	3.508	0.006
10/30/2009	−0.018	0.905	0.052	3.417	0.027
11/30/2009	0.040	0.919	0.015	3.395	0.006
12/31/2009	0.018	0.902	−0.018	3.426	−0.009
1/29/2010	−0.042	0.911	0.010	3.395	0.009
2/26/2010	0.014	0.887	−0.027	3.425	−0.009
3/31/2010	0.060	0.911	0.028	3.340	0.026
4/30/2010	0.000	0.926	0.016	3.222	0.037
5/28/2010	−0.101	0.875	−0.055	3.265	−0.013
6/30/2010	−0.035	0.854	−0.025	3.272	−0.002
7/30/2010	0.078	0.874	0.024	3.217	0.017
8/31/2010	−0.038	0.901	0.031	3.164	0.017
9/30/2010	0.089	0.934	0.037	3.117	0.015
10/29/2010	0.037	0.982	0.051	3.106	0.003
11/30/2010	−0.022	0.990	0.009	3.115	−0.003
12/31/2010	0.071	0.992	0.001	3.138	−0.007
1/31/2011	0.022	0.998	0.006	3.075	0.020

(*Continued*)

(*Continued*)

Date	World Return	$/A$	A$ FX Return	RM/$	RM FX Return
2/28/2011	0.034	1.009	0.011	3.050	0.008
3/31/2011	−0.010	1.011	0.002	3.040	0.003
4/29/2011	0.042	1.057	0.046	3.017	0.008
5/31/2011	−0.021	1.070	0.012	3.017	0.000
6/30/2011	−0.016	1.060	−0.009	3.038	−0.007
7/29/2011	−0.018	1.077	0.016	3.000	0.013
8/31/2011	−0.073	1.050	−0.025	2.989	0.003
9/30/2011	−0.090	1.029	−0.020	3.069	−0.026
10/31/2011	0.098	1.012	−0.017	3.149	−0.025
11/30/2011	−0.025	1.012	0.000	3.155	−0.002
12/30/2011	−0.001	1.013	0.001	3.166	−0.004

Notes

Chapter 1

1. See O'Brien (2013).
2. See Bergbrant, Campbell, and Hunter (2013).
3. See Pettit (2003).
4. See Adler and Dumas (1984).
5. The Finning scenario is described in Millman (1990).
6. This hypothetical scenario is adapted from Godfrey and Espinosa (1996).
7. See Pringle (1991).
8. See Maloney (1990) and Dhanani (2003).
9. See O'Brien (2010).
10. For further analysis of competitive FX exposure, see O'Brien (1998, 2010), and the references therein, plus Shapiro (1975) and Friberg and Ganslandt (2007).
11. See Adler and Jorion (1992).
12. See Oxelheim and Wihlborg (1995).
13. See Garner and Shapiro (1984).

Chapter 2

1. See Bates, Kahle, and Stulz (2009).
2. See Miller and Modigliani (1963) and Miller (1977).
3. Even if we considered debt tax shield value, there does not need to be a tax term in the levering/unlevering equation (2.2). Justification for this approach is in Miles and Ezzell (1980).
4. Bonini, Dallocchio, Raimbourg, and Salvi (2012).
5. An example is the British mining company in Dhanani (2003).
6. See Dufey and Srinivasulu (1983) and Froot, Scharfstein, and Stein (1994).
7. See Lewent and Kearney (1990).
8. For useful discussions see Aggarwal and Soenen (1989); Maloney (1990); and Allayannis, Ihrig, and Weston (2001).

Chapter 3

1. See Bartram, Brown, and Minton (2010).
2. See the survey by Graham and Harvey (2001).

3. See Allayannis and Ofek (2001); Kedia and Mozumdar (2003); and Keloharju and Niskanen (2001).
4. See McBrady, Mortal, and Schill (2010).
5. The Vulcan Materials case is in Garner and Shapiro (1984).
6. Aabo, Hansen, and Muradoglu (2013) find that Danish firms prefer to hedge FX accounting exposure over FX operating exposure.

Chapter 4

1. See Munro (2011).
2. See Kester and Allen (1991).

Chapter 5

1. See Brotherson, Eades, Harris, and Higgins (2013).
2. See Da, Guo, and Jagannathan (2012).
3. See Welch (2009).
4. See Brotherson, Eades, Harris, and Higgins (2013).
5. See Luehrman and Heilprin (2009); Welch (2009); Donaldson, Kamstra, and Kramer (2010); and Fernandez, Aguirreamalloa, and Avendaño (2012).
6. Campbell, Serfaty-de Medeiros, and Viceira (2010).
7. See Stulz (1995).
8. Bruner, Li, Kritzman, Myrgren, and Page (2008).
9. See Bryan (2007) and Maldonado and Saunders (1983).
10. See Baruch, Karolyi, and Lemmon (2007). For trends in cross-listing, see Halling, Pagano, Randl, and Zechner (2008).
11. For dual-listed shares, see Froot and Dabora (1999) and de Jong, Rosenthal, and Van Dijk (2009). For Chinese A-shares and B-shares, see Mei, Scheinkman, and Xiong (2009). Also see Arquette, Brown, and Burdekin (2008).
12. See Lustig and Verdelhan (2011).
13. Because the risk-free euro asset's return in euros is certain, we can apply equation (5.1b) to get that the linear approximation to the actual U.S. dollar rate of return on the risk-free euro asset is $R_{ef}^{\$} = r_f^{€} + x^{\$/€}$, where $r_f^{€}$ denotes the risk-free rate in euros. Taking expected values, we get $E(R_{ef}^{\$}) = r_f^{€} + E(x^{\$/€})$. Using financial market equilibrium constructs, we thus have that the required rate of return in U.S. dollars on a risk-free euro asset, $k_{ef}^{\$}$, is equal to the euro risk-free rate, $r_f^{€}$, plus the expected rate of intrinsic FX change of the euro, $E^*(x^{\$/€})$. That is, $k_{ef}^{\$} = r_f^{€} + E^*(x^{\$/€})$. We now equate this definition of $k_{ef}^{\$}$ with the $k_{ef}^{\$}$ we get by applying the global CAPM, $k_{ef}^{\$} = r_f^{\$} + \beta_e^{\$}(GRP^{\$})$. With some rearranging of terms, the result is the risk-adjusted UIRP relationship in equation (5.3), which is in a linear approximation, percentage form.

Chapter 6

1. See Bank of America Roundtable on Evaluating and Financing Foreign Direct Investment (1996).
2. This point is made in Pettit, Ferguson, and Gluck (1999) and Block (2003).
3. Weston (1973) pioneered the idea.
4. Desai (2006) uses this formula in his Harvard case on the cost of capital for AES Corporation.
5. See Reyent (2008).
6. See Perold (2004).
7. See Lessard (1996). The only difference is that the betas in the original Lessard analysis are local, relative to the U.S. market index, whereas the betas in equation (6.2) are global, relative to the global market index (in U.S. dollars).
8. See Abuaf (2011).
9. See Damodaran (2003).
10. See Damodaran, op cit. Equation (6.3) adapts ideas from diverse places in the literature, such as Zenner and Akaydin (2002); Godfrey and Espinosa (1996); and Harvey (2000).

Chapter 7

1. To formally derive equation (7.1), start with the definition, $O_N^{\$} = O_N^{\epsilon} \cdot X_N^{\$/\epsilon}$. Taking expectations, $E(O_N^{\$}) = E(O_N^{\epsilon}) \cdot E(X_N^{\$/\epsilon}) + cov(O_N^{\epsilon}, X_N^{\$/\epsilon})$. The covariance term is equal to $E(O_N^{\epsilon}) \cdot E(X_N^{\$/\epsilon})[cov(O_N^{\epsilon}/E(O_N^{\epsilon}) - 1, X_N^{\$/\epsilon}/E(X_N^{\$/\epsilon}) - 1)]$, where the new covariance term in the brackets is the covariance between the percentage deviation of O_N^{ϵ} from $E(O_N^{\epsilon})$, and the percentage deviation of $X_N^{\$/\epsilon}$ from $E(X_N^{\$/\epsilon})$. We use an Ito transformation, $X_N^{\$/\epsilon}/E(X_N^{\$/\epsilon}) - 1 = -(X_N^{\epsilon/\$}/E(X_N^{\epsilon/\$}) - 1)$, which says the percentage deviation of the exchange rate from its expectation in $\$/\epsilon$ is approximately equal to the negative of the percentage deviation of the exchange rate from its expectation in $\epsilon/\$$. Substituting, the bracketed covariance term becomes $[cov(O_N^{\epsilon}/E(O_N^{\epsilon}) - 1, -X_N^{\epsilon/\$}/E(X_N^{\epsilon/\$}) - 1)]$, which is also equal to $-[cov(O_N^{\epsilon}/E(O_N^{\epsilon}) - 1, X_N^{\epsilon/\$}/E(X_N^{\epsilon/\$}) - 1)]$. The last expression can be restated in terms of two variables that we understand better: (a) the FX operating exposure to the U.S. dollar, $\xi_{O\$}^{\epsilon}$; and (b) the volatility of the euro, σ_{ϵ}. By definition, $\xi_{O\$}^{\epsilon} = [cov(O_N^{\epsilon}/E(O_N^{\epsilon}) - 1, X_N^{\epsilon/\$}/E(X_N^{\epsilon/\$}) - 1)]/(N\sigma_{\epsilon}^{2})$. Substituting, we have that $E(O_N^{\$}) = E(O_N^{\epsilon}) \cdot E(X_N^{\$/\epsilon}) + E(O_N^{\epsilon}) \cdot E(X_N^{\$/\epsilon})[-N\xi_{O\$}^{\epsilon}\sigma_{\epsilon}^{2}]$, which simplifies to $E(O_N^{\epsilon}) \cdot E(X_N^{\$/\epsilon})[1 - N\xi_{O\$}^{\epsilon}\sigma_{\epsilon}^{2}]$, which is approximated by equation (7.1).
2. Start with the linear return-generating model, $R_i^{\$} = a_i^{\$} + \xi_{i\epsilon}^{\$}x^{\$/\epsilon} + \epsilon_i^{\$}$, where $\xi_{i\epsilon}^{\$}$ is asset i's FX exposure to the euro. Take the covariance of

both sides of this equation with the return on the global market (in U.S. dollars), $R_G^{\$}$, to get $\text{cov}(R_i^{\$}, R_G^{\$}) = a_i^{\$} + \xi_{i\epsilon}^{\$}\text{cov}(x^{\$/\epsilon}, R_G^{\$}) + \text{cov}(\epsilon_i^{\$}, R_G^{\$})$. Divide both sides by the variance of $R_G^{\$}$, and note that the definition of a beta is covariance with $R_G^{\$}$, divided by the variance of $R_G^{\$}$, to get $\beta_i^{\$} = \xi_{i\epsilon}^{\$}\beta_\epsilon^{\$} + \beta_{\epsilon i}^{\$}$. Repeat for asset j to get $\beta_j^{\$} = \xi_{j\epsilon}^{\$}\beta_\epsilon^{\$} + \beta_{\epsilon j}^{\$}$. Subtract the second beta equation from the first and note that if assets i and j have different betas only on account of FX exposure, then $\beta_{\epsilon i}^{\$} = \beta_{\epsilon j}^{\$}$. The result is equation (7.2).

Chapter 8

1. The adjustment term in equation (8.1) has the same foundation as the one in equation (7.1). To better see the connection, note that an asset's FX exposure to the euro from the U.S. dollar point of view, $\xi_{O\epsilon}^{\$}$, and the asset's FX exposure to the U.S. dollar from the euro point of view, $\xi_{O\$}^{\epsilon}$, sum to 1. That is, $1 - \xi_{O\epsilon}^{\$} = \xi_{O\$}^{\epsilon}$. See Adler and Jorion (1992).

2. To formally derive the conversion formula in equation (8.1), start with equation (5.1a): $1 + R_i^{\$} = (1 + R_i^{\epsilon})(1 + x^{\$/\epsilon})$. Multiply out the right-hand side to get $1 + R_i^{\$} = 1 + R_i^{\epsilon} + x^{\$/\epsilon} + R_i^{\epsilon}x^{\$/\epsilon}$. Take expectations to get $1 + E(R_i^{\$}) = 1 + E(R_i^{\epsilon}) + E(x^{\$/\epsilon}) + E(R_i^{\epsilon}x^{\$/\epsilon})$. The term $E(R_i^{\epsilon}x^{\$/\epsilon})$ is equal to $E(R_i^{\epsilon}) \times E(x^{\$/\epsilon}) + \text{cov}(R_i^{\epsilon}, x^{\$/\epsilon})$, so we substitute and get $1 + E(R_i^{\$}) = 1 + E(R_i^{\epsilon}) + E(x^{\$/\epsilon}) + E(R_i^{\epsilon}) \times E(x^{\$/\epsilon}) + \text{cov}(R_i^{\epsilon}, x^{\$/\epsilon})$, which simplifies to $1 + E(R_i^{\$}) = (1 + E(R_i^{\epsilon}))(1 + E(x^{\$/\epsilon})) + \text{cov}(R_i^{\epsilon}, x^{\$/\epsilon})$. The covariance term, which is an adjustment for the interaction between R_i^{ϵ} and $x^{\$/\epsilon}$, can be reexpressed in terms of two variables that we understand better: (1) the asset's FX exposure to the euro, $\xi_{i\epsilon}^{\$}$; and (2) the volatility of the euro, σ_ϵ, the standard deviation of annualized percentage changes in the spot FX price of the euro. By definition, $\text{cov}(R_i^{\$}, x^{\$/\epsilon}) = \xi_{i\epsilon}^{\$}\sigma_\epsilon^2$. Using the transformation, $\text{cov}(R_i^{\epsilon}, x^{\$/\epsilon}) = \text{cov}(R_i^{\$} - x^{\$/\epsilon}, x^{\$/\epsilon}) = \text{cov}(R_i^{\$}, x^{\$/\epsilon}) - \sigma_\epsilon^2$, we have that $\text{cov}(R_i^{\epsilon}, x^{\$/\epsilon}) = \xi_{i\epsilon}^{\$}\sigma_\epsilon^2 - \sigma_\epsilon^2 = (\xi_{i\epsilon}^{\$} - 1)\sigma_\epsilon^2$. Making this substitution, and expressing expectations in terms of *equilibrium* concepts, we get the cost of capital conversion formula in equation (8.1).

3. Luehrman and Quinn (2010) address this issue in a Harvard case. However, the case bases intrinsic FX forecasts on purchasing power parity (goods market conditions), whereas here the intrinsic FX forecasts are based on uncovered interest rate parity (financial market conditions).

4. See Harris and Ravenscraft (1991); Dewenter (1995); and Erel, Liao, and Weisbach (2012). See also Baker, Foley, and Wurgler (2009), who report that FDI flows increase sharply with source-country stock market valuations.

References

Aabo, T., Hansen, M., & Muradoglu, Y. (2013). Foreign debt usage in non-financial firms: A horse race between operating and accounting exposure hedging. *European Financial Management*, forthcoming.

Abuaf, N. (2011). Valuing emerging market equities – The empirical evidence. *Journal of Applied Finance 21*(2), 123–141.

Adler, M., & Dumas, B. (1984). Exposure to currency risk: Definition and measurement. *Financial Management 13*(2), 41–50.

Adler, M., & Jorion, P. (1992). Universal currency hedges for global portfolios. *Journal of Portfolio Management 18*(4), 28–35.

Aggarwal, R., & Soenen, L. (1989). Managing persistent real changes in currency values: The role of multinational operating strategies. *Columbia Journal of World Business 24*(3), 60–67.

Allayannis, G., & Ofek, E. (2001). Exchange rate exposure, hedging, and the use of foreign currency derivatives. *Journal of International Money and Finance 20*(2), 273–296.

Allayannis, G., Ihrig, J., & Weston, J. (2001). Exchange-rate hedging: Financial vs. operating strategies. *American Economic Review Papers & Proceedings 91*(2), 391–395.

Arquette, G., Brown, W., & Burdekin, R. (2008). Investigating US ADR and Hong Kong H-Share spreads against domestic Shanghai Stock Exchange listings of Chinese firms. *Journal of Banking and Finance 32*(9), 1916–1927.

Baker, M., Foley, F., & Wurgler, J. (2009). Multinationals as arbitrageurs: The effect of stock market valuations on foreign direct investment. *Review of Financial Studies 22*(1), 337–389.

Bank of America roundtable on evaluating and financing foreign direct investment. (1996). *Journal of Applied Corporate Finance 9*(3), 64–79.

Bartram, S., Brown, G., & Minton, B. (2010). Resolving the exposure puzzle: The many facets of exchange rate exposure. *Journal of Financial Economics 95*(2), 148–173.

Baruch, S., Karolyi, A. & Lemmon, M. (2007). Multimarket trading and liquidity: Theory and evidence. *Journal of Finance 62*(5), 2169–2200.

Bates, T., Kahle, K., & Stulz, R. (2009). Why do U.S. firms hold so much more cash than they used to? *Journal of Finance 64*(5), 1985–2022.

Bergbrant, M., Campbell, K., & Hunter, D. (2013). *Firm-level competition and exchange rate exposure: World-wide evidence from foreign-involved and purely domestic firms.* New York, NY: St John's University.

Block, S. (2003). Divisional cost of capital: A study of its use by major U.S. firms. *Engineering Economist 48*(4), 345–362.

Bonini, S., Dallocchio, M., Raimbourg, P., & Salvi, A. (2012). Do firms hedge translation risk. Retrieved April 8, 2013, from SSRN: http://papers.ssrn.com/sol3/papers.cfm?abstract_id=1063781

Brotherson, T., Eades, K., Harris, R., & Higgins, R. (2013). "Best practices" in estimating the cost of capital: An update. *Journal of Applied Finance 23*(1), 15–33.

Bruner, R., Li, W., Kritzman, M., Myrgren, S., & Page, S. (2008). Market integration in developed and emerging markets: Evidence from the CAPM. *Emerging Markets Review 9*(2), 89–103.

Bryan, A. (2007). Do ADRs violate the law of one price? Deviations in price parity in the absence of fundamental risk. Retrieved February 12, 2013, from Washington University: http://www.olin.wustl.edu/Documents/CRES/Bryan.pdf

Campbell, J., Serfaty-de Medeiros, K., & Viceira, L. (2010). Global currency hedging. *Journal of Finance 65*(1), 87–121.

Da, Z., Guo, R., & Jagannathan, R. (2012). CAPM for estimating the cost of equity capital: Interpreting the empirical evidence. *Journal of Financial Economics 103*(1), 204–220.

Damodaran, A. (2003). Country risk and company exposure: Theory and practice. *Journal of Applied Finance 13*(2), 63–75.

de Jong, A., Rosenthal, L., & Van Dijk, M. (2009). The risk and return of arbitrage in dual-listed companies. *Review of Finance 13*(3), 495–520.

Desai, M. (2006). Globalizing the cost of capital and capital budgeting at AES. Harvard Business School Case 9-204-109.

Dewenter, K. (1995). Do exchange rate changes drive foreign direct investment? *Journal of Business 68*(3), 406–433.

Dhanani, A. (2003). Foreign exchange risk management: A case study in the mining industry. *British Journal of Accounting 35*(1), 35–63.

Donaldson, G., Kamstra, M., & Kramer, L. (2010). Estimating the equity premium. *Journal of Financial and Quantitative Analysis 45*(4), 813–846.

Dufey, G., & Srinivasulu, S. (1983). The case for corporate management of foreign exchange risk. *Financial Management 12*(4), 54–62.

Erel, I., Liao, R., & Weisbach, M. (2012). Determinants of cross-border mergers and acquisitions. *Journal of Finance 67*(3), 1043–1081.

Fernandez, P., Aguirreamalloa, P., & Avendaño, L. (2012). US market risk premium used in 2011 by professors, analysts and companies: A survey with 5731 answers. Retrieved February 1, 2013, from SSRN: http://papers.ssrn.com/sol3/papers.cfm?abstract_id=1805852

Friberg, R., & Ganslandt, M. (2007). Exchange rates and cash flows in differentiated product industries: A simulation approach. *Journal of Finance 62*(5), 2475–2502.

Froot, K., & Dabora, E. (1999). How are stock prices affected by the location of trade? *Journal of Financial Economics 53*(2), 189–216.

Froot, K., Scharfstein, D., & Stein, J. (1994). A framework for risk management. *Journal of Applied Corporate Finance 7*(3), 22–33.

Garner, K., & Shapiro, A. (1984). A practical method of assessing foreign exchange risk. *Midland Corporate Finance Journal 2*(3), 6–17.

Godfrey, S., & Espinosa, R. (1996). A practical approach to calculating costs of equity for investments in emerging markets. *Journal of Applied Corporate Finance 9*(3), 80–90.

Graham, J. (2000). How big are the tax benefits of debt? *Journal of Finance 55*(5), 1901–1941.

Graham, J., & Harvey, C. (2001). The theory and practice of corporate finance: Evidence from the field. *Journal of Financial Economics 60*(2), 187–243.

Halling, M., Pagano, M., Randl, O., & Zechner, J. (2008). Where is the market? Evidence from cross-listings in the U.S. *Review of Financial Studies 21*(2), 725–761.

Harris, R., & Ravenscraft, D. (1991). The role of acquisitions in foreign direct investment: Evidence from the U.S. stock market. *Journal of Finance 46*(3), 825–844.

Harvey, C. (2000). The drivers of expected returns in international markets. *Emerging Markets Quarterly 4*(3), 32–49.

Kedia, S., & Mozumdar, A. (2003). Foreign currency denominated debt: An empirical examination. *Journal of Business 76*(4), 521–546.

Keloharju, M., & Niskanen, M. (2001). Why do firms raise foreign currency denominated debt? Evidence from Finland. *European Financial Management 7*(4), 481–496.

Kester, C., & Allen, W. (1991). *Walt Disney Co.'s Yen Financing*. Harvard Business School Case 287–058.

Lessard, D. (1996). Incorporating country risk in the valuation of offshore projects. *Journal of Applied Corporate Finance 9*(3), 52–63.

Lewent, J., & Kearney, J. (1990). Identifying, measuring, and hedging currency risk at Merck. *Journal of Applied Corporate Finance 2*(4), 19–28.

Luehrman, T., & Heilprin, P. (2009). *Midland Energy Resources, Inc.: Cost of capital*. Harvard Business School Case 4129.

Luehrman, T., & Quinn, J. (2010). *Groupe Ariel S.A.: Parity conditions and cross-border valuation*. Harvard Business School Case 4194.

Lustig, H., & Verdelhan, A. (2011). The cross section of foreign currency risk premia and consumption growth risk: Reply. *American Economic Review 101*(7), 3477–3500.

Maldonado, R., & Saunders, A. (1983). Foreign exchange restrictions and the law of one price. *Financial Management 12*(1), 19–23.

Maloney, P. (1990). Managing currency exposure: The case of Western Mining. *Journal of Applied Corporate Finance 2*(4), 29–34.

McBrady, M., Mortal, S., & Schill, M. (2010). Do firms believe in interest rate parity? *Review of Finance 14*(4), 695–726.

Mei, J., Scheinkman, J., & Xiong, W. (2009). Speculative trading and stock price: Evidence from Chinese A-B share premia. *Annals of Economics and Finance 10*(2), 225–255.

Miles, J., & Ezzell, R. (1980). The weighted average cost of capital, perfect capital markets, and project life: A clarification. *Journal of Financial and Quantitative Analysis 15*(3), 719–730.

Miller, M. (1977). Debt and taxes. *Journal of Finance 32*(2), 261–275.

Miller, M., & Modigliani, F. (1963). Corporate income taxes and the cost of capital: A correction. *American Economic Review 53*(3), 433–443.

Millman, G. (1990). The floating battlefield: Corporate strategies in the currency wars. New York, NY: Amacom Books.

Munro, A. (2011). Motivations for swap-covered foreign currency borrowing. Reserve Bank of New Zealand.

O'Brien, T. (1998). International production location and "pro forma" hedging of exchange rate risk. *Journal of Applied Corporate Finance 11*(3), 100–108.

O'Brien, T. (2010). Fundamentals of corporate currency exposure. *Journal of International Financial Markets, Institutions, and Money 20*(3), 310–321.

O'Brien, T. (2013). *Introduction to foreign exchange rates.* New York, NY: Business Executive Press.

Oxelheim, L., & Wihlborg, C. (1995). Measuring macroeconomic exposure: The case of Volvo cars. *European Financial Management 1*(3), 241–263.

Perold, A. (2004). The capital asset pricing model. *Journal of Economic Perspectives 18*(3), 3–24.

Pettit, J. (2003). FX policy revisited: Strategy & tactics. Retrieved August 14, 2008, from SSRN: http://papers.ssrn.com/sol3/papers.cfm?abstract_id=463106

Pettit, J., Ferguson, M., & Gluck, R. (1999). A method for estimating global corporate capital costs: The case of Bestfoods. *Journal of Applied Corporate Finance 8*(3), 80–90.

Pringle, J. (1991). Managing foreign exchange exposure. *Journal of Applied Corporate Finance 3*(4), 73–82.

Reyent, S. (2008). Calculating country risk observed by betas. Retrieved December 12, 2008, from Seeking Alpha: http://seekingalpha.com/article/110434-calculating-country-risk-observed-by-betas

Shapiro, A. (1975). Exchange rate changes, inflation, and the value of the multinational corporation. *Journal of Finance 30*(2), 485–502.

Stulz, R. (1995). Globalization of capital markets and the cost of capital: The case of Nestlé. *Journal of Applied Corporate Finance 8*(3), 30–38.

Welch, I. (2009). The consensus estimate for the equity premium by academic financial economists in December 2007. Retrieved June 1, 2013, from SSRN: http://papers.ssrn.com/sol3/papers.cfm?abstract_id=1084918

Weston, F. (1973). Investment decisions using the capital asset pricing model. *Financial Management 2*(1), 25–33.

Zenner, M., & Akaydin, E. (2002). *A practical approach to the international valuation and capital allocation puzzle.* New York, NY: Salomon Smith Barney.

Index

OTHER TITLES IN OUR FINANCE AND FINANCIAL MANAGEMENT COLLECTION

John Doukas, Old Dominion University, Editor

ALSO FORTHCOMING IN THIS COLLECTION

Announcing the Business Expert Press Digital Library

Concise E-books Business Students
Need for Classroom and Research

CPSIA information can be obtained at www.ICGtesting.com
Printed in the USA
BVOW06s1904210815

414470BV00003B/10/P